HORN OF THE MOON COOKBOOK

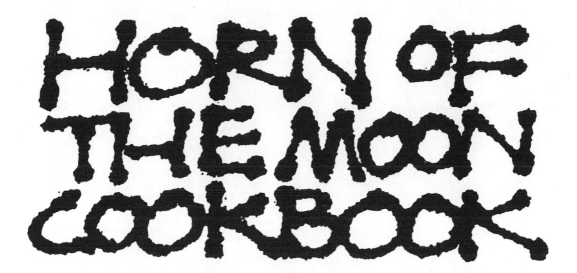

HORN OF THE MOON COOKBOOK

Ginny Callan

Illustrations by
Don Cook

PERENNIAL LIBRARY

Harper & Row, Publishers, New York
Cambridge, Philadelphia, San Francisco, Washington
London, Mexico City, São Paulo, Singapore, Sydney

*This book is lovingly dedicated
to my mother, Mary*

Design by The Laughing Bear Associates

Copyeditor: Libby Kessman

Indexer: Maro Riofrancos

Library of Congress Cataloging-in-Publication Data

Callan, Ginny.
  Horn of the Moon cookbook.

  Includes index.
   1. Vegetarian cookery.   2. Horn of the Moon Café (Montpelier,
Vt.)   3. Cookery—Vermont—Montpelier.   I. Horn of the Moon Café
(Montpelier, Vt.)   II. Title.
TX837.C325   1987   641.5′09743′4   86-45644
ISBN 0-06-055037-6   87 88 89 90 91   10 9 8 7 6 5 4 3 2 1
ISBN 0-06-096038-8 (pbk.)   89 90 91   10 9 8 7 6 5 4

Acknowledgments

To the many people who have shared time, energy, and effort and whose contributions helped to make this book possible. My special thanks to:

All those who have worked at the Horn of the Moon Café through the years and given it so much, especially Heidi Broner and Andrea Mills, who did a wonderful job running the café while I took time off to complete this book. Cort Richardson, my husband and friend, who supported me in my work, read and edited many drafts, and washed a never-ending supply of dirty dishes. Many friends who shared recipes and ate my test meals. The staff at Laughing Bear Associates, especially Mason Singer, for their inspired design work. Andrea Warnke, for years of typing and editing long after it was convenient to do so. Rebecca Davison and Andrea Chesman, for early editing help. Andrew Kline, who urged me onto the path of selling my food. David Champoux, my sandwich partner in Mother's Best. Chris Wood, for two years of hard work. The café customers who kept after me to turn my recipes into a cookbook. And especially all the café's regular customers and friends whose smiles and appreciative remarks brighten so many of my days.

Contents

Introduction

The Horn of the Moon Café sits on Langdon Street in Montpelier, Vermont, tucked against the north branch of the Winooski River. I adopted the café's name from a beautiful, mountainous area just a few miles outside of Montpelier. This area got its name, so the story goes, when an Indian lost his wife and, after searching for her, found her there under the horn of the moon.

Opened for business in the spring of 1977, the Horn of the Moon Café has become a favorite haunt of many wonderful people. Artisans, carpenters, business people, legislators, activists, senior citizens, office workers, mechanics, and families all come to the café to share meals and talk. The atmosphere is friendly and warm, and the tantalizing aromas of breads, pastries, casseroles, and pies waft in from the kitchen. Beautiful plants fill the large windows and local artworks hang on the café's walls. Shelves overflow with political leaflets and bulletin boards outside the front doors announce classes, benefit dinners, meetings, and dances.

Six months of snowy cold weather is typical of a central Vermont winter. Morning customers and staff tell hair-raising tales of getting to work after driving off the road twice or shoveling snow for an hour. "It was 20 below in Cabot," says Tony, a café regular. "Well, it was 25 below in Worcester at five this morning!" Andrea, the soup cook, brags. The café serves plenty of hot soup on these cold days and steaming bowls of chili with Vermont cheddar cheese on top. Grilled melted cheese sandwiches with our own whole wheat bread are a popular wintertime choice for the hardy souls who have braved the harsh weather.

Between winter and spring comes Vermont's special fifth season, known to us as mud season. It makes traveling in deep snow easy by comparison. Dirt roads become impassable when the snow melting off the mountains is joined with a few days of rain, and cars get mired in the mud. "The mud was up to the car's doors," complained one customer who had to be pulled out by a tow truck.

In springtime customers watch the river rise and recall the flood of 1973. "We watched people canoe down Main Street," someone tells a newcomer to the area. When the river level reaches six feet we begin to worry about the café basement. At 7½ feet the water will start coming in, so we store high rubber boots by the basement stairs just in case. But the spring also brings fresh vegetables and we celebrate by making a spanakopita for dinner with an early batch of locally grown organic spinach and Vermont feta cheese.

By summer we have an abundance of local strawberries, fresh garden vegetables, and herbs. We serve large fresh green salads with Tabouli or pasta salad on top. Pesto over freshly made pasta is a favorite summer dish, too, as are chilled fruit soups and Strawberry Cheese Pie.

Fall brings foliage enthusiasts to the café, referred to by the locals as "leaf peepers." They always order our Vermont Special, a bowl of hot soup, cold apple cider, sharp Vermont cheddar cheese, and sourdough rye rolls spread with sweet butter, often followed by freshly baked pumpkin pie with whipped cream on top.

I moved from New York City to Vermont in the fall of 1970 to go to college and found myself growing attached to Vermont despite the subzero cold temperatures and ten-foot-high snowbanks. The way of life was certainly more basic than I was used to but the difficult living conditions drew people closer together. Friends taught me how to load a wood stove so that it would burn through the night to cross-country ski across the mountains, and to milk a goat.

But the job market in Vermont was quite limited, so after finishing college I took on a job managing a clothing store. Occasionally I would go out to buy a sandwich for lunch at Montpelier's then new and only natural foods shop. It was not much bigger than a large closet. Still, it was an exciting addition to Montpelier and healthy sandwiches were sold there, made by different people in their homes.

David Champoux, a friend, took over the sandwich making but soon grew tired of it. The business, he told

me, offered barely enough income to live on, and de-
manded a lot of work. David and I decided to become
partners and expand the business, delivering as far as
fifty miles away to Burlington, Vermont. Mother's Best
Sandwiches was born in the spring of 1976 and my
food career was launched.

That first summer in business went by quickly, with
sales increasing until the cold weather arrived. By fall
David was ready to move on, and he dropped out of
the business. Mother's Best couldn't support a single
worker through the winter months, so I continued
working at the clothing shop in addition to making
sandwiches. This hectic schedule was taxing and I
knew something had to change.

I began to consider the idea of opening a real restaurant. My first step was to go to the Small Business Ad-
ministration for some free advice. They recommended
I come back to talk to them when I had at least
$10,000 in start-up money. Instead, I rented a small
storefront off Main Street in Montpelier. With my
$3,000 in savings, I bought used restaurant equip-
ment. My friend Chris Wood and I did all the renova-
tions. The space was tiny, but the close quarters made
it cozy and certainly unusual. The café could seat just
thirteen customers. The kitchen was larger than the
dining area and was left open to allow conversation to
flow among customers and cooks.

The Horn of the Moon Café opened on May 2, 1977.
Those first few weeks of business were busy and as the
café became known we grew busier and busier still.
Soon customers were jamming themselves into the
small space so tightly that it was difficult to move
around.

Two years later we moved to our present location on
Langdon Street. We expanded our service from only
lunch to breakfast, lunch, and dinner. The staff grew
to twenty. I hired people like myself with little or no
restaurant experience but with a knowledge of natural
foods. All the workers, including myself, rotated jobs
and pooled tips. Long staff meetings occurred once a
month, using consensus as a decision-making process.

The café has struggled financially over the years. It has had to compete with other restaurants that use cheap and easy options. The fresh produce that we buy costs more than the canned or frozen foods many restaurants use, and it takes more time to prepare. We avoid using food additives. We also try to help support local farmers by buying their products. Our decision, made over time, has been to buy locally, organically raised produce in season, and to cook more with root crops that store well in the winter months. The sacrifice in profit is made up for by the good feeling we have about the food we serve. Through the years, the café has grown and matured. But our special relationship with customers and friends has been maintained, giving the Horn of the Moon a warm and unique community atmosphere.

Many of the Horn of the Moon Café's customers and staff are not vegetarians, although I have been one since 1971. The majority of the café's clientele choose the Horn for its delicious, healthy food. Their reasons vary from concern about the high cholesterol, chemicals, and hormones found in animal protein to the economy of a vegetarian diet and the moral implications of killing animals. Frances Moore Lappé's book, *Diet for a Small Planet,* has taught many people that world hunger is exacerbated by eating livestock rather than grains.

My personal decision to become a vegetarian came about when I met a chicken running for its life from a neighbor's hatchet. After harboring and protecting the runaway, I came to the realization that I could not kill the bird and that I did not want anyone else to kill it either. Yet I ate chicken regularly! On that day I decided to eliminate meat from my diet.

Becoming a vegetarian forced me to make many more decisions. Should I eat seafood? Eggs? Dairy products? Wear leather? Buy a down sleeping bag? Some people choose to eliminate only red meat from their diet, and eat chicken or seafood; others choose to avoid all but seafood. I follow an ovolactarian diet, which means I include dairy products and eggs. But the café's menu also offers dishes for lactarians who eat no meat or eggs but do consume dairy products, as well as dishes for nondairy vegetarians.

The recipes in this book are a far cry from the brown rice loaves I once made. My cooking skills and styles have changed greatly over time. Years ago I would follow a recipe word for word. Now I can look at several recipes for ideas and create a new dish incorporating my own tastes, daring to add my favorite vegetables and the spices I relish.

Many of the recipes presented here have been café favorites for years. They come from many different sources, including friends, café workers, and relatives. Some are adaptations from traditional recipes; others are international in origin. We pay special attention not only to taste, but to the color and texture of foods as well.

Cooking and sharing food is for me a way of giving to others and showing that I care. It's been a wonderful, creative process. I hope you will have as much pleasure in creating these dishes as I have!

Stocking Your Pantry

At the café we need to have on hand at all times a large supply and wide assortment of grains, beans, nuts, flours, vegetables, and cheeses, for most of our menu specials are not planned in advance. Keeping up with the supply of food coming and going can be a never-ending job. Having a well-stocked pantry is helpful at home, too, and can save you numerous trips to the store or knocking on a neighbor's door to borrow something.

Basic supplies to have on hand include whole wheat, whole wheat pastry, and unbleached white flours; cereals, rice, and other grains; assorted dried beans and legumes; nuts; dried fruits; baking powder; yeast; oils; and a wide variety of herbs and spices, including fresh garlic. Stock your refrigerator with butter or margarine, milk, eggs, tofu, cheeses, and various vegetables, including potatoes, onions, carrots, and cabbage, which store well.

Each cook quickly develops his or her own style and methods of working. One, for example, may use oil for a piecrust; another, margarine, butter, vegetable shortening, or lard. Each chef will argue why the choice is best, and some may vary what they use depending on the kind of pie they are making.

These variations in a cook's style can extend to the brands selected and the quality of ingredients bought. At the café we consider flavor, appearance, and price as well as purity. We avoid the use of additives and preservatives in the foods we serve.

When I first became a vegetarian, I had little knowledge of many of the materials that I now cook with daily. Cooking with natural foods makes use of standard ingredients, but it also includes foods that are new to many of us living in the Northern Hemisphere. If you don't know what the basic *t*'s are—tofu, tahini, and tamari—I'll describe them here. But even if you are familiar with natural foods you should read on to learn more about which ingredients to avoid as well as to buy.

The Basic Ingredients

Baking Powder

Baking powder is a leavening agent used in many breads and desserts. Its rising agent works more quickly than yeast and it is typically found in quick breads, muffins, and cookies. In Ireland, for example, yeasted breads are a rarity and baking powder and soda breads are the common fare.

Baking powder is a combination of calcium acid phosphate, bicarbonate of soda, and cornstarch. Certain brands also include aluminum silicate, which should be avoided. Rumford Baking Powder, a double-acting baking powder, is a common brand found in many markets and does not contain aluminum. It is our standard baking powder at the café.

Butter

Locally available unsalted butter is the shortening most commonly used and preferred at the café. Before the days of refrigeration, butter was salted to preserve it from turning sour. Now, however, unsalted butter can last for a good month in the refrigerator, and it also freezes well. If a salted butter is being used to replace unsalted butter in a recipe, cut back the amount of salt being called for by one quarter to one half, depending on how much salted butter you are using.

We especially like to use unsalted butter for desserts and pastries at the café. Many recipes for baked goods call for little or no salt so that the natural, subtle flavors in them can be savored.

We use margarine on the griddle and for certain dishes in which we intentionally exclude dairy products. If you do use margarine, avoid those containing cottonseed oil. Many of the cheaper brands contain it because of its low cost. Cottonseed oil is derived from the cotton plant, which is not grown primarily as a food crop. Consequently, stronger pesticides and herbicides are used through the growing process, and the seeds are not protected. For this same reason, but to a lesser extent, corn oil should also be avoided. Cornfields have heavy applications of herbicides applied to them. Coconut and palm oil are saturated oils and contain high levels of cholesterol. Soy, sunflower, or safflower margarine are the best choices.

Grains and Flours

Always purchase whole, unadulterated grains, such as brown rice instead of white and whole barley rather than the pearled variety. Processing grains refines a natural product, removing the valuable outer husk, where essential vitamins, minerals, and roughage are stored.

While whole wheat flour offers roughage and a high nutritional value, it can produce a heavy, grainy-tasting loaf or cake. As a compromise, we often blend two or more flours together for lightness and health, usually including whole wheat pastry or unbleached white flour with the whole wheat. Yeast-risen baked goods need gluten to feed the yeast during the rising process. Whole wheat pastry flour does not have a high level of gluten and should be used only when yeast is not the leavening agent.

Herbs and Spices

Fresh herbs and spices, as well as the dried variety, are called for in many of the following recipes. Fresh herbs will add even more color and flavor to a meal than dried. When replacing dried herbs, substitute three times as much fresh herbs. Some herbs are particularly easy to grow and will do well in a pot on your windowsill. Many markets are beginning to carry fresh herbs as well, such as dill weed, chives, parsley, thyme, basil, and oregano.

Fresh garlic and ginger taste vastly different than the powdered variety. Elephant garlic, which has extremely large cloves, is available in some markets. We chose not to use it at the café because the flavor is much milder; therefore, more is needed. When buying garlic, select large heads that have not begun to sprout or soften, which can be a sign of rot. If purchasing dried garlic powder, pick the granulated variety, which holds more flavor than the powdered.

Avoid buying dried spices at grocery stores that sell them in cute, expensive little jars. Instead, go to a food co-op or natural foods store that sells spices in bulk. They will generally be less expensive and fresher, and you can buy the amount you want.

Legumes

We buy dried beans in bulk because it's more economical. Most beans need to be presoaked for a minimum of six hours in three times the amount of water. Soaking speeds up the cooking process. In hot weather, you can refrigerate the beans while they soak to prevent fermentation.

Some legumes, such as lentils and split peas, cook at a much faster rate and soaking is not necessary. Canned cooked beans are more convenient but costlier and some include additives to prevent discoloration. Quantities for grains and beans are always the dry uncooked amount unless otherwise noted.

Milk and Cream

When the café first opened, we served only raw milk, which was delivered to us from a local dairy farm. The milk was delicious and rich. This practice had to be changed when commercial distribution of raw milk was stopped in the state of Vermont. A mild bacteria was discovered in the state's only remaining raw milk dairy, caused by an ill cow.

Now the café uses pasteurized, nonhomogenized whole milk, though low fat milk can be substituted in any of these recipes. Vermonters who live near dairy farms can still buy raw milk from farmers, and it is not dangerous to drink as long as it comes from a healthy herd. It is a tasty and creamy treat.

Heavy cream is now found in many stores right next to the ultrapasteurized variety. Beware of ultrapasteurized cream, which has many chemical additives to extend its shelf life from the usual week to a month or more. Read a container's label before you grab it off the shelf. If your local store is not carrying real cream, ask the dairy manager to stock it.

Oil

When oil is called for, unrefined sunflower oil is used unless otherwise noted. Unrefined safflower oil can be substituted but it has a slightly more noticeable flavor in foods. Corn oil, however, is best avoided. It has a strong flavor and a tendency to foam up when it's heated to a hot temperature for deep frying.

A chilled oil will make a thicker salad dressing. When sautéing foods, always heat the pan and oil before adding your vegetables, tofu, or whatever. Set the pan over medium heat for a few minutes. If the pan begins to smoke, allow it to cool down for a minute and then try again. This procedure will allow the food to cook in the oil, rather than absorb it.

Pasta

Fresh pasta is a delight to eat and guarantees a memorable meal. Since it is still moist and soft it cooks in less than half the time it takes to cook dried pasta. Be careful not to overcook it or it will be ruined.

Fresh pasta can be made in assorted shapes and flavors. Listed are a few of the common varieties of pasta that are called for in this book. Some specialty shops now sell fresh pasta in addition to dried noodles.

Fettuccine. A long, wide, flat noodle that is a favorite for dinner at the café.

Lasagne. Much wider than fettuccine, it can be cut and rolled into a manicotti noodle, but is most commonly used for the ever popular baked lasagne.

Linguine. A long, thin noodle that is flat on all sides and similar in appearance to spaghetti.

Spaghetti. A long, round, thin noodle.

Rotini. Curly, squiggly-shaped noodles that work particularly well in casseroles and with sauces.

Vanilla Extract

Always buy the real variety rather than the cheaper imitation vanilla. Real vanilla extract tastes better and is a purer product.

The café uses fresh vegetables; local and organically grown are best. We exclude them only when they are simply not available, too costly, or take too much time and effort, like artichokes. But canned tomatoes, which have excellent taste, color, and texture, are an exception. For the home gardener, however, freezing vegetables is a good option because you can blanch the fresh produce lightly and end up with a product far superior to the commercial alternative.

Overcooking vegetables is the most common mistake of the inexperienced cook. Vegetables are lovelier to look at, tastier and healthier to eat when they still retain their bright color and crispness. If a dish is going to be baked after the vegetables have been sautéed, undercook the vegetables. Otherwise they will be soft and tasteless after baking.

Vegetables

The Less Common Ingredients

Agar-Agar, Arrowroot, or Kudzu

These are all natural thickening agents which are nutritious and processed without chemical or animal products. They are substitutes for cornstarch or gelatin and will thicken up pastries like blueberry or strawberry rhubarb pie, or a sweet and sour sauce. Arrowroot powder is less expensive than the other thickeners and is available in many natural foods stores.

Carob Powder

Also known as Saint John's bread, carob powder is made from a bean that bears a resemblance to chocolate. However, it has a unique flavor and is rich in minerals and natural sugars. It is used primarily in baking, can be substituted for chocolate, and unlike chocolate, contains no caffeine.

Hiziki

This calcium-rich seaweed looks like strands of dried-up black twine and has a salty and somewhat fishy taste. Break the hiziki up with your hands before soaking it. Hiziki should be soaked in water for fifteen minutes before it can be drained and sautéed. Once customers at the café build up the courage to try hiziki, we find that most of them really like it.

Miso

Miso, a fermented soybean paste, is Japanese in origin. Miso is high in protein and vitamin B_{12}. It is a salty seasoning that is especially good in soups. It will dissolve more easily if it is first thinned with some hot water. Avoid boiling it, as that will destroy some of the helpful bacteria miso contains. Miso can be stored in a tightly closed container in the refrigerator for months.

Nutritional Yeast

Nutritional yeast has yellow flakes that are delicious and very high in B vitamins. It can be sprinkled onto almost any food. Though I refuse to put it in my orange juice (it looks awful floating around in the glass), many people do. The café cooks shake generous amounts of it onto sautéing tofu just before the tofu is done. Even our small local movie theater in Montpelier has a shaker of it available to put on top of popcorn.

The first vegetarian cookbook I ever bought called for brewer's yeast in just about every dish, and they all had a bitter taste. Eventually I discovered that the culprit was the brewer's yeast. Though both brewer's yeast and nutritional yeast are nutritional yeasts, they are made from different strains. The yellow nutritional yeast is produced from torula yeast and has a much more pleasant, nonbitter taste to it. Be sure always to buy yeast primarily grown for supplemental purposes and not yeast that is a by-product of the brewing process.

Phyllo Dough

The café uses this ultrathin pastry dough for strudels, baklava, spanakopita, and other vegetable pies. The dough, which is Greek in origin, is difficult and time-consuming to make. We gave in to buying our dough ready-made even though it contains a mild preservative. Phyllo dough is found in the freezer section of many stores and should be allowed to thaw overnight in the refrigerator before it is used.

Be certain that the dough is thoroughly defrosted before you remove it from the package and attempt to unfold it. Otherwise you will have difficulty working with it, as the dough will crack as well as stick together.

Once a package has been opened, store the extra dough in a tightly wrapped, airtight package in the refrigerator or freezer. It will last for one or two weeks refrigerated and for months if frozen.

Tamari

Tamari, an aged soy sauce, is made from soybeans, salt, and water. It is darker in color, richer and stronger in flavor than commercial soy sauce, and has no added color or sweeteners. Commercial soy sauces may have chemical preservatives, color, or sweeteners included in their ingredients. Japanese tamari is aged for a minimum of one year and is thicker than other less aged soy sauces. Although other soy sauces are acceptable, the café uses only Japanese tamari.

Tempeh   Tempeh is made from cultured, fermented soybeans, and comes in flat, light, grainy-looking cakes. It is high in protein and B vitamins and is more flavorful than tofu. Tempeh is found in the refrigerated or frozen food sections of natural foods stores or co-ops.

Marinating sliced tempeh for a few hours in an oil, vinegar, and tamari mix adds an especially delicious taste to it.

Tahini   Middle Eastern in origin, tahini is made from crushed sesame seeds. It is used mainly for its creamy, rich, and nutty flavor, but it also helps in binding food together.

Sesame butter is a close relative to tahini, but its seeds are roasted before being ground. The flavor is stronger and delicious, but it is not as adaptable and is used more as a spread. It has a much thicker consistency than tahini. Nut butters, like tahini and sesame butter, are high in protein as well as calories.

Tofu   A versatile, cheeselike soy food, tofu is an excellent and inexpensive form of protein. It is characteristically bland in taste, but its flavor can be enhanced by many different seasonings and spices. Tofu is cut into sections or mashed and mixed into foods raw or cooked. It can be sautéed, deep fried, frozen and then defrosted, or even dehydrated for backpacking trips.

Tofu is often found in natural foods stores, floating in water in a large tub with the refrigerated foods. Since it is often sold in bulk, you can buy one square or many. Avoid the prepacked tofu, which is shipped in small plastic containers. It is usually not as fresh and will not keep as long.

After buying tofu, store it in the refrigerator in a covered container filled with water. If the water is changed every day or two, the tofu will keep for a week or more. You will be able to tell if it has gone bad by a distasteful smell, yellowish color, and sour taste.

Before sautéing tofu, allow it to drain on paper towels for fifteen minutes. Then pat it dry before adding it to hot oil. This prevents the oil from spattering.

Tools of the Trade

Cooking with natural foods requires very little exotic equipment. Basic kitchen supplies will do for preparing most meals. The few standard requirements include sharp knives for chopping and a serrated one that will glide through the chewiest of breads. Blenders are necessary for preparing some of the soups and salad dressings, though a food processor fitted with a chopping blade makes a good substitute.

The first food processor brought into our kitchen received a cold welcome. Most of the cooks wanted nothing to do with it. They simply did not want to learn how to operate yet another machine that would get in the way, break down, and conflict with a more natural way of preparing foods.

But within the first week the baker discovered how quickly butter could be cut into pie dough using the chopping blade. The soup cook began using the slicing blade for vegetables, and everyone soon learned to appreciate how quickly the tedious jobs, like chopping garlic, could be completed with a processor. A month later the staff had been won over. Today it's used at least half a dozen times daily. It is important to know, however, that this valuable instrument is most useful for large-scale food preparation, and is not as efficient in a small household.

Choosing the right kind of pots is essential. Aluminum pots and pans are found in many kitchens because of their low cost and availability. This kind of cookware should be avoided, in my view, because it reacts with acid in foods, especially tomato products, to produce a metallic flavor. The aluminum from the pots can also enter the food you are cooking and be metabolized in your body.

The café uses mostly cast-iron and stainless steel pots. There and at home I have numerous cast-iron fry pans and a four-quart Dutch oven which is wonderful for cooking rice, soups, and sauces. Enameled cast-iron pots will not rust as plain cast-iron ones can, but they are much more expensive. Drying your cast-iron pots on a medium burner after washing will prevent rusting. Once a cast-iron pot has been seasoned, it needs little washing and no scrubbing at all! In most cases a rinse under very hot water should be enough. The best way to retire aluminum cookware is to identify your most frequently used pots first and replace them one by one with one of the nonaluminum alternatives. I've found very serviceable ironware and stainless steel pots at garage sales.

Many of the cakes made at the café require the use of a ten-inch springform cake pan. The sides readily slip off these pans, which comes in very handy for serving and showing off your creation. It's best to buy a well-made, high quality springform pan, as the inexpensive ones tend to leak.

If you plan on cooking with phyllo dough, buy a good quality pastry brush. The cheaper ones sometimes lose their bristles as you brush. A pastry brush is a necessary item for spreading butter over your dough.

Finally, our pies and quiches are typically made in ten-inch Pyrex glass pie plates. The glass distributes the heat well and also allows you to see if your crust is done from the bottom up. Glass pans will cook food slightly faster than metal ones. Therefore, if you are using a metal pie tin, your pie will probably need a few minutes of extra baking time in the oven. If you prefer to buy a metal pie plate, choose a heavy gauge which will help spread the heat more evenly to your pie.

Breakfast

From the Griddle/ page 29

Blueberry Waffles
Cashew French Toast
Maple Almond Ricotta
   Crepes
Granola
Tofu, Onions,
   Mushrooms, and
   Spinach
Home Fries
Home Fries with Tofu
"Tex-Mex" Home Fries
Rice, Tofu, and
   Vegetables
Oriental Rice Cakes
Stuffed French Toast

Pancakes/page 38

Sour Cream Pancakes
Poppy Seed Pancakes
Blueberry Cornmeal
   Pancakes

Eggs/page 40

Omelettes
* *Asparagus*
* *Brie, Fresh Herb, and*
   Tomato
* *Florentine*
* *Mushroom, Onion,*
   and Monterey Jack
* *Mexican*
Scrambled Options

* *Cheese*
* *Spinach and Cheese*
* *Avocado and Cream*
   Cheese
* *Broccoli, Mushrooms,*
   Peppers, Zucchini,
   or Onions
* *Asparagus, Potatoes,*
   or Snow Peas
* *Scallions, Apples,*
   Spinach, Sprouts,
   Tomato, Avocado,
   and Fresh Herbs
* *Leftovers*
Egg McMoon
Full Moon Eggs

Breakfast Treats/ page 47

Cinnamon Rolls
Danish Pastry
* *Cheese Danish*
* *Almond Cream*
   Danish
* *Apricot Danish*
* *Date Danish*
* *Date Nut Danish*
Date Swirls
Poppy Almond Coffee
   Cake
Blackberry Buttermilk
   Coffee Cake
Sticky Buns
Maple Cornmeal Muffins
Date Nut Muffins

Maple Almond Muffins
Blueberry Muffins
Fresh Grape Walnut
   Muffins
Carrot Walnut Raisin
   Muffins
Pineapple Muffins
Maple Walnut
   Buttermilk Muffins
Poppy Seed Muffins
Sourdough English
   Muffins
Cinnamon Raisin
   English Muffins

Sweet Breads/ page 64

Apple Bread
Cranberry Bread
Blueberry Nut Bread

Breads/page 66

Raisin Bread
Whole Wheat Bread
Chapatis
Bedouin Bread
Corn Bread

Breakfast Drinks/ page 69

Hot Carob Mix
Hot Cocoa Mix
Mocha Coffee

Breakfast is a favorite meal of mine. I especially enjoy it on weekends and vacations when I have the time to prepare a delicious recipe and to relax and enjoy it. Choosing among Poppy Seed Pancakes, Mushroom, Onion, and Monterey Jack Omelette, Blueberry Waffles, Cinnamon Rolls, and hot, freshly baked muffins can be a delightful dilemma.

Normally, though, the first meal of the day must be the simplest and least pretentious. On most occasions there is too much to do at the beginning of the day, so meal preparation time needs to be short. Quick breakfast options include a bowl of yogurt with fruit or granola mixed in, hot or cold cereal, or scrambled eggs with some onion or cheese tossed into them while they cook.

Mornings at the café are special. Customers and workers share the beginning of their day together. Café regulars get to know each other in the morning and more than one romance has begun from a casual conversation at the counter. The wait people quickly learn who drinks their coffee black and who likes peppermint tea or prefers Earl Grey. This familiarity creates an advantage that enables them to bring customers their favorite hot drinks practically as they sit down.

In summertime the café fills up early since there are no snowy or muddy roads, or cars that refuse to start. It is also light and warm outside, which encourages early rising. Thinking about locally made whole milk yogurt from Jersey cows topped with fresh blueberries, strawberries, peaches, or grapes or a glass of freshly squeezed orange juice is difficult to resist.

At these times coffee sells as quickly as we make it. The café is known for having the best cup of coffee in town and it brings in some of the most confirmed carnivores. It's the blend of French roast and Colombian beans, freshly ground, that gives our coffee its rich flavor. Our decaffeinated coffee is made with a Swiss water process, and no chemicals are added during production. Many commercial decaffeinated coffees, however, use harsh chemicals to separate the caffeine from the coffee.

On holidays, the café serves special breakfasts. I like to do the same thing at home to celebrate a birthday or gathering of old friends. Date Swirls or a Poppy Almond Coffee Cake might be baked and served with an Asparagus Omelette and a side of Home Fries.

If breakfast begins later than usual, make it into brunch. You can include quiche in the menu instead of scrambled eggs or an omelette, or have Maple Almond Ricotta Crepes. A green salad and a fresh baked Blackberry Buttermilk Coffee Cake can complete the meal.

Breakfast creates the opportunity for establishing new traditions. There are many selections you can choose from by introducing recipes typically reserved for meals later in the day. When the café began serving tofu for breakfast, no one ordered it at first except the staff. Now it has become a popular breakfast item.

Though some friends of mine have been known to eat cold pizza or eggplant parmigiana in the morning, it's a bit too heavy for me. But I've had miso soup or pita bread stuffed with melted cheese. If you're famished when you wake up and there are leftovers to be eaten, you might be pleasantly surprised at how good they are.

From the Griddle

Blueberry Waffles

W e don't have a commercial waffle iron at the café yet, though we have thought about where we could fit one. I make my waffles at home on relaxing weekend mornings; blueberry waffles are my favorite.

A few of the staff are hard-core waffle fanatics and have brought their waffle irons to work in the morning. By 6:00 A.M. the rest of the morning crew came in to find waffles awaiting them. These same waffle lovers brought their waffle irons to the café's potluck Christmas party. Waffles à la mode, along with eggnog and rum, were enjoyed by all.

Mix together dry ingredients. Add wet ingredients, stirring the oil and the berries in last. Don't overstir. Preheat waffle iron and butter it lightly. Cook until waffle iron stops steaming and waffles are golden brown (4 to 7 minutes).

4 to 5 waffles

Plain Waffles. Omit the blueberries.

Poppy Seed Waffles. Add 2 tablespoons poppy seeds with the oil.

Nut Waffles. Add ½ cup chopped walnuts or almonds with the oil.

1¾ cups flour (1 cup whole wheat pastry, ½ cup unbleached white, ¼ cup corn or rice or soy flour)

3 teaspoons baking powder

¼ teaspoon salt

½ teaspoon cinnamon

2 eggs, beaten

1¼ cups milk

1 teaspoon vanilla extract

½ cup sunflower oil

2 cups blueberries

Butter

Maple syrup

Cashew French Toast

½ *cup cashew nuts*

*2 tablespoons sunflower
seeds*

2 tablespoons sesame seeds

1½ *cups milk*

¼ *teaspoon vanilla extract*

6 slices whole wheat bread

Butter

Hot maple syrup

S *ome café customers include dairy products but not
eggs in their diets. They asked for some eggless
breakfast items. This is a delightfully nutty and eggless
version of French toast.*

In a blender, puree the cashews, sunflower seeds, and
sesame seeds until they are ground into a paste. Pour the
milk and vanilla into the blender, cover, and run until
mixture is smooth.

Pour this mixture into a large but shallow bowl. Dip a
slice of bread into the batter. Allow it to soak for 1 minute. Then gently pierce the bread with a fork 5 or 6 times
around the surface. This will allow the bread to absorb
more batter. Turn bread over and allow it to soak for a
minute again to absorb batter.

Meanwhile, preheat a 10-inch cast-iron skillet or griddle over medium heat. Add 1 teaspoon butter to the pan
and swirl it around so that the surface of the pan is covered. Add 2 slices of the dipped bread and cook over low
to medium heat until nicely browned. Using a spatula,
flip the bread over and cook remaining sides until done.
Repeat, using up all the bread and batter. Cut each slice
in half diagonally, allowing 3 pieces per serving. Serve
with hot maple syrup and a dot of butter on top.

4 servings

Maple Almond Ricotta Crepes

*E*llie, *a breakfast cook at the café, created these one morning when she wanted to use up crepes from a previous night's dinner. The result proved delicious.*

Follow Basic Crepes recipe (page 220) and make crepes. Put almonds into food processor or blender and grind very fine. Add water and blend until a smooth paste is formed. In medium-sized bowl, mix ground almonds with ricotta cheese, maple syrup, and almond extract. Put ⅓ cup filling across the middle of each crepe. If desired, sprinkle fresh blueberries or strawberries, or peach or apple slices on top of filling. Roll each crepe up. Bake 10 minutes at 375° in a buttered 9 × 12-inch pan. Serve garnished with sour cream on top and a few fresh berries.

5 servings

10 crepes

¾ cup almonds

2 tablespoons water

3 cups ricotta cheese

½ cup maple syrup

1 teaspoon almond extract

Fresh fruit in season

Sour cream for garnish

Granola

*F*reshly made granola is a far cry from the soggy variety sold in most stores. It's delicious with milk, in yogurt and fruit, and sprinkled in pancakes. For granola pancakes, simply sprinkle a tablespoonful of granola onto a pancake after it has gone on the griddle and before the pancake has been flipped.*

Preheat oven to 300°. In medium-sized bowl, mix together the oats, sesame seeds, and sunflower seeds or almonds. Pour honey, oil, and water over this mixture and stir well. Spread on a large cookie sheet and bake 35 to 40 minutes until nicely browned on top. Stir the granola often while baking, every 5 to 10 minutes.

Remove from oven and allow to cool. Add dried fruit, stir, and store in a tightly sealed jar to keep fresh.

6 cups

Variation: In place of the ¾ cup each raisins and shredded coconut, substitute ½ cup each raisins, shredded coconut, and chopped dried apricots.

4 cups uncooked rolled oats

½ cup sesame seeds

¾ cup sunflower seeds or chopped almonds

⅓ cup honey

⅓ cup sunflower oil

2 tablespoons water

¾ cup raisins

¾ cup shredded coconut

Tofu, Onions, Mushrooms, and Spinach

5 tablespoons sunflower oil

4 squares tofu, cut in ½-inch cubes (2 pounds)

2 teaspoons tamari

2 tablespoons nutritional yeast

1 cup chopped onion (approximately 2 onions)

¼ teaspoon dried leaf thyme

2 cups sliced mushrooms

2 cups chopped fresh spinach

Tahini

A *popular high-protein breakfast at the café. Serve it with toast or a hot muffin on the side.*

Heat 2 tablespoons oil in a 10-inch fry pan over medium heat. Add half the tofu to the pan. Fry, tossing tofu occasionally until it is lightly browned and crispy. This will take around 15 minutes. Pour on 1 teaspoon tamari, stir in quickly, and sprinkle on 1 tablespoon nutritional yeast. Place sautéed tofu on paper towels to drain. Pour 2 more tablespoons oil into pan; fry the remaining tofu, repeating the tamari and nutritional yeast coating, and set it aside.

Heat the remaining tablespoon of oil in the same fry pan over medium heat. Add the onion and thyme. When the onion begins to brown, add the mushrooms and cook for 2 minutes more until mushrooms are barely tender. Add the sautéed tofu to the mushroom-onion mixture, then add the chopped spinach. Cook for a few minutes until spinach is tender but still green. Serve with tahini on the side.

4 servings

Home Fries

The trick to making great home fries is to have the potatoes tender but not overcooked on the inside and nicely browned and crispy on the outside. Leftover baked potatoes can make great home fries.

For a delicious option, just before serving spread home fries with a cup of grated cheddar or Jack cheese. Cover pan with a lid and serve when the cheese is melted all over the potatoes.

Bring water to a boil in 3-quart pot. Add potatoes and cover. Cook over medium heat for 10 to 15 minutes until potatoes are just tender and a fork goes into them easily. Drain water and save for soup stock.

In medium-sized bowl, mix potatoes with the salt, pepper, parsley, and green pepper. Preheat a 10- or 12-inch cast-iron fry pan. Add oil; sauté onions and dill. When onions begin to brown and get tender, add potato mixture. Cook, uncovered, until potatoes are browned on bottom. Turn with a spatula and continue to cook until brown on all sides. Serve with tahini and ketchup on the side.

4 servings

1 quart water

4 cups cubed unpeeled potatoes (approximately 4 potatoes)

½ teaspoon salt

Dash of black pepper

½ cup minced fresh parsley

¾ cup diced green pepper

1 tablespoon sunflower oil

1½ cups diced onion (approximately 3 onions)

1 teaspoon dried dill weed

Tahini

Ketchup

Home Fries with Tofu

Preheat a 10-inch cast-iron fry pan; add oil. Add tofu to hot oil; sauté tofu for 10 to 15 minutes over medium heat, tossing occasionally. Tofu should be lightly browned. Sprinkle on tamari, then nutritional yeast; stir quickly and set aside.

Mix tofu in with potato mixture before adding to onions in Home Fries.

4 servings

3 tablespoons sunflower oil

2 squares tofu, drained, cut into ½-inch squares (1 pound)

2 teaspoons tamari

1 tablespoon nutritional yeast

1 recipe Home Fries

"Tex-Mex" Home Fries

1 quart water

4 cups cubed unpeeled potatoes (approximately 4 potatoes)

½ teaspoon salt

Dash of black pepper

¼ cup chopped fresh cilantro (also known as Chinese parsley)

2 tablespoons chopped fresh dill weed

¾ cup diced green pepper

1 medium-size ripe red tomato, coarsely chopped

1 tablespoon sunflower oil

2 large cloves garlic, minced

1 tablespoon minced fresh Jalapeño pepper

1½ cups chopped onion (3 onions)

1 cup grated sharp cheddar cheese

½ cup sour cream

½ cup Salsa (p. 145)

I've added a few more vegetables, spices, and some hot pepper to the basic Home Fries recipe. Patti, a breakfast cook at the café, came up with the idea of topping home fries with cheese, salsa, and sour cream one morning. Everyone had it for breakfast that day and loved it.

Bring water to a boil in 3-quart saucepan. Add potatoes and cover. Cook over medium heat for 10 to 15 minutes until potatoes are just tender and a fork goes into them easily. Drain.

In medium-sized bowl, mix potatoes with salt, pepper, cilantro, dill weed, green pepper, and tomato. Stir well. Preheat a 10-inch cast-iron skillet; add oil. Sauté garlic, hot pepper, and onion over medium heat. When onions begin to brown, add potato mixture. Continue to cook over low heat until potatoes are nicely browned. Sprinkle grated cheese over potatoes. Cover and cook for 5 minutes. Turn off heat and serve with sour cream and Salsa on the side.

4 servings

Rice, Tofu, and Vegetables

Known to café workers and regular customers as R.T.V., this menu item sells for breakfast, lunch, and dinner.

Bring 2 cups water to a boil in a 1-quart saucepan, add rice, and lower heat to a simmer. Cover and cook until all water evaporates and rice is tender (about 40 minutes). Meanwhile, cut tofu into small squares. Heat oil in a 10-inch cast-iron fry pan over medium heat, add tofu, and cook over medium heat, stirring occasionally until nicely browned. Then add nutritional yeast, tamari and ginger, and stir until tofu is well coated. Turn off heat.

Meanwhile, bring 1 cup water to a boil in a 3-quart saucepan. Set a vegetable steamer inside pan, add carrot sticks, cover, and simmer for 3 minutes. Put onions and broccoli on top of carrots and continue to simmer for 3 minutes more. Add zucchini and cook for 3 minutes more until just barely tender. Turn off heat. Toss vegetables and tofu with cooked rice and serve with tahini on the side. The mixture will hold well if refrigerated and can be reheated in a fry pan.

4 servings

3 cups water

1 cup uncooked brown rice

2 squares tofu, well drained (1 pound)

3 tablespoons sunflower oil

1 tablespoon nutritional yeast

2 teaspoons tamari

1 teaspoon ground ginger

1 large carrot, cut into thin sticks approximately 2 inches long

1 cup chopped onion (approximately 2 onions)

2 cups coarsely chopped broccoli, stems and florets

1¾ cups zucchini, cut into ¼-inch-thick slices (approximately 1 medium zucchini)

Tahini

Oriental Rice Cakes

2 cups water

1 cup uncooked brown rice

6 tablespoons sunflower oil

1 square tofu, cut into
small pieces (½ pound)

½ cup chopped onion
(approximately 1 onion)

1 tablespoon peeled and
minced fresh ginger root

1 cup sliced mushrooms

1 cup chopped bok choy
(or Chinese cabbage or
celery)

2 teaspoons sesame seeds

4 teaspoons tamari

¼ teaspoon cayenne
pepper

4 eggs, beaten

3 scallions, sliced

Bring water to a boil in a 2-quart saucepan, add rice, cover, and lower heat to a simmer. Cook until rice is tender and all the water has evaporated (around 40 minutes). When rice is done, mash slightly and set aside.

Meanwhile, set a 10-inch cast-iron fry pan over medium heat and add 3 tablespoons oil. When hot, add tofu and cook until browned on all sides, stirring occasionally. When tofu is browned, add onion and ginger. When onion begns to brown, add mushrooms, bok choy, and sesame seeds. When mushrooms are just barely tender, turn off heat and pour 2 teaspoons tamari over the mixture, stirring in quickly. Combine tofu-vegetable mixture with rice in medium-sized bowl. Add the remaining 2 teaspoons tamari and the cayenne. Mix well. Stir in eggs and scallions.

Heat the remaining 3 tablespoons oil in cleaned fry pan over medium heat. Use ½ cup of mixture per rice cake. When oil is hot, add the measured mix and pack each patty down into a round shape approximately 1 inch thick. Fry until nicely browned on one side. Carefully flip over the cakes and cook other side until browned. Repeat until all the cakes are done.

4 servings
(8 cakes)

Stuffed French Toast

In a medium-sized bowl, mix together the ricotta cheese, egg yolks, ¼ teaspoon vanilla, maple syrup, lemon rind, and lemon juice. Set aside.

In a shallow dish, beat the 2 eggs with the cinnamon and remaining ¼ teaspoon vanilla extract. Add milk and beat again.

Put 2 slices of bread in the egg batter. Allow them to soak up the batter, then turn bread over. Meanwhile, pre-heat a 10-inch skillet over medium heat; add ½ table-spoon butter to it. When melted, add the soaked bread. Cook until bread is crisp and browned on one side.

Flip bread over and spread ½ cup ricotta mix over every other piece. Continue to cook bread until crispy and brown on remaining side. Set a piece of the French toast without the cheese on top of the piece with cheese. Place on a plate, top with whipped cream, strawberry slices, and hot maple syrup. Repeat with remaining bread.

4 servings

1 pound ricotta cheese

2 egg yolks, beaten

½ teaspoon vanilla extract

1 tablespoon maple syrup

1 teaspoon grated lemon rind

2 teaspoons lemon juice

2 eggs, beaten

¼ teaspoon ground cinnamon

⅔ cup milk

8 large slices French bread

1 tablespoon butter

1 cup whipped cream

2 cups sliced fresh strawberries

Hot maple syrup

Pancakes

Sour Cream Pancakes

1¼ cups whole wheat flour

¾ cup unbleached white flour

½ teaspoon salt

2 teaspoons baking powder

¾ teaspoon baking soda

1¾ cups sour cream

1 tablespoon honey

2 tablespoons butter, melted

½ teaspoon vanilla extract

1¾ cups milk

1 egg yolk

1 egg white, beaten well

1 to 2 tablespoons butter

Hot maple syrup

Mix dry ingredients together in medium-sized bowl. In a separate bowl, mix sour cream, honey, melted butter, and vanilla together. Add milk and egg yolk. Mix again. Pour dry ingredients into wet and stir well. Add egg white and stir.

Preheat a griddle or fry pan over medium-low heat. When pan is hot add 1 teaspoon butter, quickly spread over pan, and pour in a ½-cup ladle of pancake batter for each pancake. Cook the pancakes until bubbles appear on the surface. Flip the pancakes and cook for another 1 to 2 minutes. Repeat until all the batter has been used, adding more butter as needed to pan. Serve with hot maple syrup.

9 large
pancakes

Poppy Seed Pancakes

Bring 1 cup milk to boil in a 1-quart saucepan. When it boils, turn off heat and add the poppy seeds and honey. Allow mixture to stand and cool for 20 minutes. Mix flour, baking powder, soda, and salt in a medium-sized bowl. In separate medium-sized bowl, mix eggs, remaining 1 cup milk, poppy seed mixture, and oil. Add dry ingredients to wet and stir.

Preheat griddle or fry pan over medium heat. When hot, add 1 teaspoon butter, spread over pan, and pour in a ½-cup ladle of pancake batter for each pancake. This makes a nice large pancake. Cook the pancakes until bubbles appear on top, flip over, and cook for another 1 to 2 minutes until done. Add more butter as needed to pan. Serve with hot maple syrup and butter on top.

9 large
pancakes

2 cups milk

½ cup poppy seeds

2 teaspoons honey

2 cups whole wheat pastry flour

2 teaspoons baking powder

½ teaspoon baking soda

½ teaspoon salt

2 eggs, beaten

2 tablespoons sunflower oil

2 tablespoons butter

Hot maple syrup

Butter

Blueberry Cornmeal Pancakes

Mix dry ingredients together in medium-sized bowl. In separate medium-sized bowl, beat eggs. Add milk and oil to eggs. Mix dry ingredients into wet; stir enough to moisten. Add blueberries and mix in gently.

Heat griddle or fry pan over medium heat. When hot, add 1 teaspoon butter, quickly spread over pan, and pour in a ½-cup ladle of pancake batter for each pancake. Cook the pancakes until bubbles appear on top, flip over, and cook for another 1 to 2 minutes until done. Add more butter as needed to pan. Serve with hot maple syrup. A dollop of yogurt on top is delicious.

9 large
pancakes

¾ cup cornmeal

½ cup whole wheat pastry flour

¾ cup unbleached white flour

2 teaspoons baking powder

½ teaspoon baking soda

½ teaspoon salt

2 eggs

2 cups milk

2 tablespoons sunflower oil

1 cup blueberries, fresh or frozen

2 tablespoons butter

Hot maple syrup

Yogurt (optional)

Eggs

Omelettes

1 tablespoon butter

4 eggs

3 teaspoons water

Dash of salt and pepper

¾ cup grated cheese

1 cup vegetables

Omelettes are quick, relatively easy to prepare, and delicious as well as quite satisfying to eat. They may be served for breakfast, lunch, or dinner, and there is no end to what can be put into them. Omelettes are especially popular at the café on weekend mornings when customers have time to relax and feel like treating themselves to something extra special.

The secret to preparing a good omelette is to cook it in a preheated heavy-gauge pan, add a splash of water in with your beaten eggs, and be fast. All your filling ingredients should be prepared before you begin to cook the eggs. Nothing is worse than a dry, overcooked omelette. So have your table set, toast ready to pop in the toaster, and hungry people sitting at the table anxiously awaiting their meal before the eggs begin to cook.

Preheat a 10-inch omelette pan over medium heat. When hot, add 1 tablespoon butter to the pan. Quickly swirl the pan around until butter covers the bottom. Add the eggs, which have been beaten well with 2 teaspoons water, salt, and pepper. Cover. The heat should not be so hot that the eggs immediately begin to set. If they do, pull the fry pan off the heat for 1 minute, lower heat a bit, and set fry pan once again on heat. Allow eggs to cook until almost set but still just a little runny on top.

Add filling ingredients (¾ cup of your favorite grated cheese and 1 cup vegetables of your choice) over ½ the omelette. Lower heat. With a spatula, fold ½ the omelette over the filled half. Add 1 teaspoon water to the empty side of fry pan and quickly cover. Allow eggs to cook just long enough for cheese to melt and filling to be hot. Cut in half and serve.

2 servings

For 1 serving. Follow the same directions. Use 2 eggs instead of 4, and cut back your filling ingredients by ⅓ to ½. Be more cautious about not overcooking the eggs, as they will cook more quickly.

Asparagus Omelette

Cut off the tough ends of asparagus. Cook asparagus in 2 cups water in pan. When tender, remove from heat and drain well.

Beat eggs, 2 teaspoons water, salt, and pepper until light and frothy. Add butter to preheated omelette pan. Follow general directions for cooking an omelette. Add asparagus, dill, and Swiss cheese in that order for a filling.

2 servings

8 to 10 thin stalks fresh asparagus

2 cups boiling water

4 eggs

3 teaspoons water

Dash of salt and pepper

1 tablespoon butter

1 teaspoon chopped fresh dill weed

¾ cup grated Swiss cheese

Brie, Fresh Herb, and Tomato Omelette

Beat eggs, 2 teaspoons water, salt, and pepper until light and frothy. Follow general directions for cooking an omelette. Lay out the herbs, tomato, and Brie cheese in that order over ½ the omelette. Fold over omelette, add 1 teaspoon water to pan to quicken melting process of cheese, cover, and cook until just done.

2 servings

4 eggs

3 teaspoons water

Dash of salt and black pepper

1 tablespoon butter

1 tablespoon chopped fresh chives

1 tablespoon chopped fresh dill weed

1 tablespoon chopped fresh parsley

½ medium tomato, coarsely chopped

Four to six ¼-inch slices of Brie cheese to cover half the omelette

Florentine Omelette

1 tablespoon butter

3 teaspoons water

Dash of salt and black pepper

⅛ teaspoon dried dill weed

4 eggs, well beaten

1 packed cup chopped fresh spinach

¾ cup grated havarti cheese

Preheat a 10-inch omelette pan over medium heat. When hot, add the butter to the pan. Quickly swirl the pan around until the butter covers the bottom. Add the water, salt, pepper, and dill weed to the eggs. Follow general omelette directions, adding the spinach and cheese when the filling is called for. Cook until cheese has melted.

2 servings

Mushroom, Onion, and Monterey Jack Omelette

2 tablespoons butter

½ cup chopped onion (1 onion)

¼ teaspoon dried leaf thyme

2 cups sliced mushrooms

3 teaspoons water

Dash of salt and black pepper

⅛ teaspoon dried dill weed

4 eggs, well beaten

¾ cup grated Monterey Jack cheese

K*nown as a M.O.M. omelette by regular customers and staff, this is a café favorite.*

Set 10-inch fry pan over medium heat. When hot, add 1 tablespoon butter, then onions and thyme. When onions begin to brown, add sliced mushrooms and cook until just tender. Remove from pan and drain if necessary.

Add water, salt, pepper, and dill weed to beaten eggs and mix in. Again, set fry pan over medium heat. Add 1 tablespoon butter. When melted, add eggs. Follow general omelette directions. When set, add mushroom-onion mix topped with cheese over half the omelette. Fold over and cook until done.

2 servings

Mexican Omelette

Set fry pan over medium heat. When hot, add 1 tablespoon butter. When butter is melted, add the onion and garlic. Cook for a few minutes. When garlic begins to brown, add hot and green peppers and cook for 2 or 3 minutes more until tender. Remove from pan and set aside.

Beat eggs with salt, water, and chili powder. Again set fry pan over medium heat. Add remaining 1 tablespoon butter. Pour eggs into fry pan. When eggs are almost set, place onion mixture over half the omelette; follow with tomato and avocado slices, then the cheese on top. Fold over the omelette to cover the filling. Lower heat, add a dash of water to pan, and quickly cover. Serve when cheese is melted.

2 servings

2 tablespoons butter

⅓ cup chopped onion (1 small onion)

2 cloves garlic, minced

1½ tablespoons finely chopped fresh Jalapeño pepper

½ cup chopped green pepper

4 eggs, well beaten

Dash of salt

2 teaspoons water

¼ teaspoon chili powder

½ cup chopped fresh tomato

½ medium avocado, sliced

¾ cup grated Jalapeño pepper Jack cheese

Scrambled Options

Butter

Eggs

Cheese and/or vegetables
as desired

Scrambled eggs are a quick and easily prepared meal, but many people habitually eat plain scrambled eggs for breakfast every morning. My father-in-law has had the same breakfast almost every day of his life, and he loves it. If, however, you are not one of these predictable people and enjoy some variety in your morning meal, you will find some not-quite-so-ordinary breakfasts here that can still be prepared in a small amount of time.

Scrambling an egg can be done well or badly, and of course everyone has a special preference. Often at the café we get very specific orders on just how a customer wants eggs cooked. People can be very particular about eggs. I've been unable to conclude if this is because they are grouchy in the morning or if eggs are one of those dishes that demand perfection. Maybe it's a little of both.

This is how we like to scramble eggs at the café. Preheat your fry pan over medium heat. Add 1½ teaspoons butter to the pan. Swirl it around until it is melted. Now add your well-beaten eggs. The pan should be hot enough to begin to cook the egg but not have it instantly set. If this begins to happen, pull the pan off the heat until it cools down.

After the eggs have cooked for about half a minute, add your choice of ingredients—grated cheese first, then vegetables on top. Now gently toss the eggs with a spatula. Do not stir the eggs constantly; allow them to cook undisturbed for 20 or 30 seconds, then gently toss them over. Repeat this process until eggs are at the desired consistency.

Scrambled Variations

Scrambled Eggs with Cheese. This is a good way to break into not-so-plain eggs. For every 2 eggs that you scramble, add ¼ cup of your favorite cheese, grated. Or combine 2 cheeses. Monterey Jack and cheddar are especially good together.

Scrambled Eggs with Spinach and Cheese.
Have ready ¼ cup grated cheddar cheese, ½ cup
chopped fresh spinach (slightly packed), and a pinch
dried leaf thyme for every 2 eggs you scramble.

**Scrambled Eggs with Avocado and Cream
Cheese.** Cut cream cheese up into ¼ cup small
pieces and slice ¼ medium-sized avocado for every 2
eggs, along with a pinch of dried dill weed.

**Scrambled Eggs with Broccoli, Mushrooms,
Red, Green, or Hot Peppers, Zucchini, or
Onions.** These vegetables should be chopped and
lightly sautéed with some dried or fresh dill weed,
basil, or dried leaf thyme before adding them to the
eggs. Use no more than ½ cup of combined sautéed
vegetables for every 2 eggs.

**Scrambled Eggs with Asparagus, Potatoes, or
Snow Peas.** These vegetables should be lightly
steamed until they're just tender, then added to the
eggs. Use no more than ½ cup total of steamed vegetables for every 2 eggs.

**Scrambled Eggs with Scallions, Apples, Spin-
ach, Sprouts, Tomato, Avocado, and Fresh
Herbs.** In their raw state and chopped slightly, these
can be combined with the eggs. Choose no more than
3 fillings. Plan on 1 chopped scallion, ¼ chopped or
grated apple, ¼ cup chopped fresh spinach, ¼ cup
sprouts, ¼ medium sliced avocado, ½ medium tomato,
chopped, and 1 tablespoon chopped fresh herbs for
every 2 eggs.

Scrambled Eggs with Leftovers. If you have some
leftover cooked vegetables or tofu, try adding some to
your eggs. Use no more than ½ cup of leftovers for
every 2 eggs. Leftover cheese sauce is a delicious
breakfast treat. Warm it up and serve it on top of your
cooked eggs over toasted bread or English muffins.

Egg McMoon

3 tablespoons butter

2 cups sliced mushrooms

1 teaspoon dried dill weed

2 tablespoons unbleached white flour

1¼ cups milk

1 cup grated sharp cheddar cheese

Pinch of salt

Dash of black pepper

8 eggs

4 English muffins, split in half

A *delicious and hearty New England breakfast.*

Melt 2 tablespoons butter in 2-quart saucepan over medium heat. Add sliced mushrooms and dill weed. When mushrooms are just tender, add flour and brown. Slowly add milk; lower heat to a simmer. When all of milk is added, add cheddar cheese and stir in with a whisk. Add salt and pepper. Simmer the cheese sauce on very low heat while cooking eggs.

Heat a 10-inch fry pan over medium heat. Swirl remaining butter over bottom of pan. Crack 4 eggs into it and fry. Toast 2 split English muffins. Fry eggs to desired texture. (I usually do this over light on the other side when flipped.) Put fried eggs over toasted English muffin halves. Top with hot cheese sauce. Repeat process with remaining eggs and muffins, and serve.

4 servings

Full Moon Eggs

1½ teaspoons butter

2 slices whole wheat bread

2 eggs

¼ teaspoon dried dill weed

Dash of salt and black pepper

A *t the Horn of the Moon, we call these Full Moon Eggs, but you might know them as a bird in the nest or a hole in a pocket or by some other name. They are easy to prepare and a good choice when you're hungry but have little time.*

Set fry pan over medium heat. Add butter and swirl pan until butter coats the bottom. Cut a circle about 2½ inches in diameter (the width of a large lemon slice) out of the center of each slice of bread. Set bread slices and the cut-out circles into the fry pan. Toast for 1 minute and flip. Now crack an egg into each hole in the bread. Sprinkle dill weed, salt, and pepper over egg and bread. Allow egg to fry until set. Flip and cook ½ minute more and serve, accompanied by the fried bread circles.

1 serving

Breakfast Treats

Cinnamon Rolls

*T*hese rolls are a Sunday brunch favorite at the café. They are light and wonderfully good. The dough freezes well; so make a double batch and be ready for unexpected friends stopping by. Serve them hot from the oven.

To freeze: place the unbaked rolls on a baking sheet, put in a large plastic bag, and secure tightly. Freeze. Defrost rolls at room temperature for 2 hours before baking. Follow directions for baking.

Bring milk to a boil in a 1-quart saucepan. Turn off heat and add potato, butter, and honey. Set aside. In medium-sized bowl combine the yeast with warm water. Stir and allow to dissolve. Add the potato mixture to yeast and water; mix and beat in egg and salt. Add ½ cup unbleached white flour. Mix in well, add remaining flour, and turn onto floured board, kneading until smooth and elastic. Set into buttered bowl, cover, and let rise until doubled in size (about 1 hour).

Preheat oven to 375°. Punch dough down and knead once again on lightly floured surface. Let dough sit for 10 minutes. Roll out to ¼-inch thickness in a rectangular shape about 9 × 15 inches. Brush 1 tablespoon melted butter over the dough, then drizzle with the honey. Sprinkle the cinnamon, followed by walnuts and currants or raisins, over the surface. Now roll the dough up by its shorter end so that you have a short but thick roll. Cut in 1-inch-thick slices and set onto buttered baking sheet, placing rolls about 1 inch apart. You should have 8 slices. Bake 15 minutes until lightly browned. Brush with remaining tablespoon melted butter and serve.

8 rolls

Dough

¼ cup milk

¼ cup mashed peeled potatoes

2 tablespoons butter

2 tablespoons honey

1½ teaspoons dry baker's yeast

2 tablespoons warm water

1 egg

½ teaspoon salt

1 cup unbleached white flour

¾ cup whole wheat flour

Filling

2 tablespoons butter, melted

2 tablespoons honey

1 teaspoon cinnamon

¼ cup chopped walnuts

Danish Pastry

Dough

½ cup butter

¾ cup unbleached white flour

¾ cup whole wheat pastry flour

½ cup sour cream

2 tablespoons water

1 Danish filling (your choice) (have this ready)

1 egg, beaten

W*e make Danish at the café early in the morning and serve them hot from the oven. The smell of freshly baked Danish is irresistible.*
Rewarming a day-old Danish in an oven will bring the flavor and softness right back into it.

Cut butter into mixed-together flours with pastry cutter or food processor's chopping blade. When the texture resembles cornmeal, add sour cream and just enough water to hold dough together. Chill for at least 4 hours or overnight. The dough will hold well in the refrigerator for a few days.

Preheat oven to 375°. (Prepare desired filling and have ready.)

Roll out dough on generously floured board. Roll into rectangle approximately 12 × 24 inches. Try to keep a rectangular shape as much as possible. When rolled out, trim edges to form an even-edged rectangle. Cut in half lengthwise down the middle. Then cut each long piece into 5 equal pieces, each about 4½ × 6 inches (figs. 1 and 2). If a piece is not quite wide enough, roll out just a touch wider, being careful not to end up with too thin a dough.

Place 1 generous tablespoon of filling into center of a piece of dough and spread out a thin line of filling from corner to corner diagonally across the dough (fig. 3). Place fruit or nuts on top of this if desired.

Fold the corners of dough opposite filling line toward the center where filling sits. Pinch corners together just so that the ends barely meet (fig. 4). Repeat until all 10 Danish are done.

Place on buttered cookie sheet. Brush each Danish lightly with beaten egg and bake 18 to 20 minutes until golden brown.

10 Danish

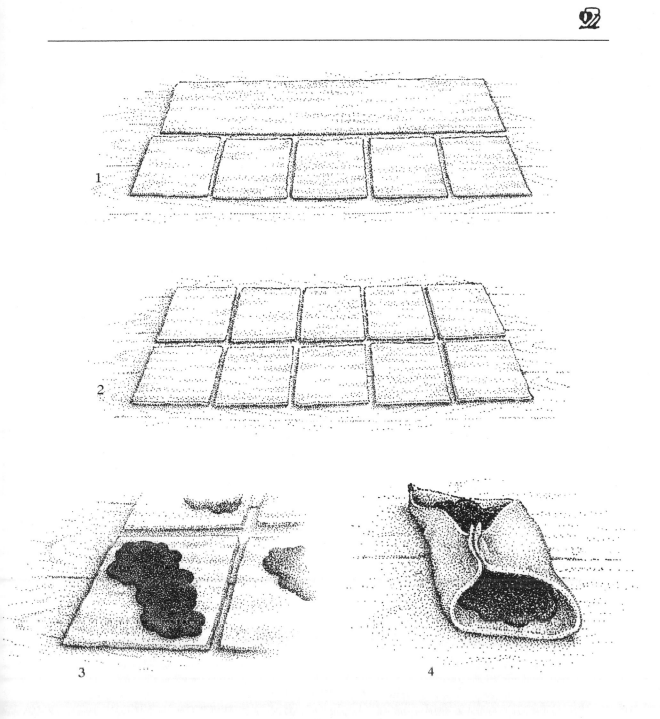

Danish Pastry Fillings

¾ cup cottage cheese

2 egg yolks

2 tablespoons honey

1 tablespoon butter

½ teaspoon grated lemon peel

1½ cups blackberries or blueberries, fresh or frozen (optional)

Cheese Filling for Danish Pastry

Puree all ingredients except berries in blender until smooth. This mix freezes well. For blackberry or blueberry cheese Danish, place frozen or fresh berries on top of cheese filling. Fold and bake as directed.

Filling for
10 Danish

1 cup almonds

¼ cup butter, softened

¼ cup honey

1 egg

2 tablespoons unbleached white flour

Almond Cream Filling for Danish Pastry

Preheat oven to 375°. Toast almonds on cookie sheet in oven 5 to 7 minutes until lightly browned. Allow to cool slightly, then grind nuts in blender until they resemble cornmeal.

In small mixing bowl, blend butter and honey until smooth. Add the egg and mix well. Stir in ground almonds, then mix in flour.

Filling for
10 Danish

½ cup water

3 tablespoons butter

⅓ cup honey

2 cups chopped dates or dried apricots

Date or Apricot Filling for Danish Pastry

Set a 1-quart saucepan over low heat. Add water, butter, and honey, and cook until smooth. Add dates or apricots and continue to cook, stirring occasionally until a thick, smooth paste is formed. Turn off heat and allow to cool before using.

Filling for
10 Danish

Date Nut Danish. Sprinkle 1 heaping teaspoon chopped walnuts over date filling after spreading over Danish dough but before folding.

Date Swirls

Dough

1 cup butter

1½ cups unbleached white flour

½ cup sour cream

Filling

2 cups chopped dates

½ cup water

⅓ cup honey

3 tablespoons butter

The baker at the café has to protect these from the kitchen crew when the swirls come out of the oven. We all want to make sure that they are "all right."
    These small, delicious treats are made with a rich pastry dough. It's difficult to eat just one. They will make any breakfast or brunch extra special.

Cut butter into flour until well blended (a food processor will do this in 10 seconds with the chopping blade). When the texture is that of cornmeal, add sour cream and mix well until thoroughly blended.

Cut dough evenly in half, wrap in plastic, and chill for at least 4 hours (set dough in the freezer for the first half hour if you're pinched for time) or overnight.

Set 1-quart saucepan over medium heat and add dates, water, honey, and butter. Bring to a boil and simmer, stirring occasionally until mixture is relatively smooth. Remove from heat and set aside to cool.

Preheat oven to 350°. Roll pastry out on well-floured board into a rectangle approximately 18 × 14 inches by ¼ inch thick. Spread half of date filling over dough to 1 inch from edges on all sides. If date filling is too thick and doesn't spread easily, thin with a little water.

Roll dough up tightly lengthwise into a long, thin log. Cut into 20 slices approximately ¾ inch thick. Set on buttered cookie sheet at least 1 inch apart. Bake 20 minutes. Repeat with second batch of dough.

40 swirls

Poppy Almond Coffee Cake

Dough

1½ teaspoons dry baker's yeast

¼ cup warm water

¼ cup warm milk

½ teaspoon salt

¼ cup honey

1 egg

¼ cup butter, at room temperature

3 cups flour (1½ cups unbleached white, 1½ cups whole wheat)

Filling

¾ cup poppy seeds

¾ cup chopped almonds

½ cup honey

⅓ cup milk

1 teaspoon grated lemon peel

1 tablespoon lemon juice

3 tablespoons butter

1 tablespoon butter, melted

2 tablespoons sliced almonds

*T*he Interstate Gourmet *guidebook reviewed the Horn of the Moon Café very favorably in their New England book. They said, "The poppy seed pastry alone will make the trip memorable."*

In a medium-sized bowl mix yeast and water. Blend milk, salt, honey, egg, and butter. Add to yeast mixture, then add 2½ cups flour. Turn onto floured board, adding the remaining ½ cup flour as needed. Knead dough until smooth (approximately 10 minutes). Place in buttered bowl, cover with damp cloth, and let rise 1 to 1½ hours until doubled.

While the dough rises, make the filling. Grind the poppy seeds in a blender. Combine the poppy seeds, almonds, honey, milk, lemon peel, lemon juice, and 3 tablespoons butter in a small pan. Cook over low heat for 10 minutes. Let cool.

When the dough has doubled, punch down and roll out on a floured board to a 10 × 15-inch rectangle. Lift onto a buttered cookie sheet.

Spread filling down the center of dough vertically (figure 1). With knife, cut 9 diagonal slashes on each side section to make 9 strips of dough (figure 2). Lift the strips and close over filling (figure 3), overlapping the strips until all are folded (figure 4). Let rise again for 30 minutes on top of stove while preheating oven to 350°. Brush with melted butter. Sprinkle with sliced almonds. Bake 20 to 25 minutes until browned.

10 servings

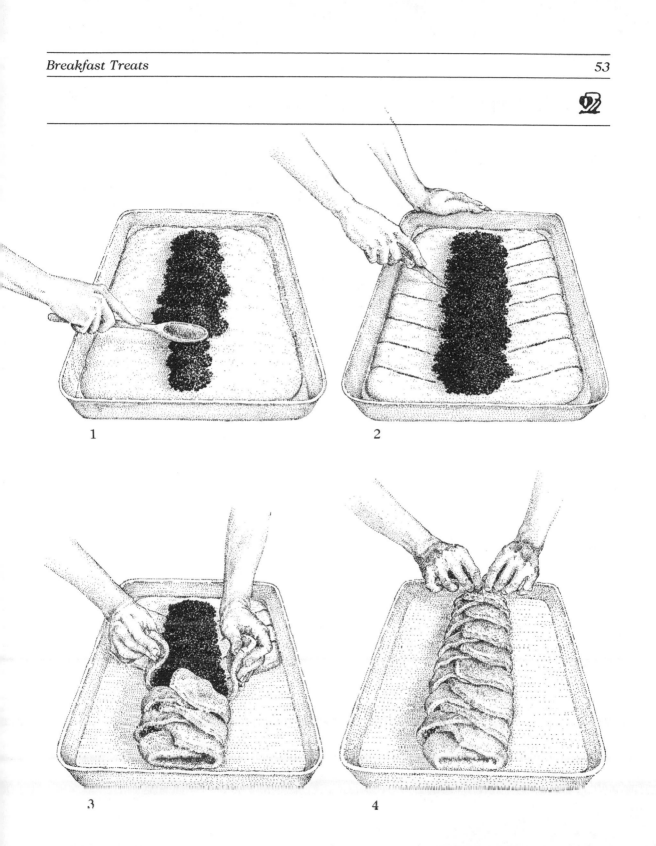

1

2

3

4

Blackberry Buttermilk Coffee Cake

2 cups whole wheat pastry flour

2¾ cups unbleached white flour

1 teaspoon baking powder

1 teaspoon baking soda

¼ teaspoon salt

1 cup butter, softened

1½ cups honey

1 teasooon vanilla extract

4 eggs

1 cup buttermilk

2 cups blackberries, fresh or frozen

Preheat oven to 350°. In medium-sized bowl, combine flours, baking powder, soda, and salt. In a large mixing bowl, blend butter and honey with an electric mixer until smooth and creamy. Add vanilla and eggs. Mix well. Add dry ingredients to butter mixture in batches alternately with buttermilk until all the flour and buttermilk are blended smoothly with the butter mix. Fold in blackberries. Butter a 10-inch tube pan and pour in batter. Bake 1¼ hours until golden on top and toothpick comes out clean when stuck into center of cake.

12 servings

Sticky Buns

These sticky buns are just beautiful when they're turned upside down after baking. But they are also incredibly good to eat, and won't last long.

The dough can be made a day in advance and refrigerated.

In a small bowl, combine the yeast, sour cream, and honey. Stir gently and allow to sit for 10 minutes.

In a medium-sized bowl or food processor using the steel blade, combine the whole wheat and white flours with the butter, eggs yolks, and salt. Add the yeast mixture and work dough until it is smooth and well mixed. Cover and refrigerate for at least 4 hours or overnight.

In a medium-sized bowl, combine the butter, honey, cinnamon, vanilla, and cloves. Mix until smooth. Add walnuts and stir well.

Set a 1-quart saucepan over low heat. Add the honey, butter, lemon juice, and cinnamon. Bring slowly to a boil and simmer for a few minutes. Turn off heat and add vanilla.

Butter a 9 × 12-inch cake pan. On a lightly floured board, roll out the chilled dough into a 12 × 15-inch rectangle. Spread walnut filling lightly over the dough, leaving a 1-inch border on the long sides of the dough. Now sprinkle the currants over the walnut mixture. Roll the dough up tightly jelly roll fashion, starting at the long side. Cut into fifteen 1-inch pieces.

Pour the syrup into the cake pan. Set slices of dough into the pan 3 wide and 5 lengthwise. Cover and allow to rise in a warm place for 45 minutes, until doubled in size. Preheat oven to 375° after 30 minutes.

Remove cover from rolls and bake 20 minutes on the middle rack of oven until lightly browned. Set a 9 × 12 inch cookie sheet over the cake pan and immediately invert the sticky buns onto the sheet. Spread any excess syrup on top of the buns. Allow to cool for a few minutes before serving.

15 buns

Dough

1 tablespoon dry baker's yeast

1 cup sour cream (heat until warm but not hot over low flame)

1 tablespoon honey

1¼ cups whole wheat flour

¾ cup unbleached white flour

½ cup butter

3 egg yolks

½ teaspoon salt

Filling

½ cup butter, softened

½ cup honey

2 teaspoons cinnamon

1 teaspoon vanilla extract

¼ teaspoon ground cloves

1¼ cups finely chopped walnuts

½ cup currants

Syrup

¾ cup honey

4 tablespoons butter

2 teaspoons lemon juice

½ teaspoon cinnamon

1 teaspoon vanilla extract

Muffin Tips

Muffins are quick and easy to prepare, and will add a special touch to a meal. Two helpful hints will aid you in making good muffins. Preheat your oven to the correct temperature. Too cool an oven will give your muffins a flat top. Do not overmix your muffin batter. Stir just enough to add in your ingredients and no more. Overmixing will create a heavy, small muffin, instead of a delicious, light, airy one.

Maple Cornmeal Muffins

Mix dry ingredients together. Beat eggs and add maple syrup, milk, and butter. Stir in dry ingredients. Fill oiled muffin tins ⅔ full. Bake 20 minutes at 400° or until golden.

12 muffins

1 cup whole wheat pastry flour

¾ cup unbleached white flour

⅔ cup cornmeal

1 tablespoon baking powder

½ teaspoon salt

2 eggs

⅓ cup maple syrup

¾ cup milk

½ cup butter, melted

Date Nut Muffins

Preheat oven to 375°. Oil muffin tins. Mix the flours, baking powder, and salt together. Beat eggs with honey. Add milk and oil, along with vanilla. Mix dates with dry ingredients and stir in well. Mix dry ingredients with wet, then add walnuts. Put approximately ½ cup mix into each muffin cup. Sprinkle a few walnuts on top if you like. Bake 25 minutes.

12 muffins

1¼ cups whole wheat pastry flour

1½ cups whole wheat flour

1 tablespoon baking powder

¼ teaspoon salt

2 eggs

½ cup honey

1 cup milk

½ cup sunflower oil

1 teaspoon vanilla extract

1 cup dates, chopped

½ cup chopped walnuts

Maple Almond Muffins

Muffins

1¼ cups whole wheat
pastry flour

1 cup whole wheat flour

2 teaspoons baking powder

¼ teaspoon salt

1¼ cups milk

¼ cup sunflower oil

¼ cup maple syrup

½ teaspoon almond extract

1 egg, beaten

Filling

½ cup maple syrup

½ cup finely chopped or
ground almonds

6 tablespoons whole wheat
pastry flour

2 teaspoons cinnamon

2 tablespoons butter,
melted

These muffins have a maple almond filling in the center that makes them very popular at the café. Some of the regular customers would like us to make them every morning. They are a bit more work than most muffins but are worth the extra effort.

Preheat oven to 400°.

Mix together the flours, baking powder, and salt.

In a separate bowl, mix together the milk, oil, maple syrup, almond extract, and egg.

For the filling, stir together the maple syrup, almonds, 6 tablespoons pastry flour, cinnamon, and melted butter.

Combine dry flour mixture and wet egg mixture and stir just until moist. Put into oiled muffin tins, making 3 layers:

1 tablespoon muffin batter
1 tablespoon almond mixture
1 tablespoon muffin batter (spread over almond mixture to cover it well)

Bake 20 minutes at 400°.

12 muffins

Blueberry Muffins

Preheat oven to 400°. Mix dry ingredients together in a bowl. In a separate bowl, beat eggs, then add milk, oil, honey, and vanilla. Beat well. Add dry ingredients and stir. Add blueberries. Stir just enough to moisten; do not overmix.

Fill buttered muffin tins ⅔ full. Bake 20 minutes.

12 muffins

2 cups whole wheat pastry flour

¾ cup unbleached white flour

1 tablespoon baking powder

½ teaspoon salt

2 eggs

1 cup milk

½ cup sunflower oil

½ cup honey

½ teaspoon vanilla extract

1½ cups blueberries, fresh or frozen

Fresh Grape Walnut Muffins

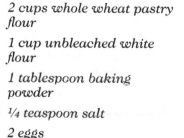

*N*ot to be confused with Grape-Nuts cereal, these are delightfully fresh and moist muffins with an occasional crunch of walnuts mixed in.

Preheat oven to 375°. Mix dry ingredients in medium-sized bowl. Beat eggs in another medium-sized bowl; add rest of liquid ingredients. Stir dry ingredients into wet. Don't overstir. Add nuts and grapes. Pour approximately ½ cup mix per muffin into oiled tin. Bake 20 minutes until golden brown.

12 muffins

2 cups whole wheat pastry flour

1 cup unbleached white flour

1 tablespoon baking powder

¼ teaspoon salt

2 eggs

¾ cup honey

1¼ cups milk

½ cup sunflower oil

¾ cup chopped walnuts

1½ cups fresh green seedless grapes, cut in half

Carrot Walnut Raisin Muffins

2 cups whole wheat pastry flour

½ cup unbleached white flour

2 teaspoons baking powder

¼ teaspoon salt

2 eggs, beaten

1 cup milk

⅓ cup sunflower oil

½ cup honey

1¼ cups grated carrots

½ cup chopped walnuts

½ cup raisins

Preheat oven to 400°. Combine flours, baking powder, and salt in a medium-sized bowl. Mix eggs, milk, oil, and honey together. Combine wet ingredients with dry. Fold in carrots, walnuts, and raisins. Spoon approximately ½ cup mixture for each muffin into oiled muffin tins. Place immediately in oven. Bake 20 minutes until lightly browned on top.

12 muffins

Pineapple Muffins

½ cup butter, softened

¾ cup honey

2 eggs, beaten

1 teaspoon vanilla extract

1 cup unsweetened pineapple juice

2 cups whole wheat pastry flour

¾ cup unbleached white flour

1 tablespoon baking powder

¼ teaspoon baking soda

½ teaspoon salt

1 cup finely chopped fresh pineapple

Preheat oven to 400°. Oil muffin tins. In medium-sized bowl, beat butter and honey together until creamy. Add eggs and vanilla and mix; then add pineapple juice. In separate medium-sized bowl, combine the dry ingredients. Mix the wet ingredients with the dry until just moist. Gently stir in the fresh pineapple. Put approximately ½ cup mix into each tin. Bake 20 minutes until golden brown.

12 muffins

Maple Walnut Buttermilk Muffins

Preheat oven to 400°. In medium-sized bowl, mix together flours, baking powder, soda, salt, and cinnamon.

In separate medium-sized bowl, beat eggs. Add buttermilk, maple syrup, and oil; stir well. Combine wet with dry ingredients. Add walnuts and stir just enough to moisten. Put approximately ½ cup batter into each oiled muffin tin. Sprinkle the reserved 1 tablespoon walnuts on the muffins and bake 20 minutes until browned.

12 muffins

2 cups whole wheat pastry flour

½ cup unbleached white flour

2 teaspoons baking powder

1 teaspoon baking soda

½ teaspoon salt

1 teaspoon cinnamon

3 eggs

1 cup buttermilk

½ cup maple syrup

½ cup sunflower oil

½ cup chopped walnuts (reserve 1 tablespoon)

Poppy Seed Muffins

Preheat oven to 375°. Heat poppy seeds and 1⅓ cups milk, bringing to a boil. Let cool 20 minutes. Combine cooled poppy seed mixture with other liquids, including remaining ⅓ cup milk and eggs. In a large bowl, combine the flours, salt, and baking powder. Add the liquid ingredients to dry ingredients. Stir until just moist. Fill buttered muffin tins ⅔ full. Bake 20 minutes.

12 muffins

1 cup poppy seeds

1⅔ cups milk

⅔ cup honey

⅔ cup sunflower oil

2 eggs

2 cups whole wheat pastry flour

1 cup unbleached white flour

½ teaspoon salt

4 teaspoons baking powder

About Sourdough
English Muffins

These are quite delicious and relatively easy to make, though time-consuming. The process takes 2 days, but the first day requires only a few minutes' time. The second day the muffin dough must rise twice before being cooked.

At the café we bake our English muffins on a large 3-burner grill. At home I use a cast-iron griddle that sits over 2 burners. If you don't have one of these, a large, thick, cast-iron fry pan will be the best substitute.

Sourdough starter can be bought commercially, though you might have to look around a bit or special-order it. The sourdough that the café uses was taken from a culture that Upland Bakers in Marshfield, Vermont, gave us. They are a sourdough bread bakery and bake all of their bread in a wood-fired oven. It is exceptionally good. If you have a friend who has a starter going that you can begin your starter from, so much the better.

A starter will continue to be good as long as you use it around once a week and feed it after you have taken some of it out. We feed our starter 1 cup of water and 1 cup of unbleached white flour every time we use some. This keeps the natural yeast bacteria alive by giving it something to eat. A smaller amount of starter will eat less; ¼ cup each of flour and water should be enough.

Jules Rabin of Upland Bakers told me that bread has been baked for over 1,000 years using the sourdough method, while baker's yeast is a relatively new process only in existence for around 100 years.

Sourdough English Muffins

This mixture of flour, milk, and starter needs to rise overnight in the warm air. The mixture will actually absorb additional yeast particles from the air. The next day it will have a spongy texture.

Mix all the sponge ingredients together and beat for 100 strokes. Cover. Leave this mixture out overnight if the room is cool (wintertime) or refrigerate it after a few hours if the air is warm.

The next day stir the baking soda, powder, salt, and honey directly into the sponge mix. Allow it to sit for 3 minutes or so until it begins to rise and bubble. Stir in enough flour (approximately 1½ cups) to make a non-sticky dough. Then move it to a floured breadboard and knead in the remaining flour until smooth, adding additional flour if necessary to keep dough from being sticky. Cover this dough and allow it to rise for ½ hour.

Now roll the dough out on a lightly floured board to ½-inch thickness. Cut rounds 3½ inches in diameter (try to find a lid or jar of about this dimension). You will need to re-roll the dough a few times, as your piece of dough slowly shrinks when the circles are cut out of it.

Oil 2 cookie sheets, then sprinkle with the cornmeal. Lay the circles of dough out on the cookie sheets. Cover with towels and allow to rise for 1 hour.

Preheat a cast-iron griddle or pan (do not oil it) over low heat. Set as many muffins as will fit without touching on the griddle or pan. Allow them to bake undisturbed until they have begun to brown nicely. This should take around 10 minutes, depending on the position of the muffins to the heat. Now turn the muffins over and bake until the other sides brown. They should cook slightly faster than the first sides. When browned, place on racks to cool and cook the remaining muffins.

Cinnamon Raisin English Muffins. Add ½ cup raisins (that have been soaked in ½ cup boiling water for 15 minutes and drained) and 1 tablespoon cinnamon before the flour is added to the sponge.

15 muffins

First day. The sponge:

¾ cup sourdough starter (after removing the starter you will be using, feed the remaining starter with ½ cup water and ½ cup unbleached flour)

1½ cups milk

1½ cups whole wheat bread flour

¾ cup unbleached white flour

Second day. The dough:

1½ teaspoons baking soda

1½ teaspoons baking powder

1½ teaspoons salt

1½ tablespoons honey

2 cups unbleached white flour, or as needed

1 tablespoon sunflower oil

2 tablespoons cornmeal

Sweet Breads

Apple Bread

½ cup butter, softened

⅔ cup honey

2 eggs

2 cups whole wheat pastry flour

¼ teaspoon salt

1½ teaspoons baking powder

2 tablespoons milk

¾ cup chopped walnuts or pecans

2½ cups coarsely chopped unpeeled apples

Cream butter and honey. Add eggs, then flour, salt, baking powder, and milk, adding nuts and apples last, and mix well. Pour into oiled 9 × 5-inch loaf pan. Bake 1 hour at 350° or until golden and toothpick comes out clean. Cool for 10 minutes in pan, then use a knife around edges to loosen before removing from pan.

8 servings

Cranberry Bread

1½ cups unbleached white flour

1½ cups whole wheat pastry flour

1 teaspoon baking powder

½ teaspoon salt

2 eggs

¾ cup honey

¼ cup butter, melted

¾ cup milk

½ cup orange juice

1¼ cups chopped raw cranberries

¾ cup chopped walnuts

The cranberry and orange juice combination gives this bread just the right amount of tartness. The red berries make it festive for the Christmas holidays.

Mix dry ingredients together. Beat eggs in separate bowl; add honey and melted butter, then milk and orange juice. Mix dry and wet ingredients together. Fold in berries and nuts. Pour into oiled 9 × 5-inch loaf pan. Bake 1 hour at 325°. Cool in pan for at least 10 minutes. Loosen around edges of pan with a knife before removing.

8 servings

Blueberry Nut Bread

Butter and flour 9 × 5-inch loaf pan. Wash berries and dry well. Preheat oven to 350°. Mix flours in bowl. Remove 1 teaspoon flour and toss with berries. Add salt, baking powder, and soda to remaining flour. In a large bowl with an electric mixer, beat egg and honey, then beat in butter and orange juice. On low speed, add dry ingredients. Remove mixer. Fold in orange peel, nuts, and blueberries. Pour batter into loaf pan. Bake 1 hour until toothpick comes out dry. Bread will crack on top, showing off its berries. Let cool 10 minutes in pan, but no longer, and remove from pan after loosening the edges with a knife.

8 servings

1¼ cups blueberries, fresh or frozen

1 cup whole wheat pastry flour

1 cup unbleached white flour

¼ teaspoon salt

1½ teaspoons baking powder

½ teaspoon baking soda

1 egg

¾ cup honey

2 tablespoons butter, melted

¾ cup orange juice

2 tablespoons grated orange peel

1 cup chopped walnuts

Breads

Raisin Bread

3 cups warm water

2 tablespoons dry baker's yeast

2 tablespoons honey

6 to 6½ cups whole wheat bread flour

2 tablespoons sunflower oil

2 teaspoons cinnamon

1 tablespoon salt

2 cups raisins

1 tablespoon butter, melted

In a large mixing bowl, combine the water with the yeast and honey. Stir and allow to dissolve for 5 minutes. When yeast begins to foam, add 3 cups flour to form a moist sponge and stir in well. Cover with a towel and set aside in warm place for 1 hour or until doubled in size.

Add the oil, cinnamon, salt and raisins to dough, and mix in. Add 3 cups more flour and knead dough about 10 minutes or until smooth and elastic, adding more flour as needed to keep it from sticking.

Divide dough in half, form into loaves, and set in oiled 9 × 5-inch loaf pans. Cover and allow to rise for 1 hour. Preheat oven to 375° after bread has risen in pans for 30 minutes.

Bake 50 minutes, or until bread is golden on top. Remove bread from pans and knock on the bottom of the loaf; if the bread sounds hollow in the center, it is done. Brush tops of bread with melted butter.

2 loaves

Whole Wheat Bread. Cut back honey to 1 tablespoon. Omit cinnamon and raisins.

Chapatis

Chapatis are a flat bread that originated in India. At the café we make a whole wheat version and serve them stuffed with various fillings. If you have an electric stove you will have difficulty in getting the chapatis to puff up on your coils. An open flame is the secret to cooking the insides while keeping the chapati soft and flexible.

These freeze well when wrapped tightly in plastic wrap. They thaw out quickly.

2½ cups whole wheat bread flour

2½ cups whole wheat pastry flour (more if needed)

½ teaspoon sea salt

2 cups cold water

Mix 2 cups whole wheat bread flour, 2 cups whole wheat pastry flour, and the salt with the water. Add more flour (another ½ cup or so), beating with a wooden spoon until dough is smooth and elastic. Put onto floured board and knead for a few minutes. Let dough rest for 5 minutes and knead again, adding flour as needed. The dough consistency should feel like an ear lobe when you pinch it. Pinch pieces off and roll these into 15 balls about the size of a lime or small lemon. Dip each ball into flour and set on the board, flour side down. When all the dough is used up, roll out each ball, rolling from the center out to form a circle about ⅛ inch thick. Use additional flour when needed to keep chapatis from sticking to board— be liberal with it!

When all chapatis are rolled out, heat a griddle or cast-iron pan on medium heat. When hot, put a chapati into pan or griddle. Cook for 1 to 2 minutes on one side and about 1 minute on the other until it forms little bubbles but is still soft, not stiff. Then set over the stove burner on an open flame on low to medium heat. (The chapati should sit on top of the stove burner.) Let the chapati sit on burner for a minute and flip. Allow it to fill with hot air. A perfect chapati will puff up like a balloon. Using tongs, pull off heat and stack hot chapatis on top of one another. They'll stay hot for a while this way. To cool, spread out and allow steam to rise. Don't allow chapatis to sit longer than 10 minutes after cooking or they will dry out. Wrap them well in a plastic bag or plastic wrap and they'll last for days refrigerated. Or freeze some and pull out a few hours before needed. Delicious with curry, or make a sandwich with them.

15 chapatis

Bedouin Bread

1 tablespoon dry baker's yeast

1 tablespoon honey

1¼ cups warm water

3½ cups mixed flour (combine several flours in any proportions: for example, 2 cups whole wheat, ¾ cup rye, ¼ cup rice, ½ cup whole wheat pastry or soy)

2 teaspoons salt

Friends traveling in Morocco came back and shared this recipe with me. Serve Bedouin Bread hot from the oven with a hearty bowl of soup and a green salad for a simple but wonderful dinner.

Dissolve yeast and honey in water; let sit 5 minutes. then mix the flour and salt into yeast mixture.

Knead the dough on a floured board. Cut into 8 pieces. Shape into rounds and roll until about 5 inches across and ¼ inch thick. Put on lightly greased cookie sheet. Cover with damp towel and let rise in warm place for 1 to 2 hours, or until ½ to ¾ inch thick. Preheat oven to 500° one-half hour before baking the bread. Bake 5 to 8 minutes at 500° until done. These breads should be served warm with butter.

8 servings

Corn Bread

1 cup cornmeal

1 cup flour (½ cup whole wheat pastry, ½ cup unbleached white, or your choice)

5 teaspoons baking powder

¼ teaspoon salt

2 tablespoons sunflower oil

1¼ cups water

2 tablespoons blackstrap molasses

1 teaspoon poppy seeds

Butter

Tahini

This is a nondairy recipe that I worked up for friends who were trying to exclude dairy products from their diet. This bread is especially good hot from the oven. Serve it with split pea soup for a simple but delicious meal.

In separate bowls, mix together dry ingredients (cornmeal, flour, baking powder, and salt) and wet ingredients (oil, water, and molasses). Then stir together until moist, adding a bit more water if needed to make a smooth consistency. Pour into 10-inch oiled pie plate and sprinkle top with poppy seeds. Bake 20 minutes at 400°. Delicious served warm with butter or tahini.

6 servings

Breakfast Drinks

I tried to find a coffee substitute a few years ago when I stopped drinking coffee. Nothing could really compare or compete with the richness of coffee beans which had been a part of my morning routine.

However, after my withdrawal symptoms cleared I was able to start enjoying other hot breakfast drinks. There are some mixes of ground barley, chicory, and rye roots that can be quite delicious when made with boiling water or hot milk, especially with a dash of cinnamon on top. A mug of hot apple cider with a cinnamon stick is also a treat on a cold morning. And the variety of herb teas is constantly increasing. Hot Cocoa and Hot Carob mixes with milk are great drinks for children and adults alike.

But if you are hooked on coffee and have no plans of giving it up, try experimenting with different blends of coffee beans if you haven't already. French roast beans are very strong and should be mixed with other beans in a 1 to 4 proportion. Special blends on the market now include roasted almonds in with beans, as well as chocolate, mint, and more. Organic coffee beans are now also available along with a large variety of decaffeinated beans. Try making your coffee with milk instead of water. The milk makes the coffee deliciously rich and it also takes away some of the acidic quality of the coffee.

Combinations of juice and sparkling water or champagne can make a brunch with friends extra special. Pour equal portions of orange juice and champagne together for a Mimosa and garnish with fresh strawberry slices. Or try mixing 1 quart orange juice in a blender with ice cubes and ½ pint heavy cream for a frothy, creamy drink. Grape juice, orange juice, and sparkling water combined in equal amounts make a refreshing drink called a We-Drink-It at the café.

Another drink option is mixing fresh fruits, yogurt, ice cubes, and protein powder into a fruit smoothie using a blender. These drinks can be filling enough to be a meal in themselves if you include too many rich ingredients like bananas, milk, yogurt, or ice cream, so be careful, and have fun experimenting.

Hot Carob Mix

¾ *cup hot water*

½ *cup carob powder*

1 *cup milk powder (noninstant)*

½ *teaspoon cinnamon*

½ *cup honey*

Whipped cream (optional)

Hot Carob Mix is a delicious noncaffeine option to hot cocoa. The mix will hold for many weeks in the refrigerator, and is a treat to have on a wintry cold day.

In a blender, combine hot water, carob powder, milk powder, cinnamon, and honey. Run until smooth, turn off blender and scrape any powder off sides of blender into mix. Blend again. Cover and store in the refrigerator. Use 3 tablespoons mix per cup of hot carob. Heat 1 cup water or milk for each serving and blend with the mix. Top with whipped cream if using water.

2 cups (10 servings)

Hot Cocoa Mix

1 *cup hot water*

½ *cup cocoa powder*

1½ *cups milk powder (noninstant)*

½ *cup honey*

Whipped cream (optional)

In a blender, mix all the ingredients together. Run until smooth. Turn off blender, scrape insides, and blend again.

To make a cup of hot cocoa, put 3 tablespoons cocoa mix in a cup. Add 1 cup hot water or hot milk for each serving. Top with whipped cream if using water to make cocoa richer. The mix will hold for weeks in the refrigerator.

2 cups (10 servings)

Mocha Coffee. Add 1 cup hot coffee instead of water. Top with whipped cream and a few chocolate shavings.

Soups

Soups, page 76

Butternut Bevy

Creamy Ginger Harvest
Vegetable Soup

Hubbard Vegetable
Bisque

Mushroom Barley Soup

Mushroom Bisque

Potato Cauliflower Soup

Mushroom Rice Soup

Potato Mushroom Soup

Potato Cheddar Soup

Corn and Cheese
Chowder

Potato Leek Soup

Tomato Corn Chowder

Tomato Barley Soup

Alphabet Vegetable Soup

Russian Tomato
Cabbage Soup

Creamy Tomato Soup

Creamy Broccoli Soup

Cream of Spinach Soup

Creamy Green Bean
Soup

Asparagus Medley Soup

Primavera Soup

Spinach Leek Neufchâtel
Soup

Miso Vegetable Soup

Oriental Bean Thread
Soup

Chili

Black Bean Soup

Butternut White Bean
Ginger Soup

Indian Split Pea Soup

Canadian Split Pea
Soup

Split Pea Vegetable Soup

Lentil Vegetable Soup

Garden Bean Soup

Gypsy Vegetable Stew

Chilled or Hot Potato
Zucchini Soup

Chilled Avocado
Cucumber Soup

Chilled Spicy Tomato
Avocado Soup

Chilled Fruit Soup

Chilled Summer
Strawberry Melon
Soup

Chilled Peachy Keen
Soup

We take special care in preparing soups at the café, making them well seasoned, thick, and hearty. Soups are started first thing in the morning, and few shortcuts are taken. Hours of effort have been devoted to determining the best combinations of vegetables, grains, legumes, and herbs. We have created the following soup recipes, which have been eaten and enjoyed by multitudes of our customers.

Selecting a soup recipe is determined by the season and what we have on hand in the café's cooler. In the winter months, legumes and root crops are favored because they store well and are relatively inexpensive. Potatoes, winter squash, onions, and carrots can be combined to become Butternut White Bean Ginger Soup, Creamy Ginger Harvest Vegetable, Potato Cheddar, or Hubbard Vegetable Bisque. In springtime we might choose Asparagus Medley, Potato Leek, or Primavera Soup with fresh fiddleheads. On a hot, muggy summer's day, a chilled soup can be a cool, quick, and refreshing alternative. Garden vegetables and fruits can be combined to make Chilled Potato Zucchini Soup, Strawberry Melon, or Avocado Cucumber Soup. Fall is harvest time for local growers, and soups are made with freshly picked corn, cauliflower, broccoli, spinach, and green beans.

A bowl of soup can be a meal in itself. Serve it with some crusty bread and perhaps a green salad. Prepare a hearty soup like Chili, topped with cheddar cheese, Garden Bean, Gypsy Vegetable Stew, Alphabet Vegetable, or Black Bean with sour cream on top when the soup is to be the main course of the meal. If the soup will be served as an appetizer, choose a lighter soup like Creamy Broccoli, Creamy Tomato, Creamy Green Bean, or Miso Vegetable.

All of the soup recipes typically produce six to eight servings. If your household is small, try cutting the recipe in half rather than eating the same soup every day for a week.

Leftover bean soups such as split pea, black bean,

lentil, white bean, or chili can be frozen. Cool them down to room temperature and leave one quarter of the space in your container empty for expansion. Plastic containers with tight-fitting lids are best to use, as glass ones can crack.

In many cases the flavor of soup is even better the second day, which is good reason to make a large amount initially. When refrigerating a soup, choose a stainless steel pot rather than aluminum, which will affect the flavor. Once it is cooled you can store it in a plastic container as well. To reheat soup, warm it over very low heat or in a double boiler. Stir the soup frequently to keep it from sticking and scorching. Be cautious when reheating bean and starchy soups containing rice, potatoes, barley, or pasta. They burn easily, which ruins their taste. Don't cover a cream soup when reheating it. Overheating separates the milk and requires reblending to restore the damaged appearance.

Soup Stocks

At the café we save our vegetable ends and peelings for soup stock. A stock can add extra flavor as well as nutrients to your broth. This is particularly helpful to basic vegetable soups like miso, broccoli, or spinach, which tend to have a light and thin consistency. Beans themselves, however, predominate a soup's flavor and thicken it sufficiently.

Prepared soup stock is sold in stores and many now carry vegetarian stock as well as beef and chicken. But this is more expensive and less satisfying than making your own.

To make a stock, save the typically unwanted parts of your vegetables, the carrot ends and peelings, broccoli stems, onion skins, celery leaves, pea pods and ends, zucchini and mushroom ends, parsley and spinach stems, etc. Old, limp vegetables that would otherwise get thrown out are a fine addition to soup stock.

Certain vegetables, however, can discolor a stock or add a bitter taste. Do not use red cabbage leaves, beets, dirty, moldy, or rotten vegetables, or too much of one variety. Water from steaming or boiling vegetables can be saved for a stock. But don't use water that beans have been cooked in, as it causes flatulence.

During preparation, use enough water to cover your vegetables (one quart is usually sufficient). The stock should be brought to a boil and simmered for twenty minutes in a covered pot. Overcooking can create a bitter taste, which a tablespoonful of honey can sometimes correct. Drain vegetables from water and your stock is ready to use or freeze.

A small amount of vegetable scraps can be saved in plastic bags in the freezer and added to until a sufficient quantity is available to make a stock. About four cups of vegetables are needed. The frozen stock vegetables can be added directly to boiling water, increasing the cooking time of the stock by five minutes.

Butternut Bevy

6 cups peeled and cubed
butternut squash (1
medium squash)

5 cups water or stock

2 tablespoons sunflower oil

2 cups chopped onion (4
onions)

1 teaspoon dried leaf thyme

4 tablespoons butter

⅓ cup unbleached white
flour

¾ cup heavy cream

½ teaspoon ground ginger

1 teaspoon salt

1 tablespoon tamari

Black pepper to taste

½ cup sliced or chopped
roasted almonds

*W*inter squashes are inexpensive, easy to grow,
and store well into spring if kept in a cool, dry
place. Butternut squashes are a favorite for soup at the
café particularly because of their deep golden color
and rich flavor.

Combine squash and water or stock in 4-quart soup
pot. Bring to a boil, then lower heat, cover, and cook
until tender (approximately 25 minutes). Meanwhile,
heat oil in fry pan and sauté the onions and thyme until
tender and lightly browned. Add to squash. Puree the
squash and onions in blender until almost smooth, leaving a few chunks. Return to soup pot.

In the fry pan, melt the butter over low heat, add the
flour, and stir 1 to 2 minutes until well mixed and lightly
browned. Add cream and mix with a whisk until blended.
Add to the soup, then return the soup to a simmer. Add
ginger, salt, tamari, and pepper. Simmer 15 minutes uncovered and serve, garnished with almonds.

6 to 8 servings

Creamy Ginger Harvest Vegetable Soup

Known *to soup cooks at the café as I Hate Turnip Soup. Many people who loathe turnips are surprised to learn of their presence after enjoying a bowl of this soup. A wonderful soup to make in the fall as gardens are being harvested.*

Bring 4 cups water or stock to a boil in a 4-quart soup pot. Add squash, turnip, cauliflower, cabbage, and celery. Cook on medium heat covered until tender (approximately 30 minutes). Turn off heat.

In a 1-quart saucepan, melt butter. Add flour, garlic, and ginger. Cook 5 minutes on low heat until garlic is lightly browned, stirring occasionally. Turn off heat, add cream, and stir well with a whisk. Add 1 cup milk to cream mixture, then add cream mixture to soup. Add parsley, salt, pepper, and remaining 1 cup milk to soup. Simmer 15 minutes more uncovered and serve.

8 servings

4 cups water or stock

3 cups peeled and cubed butternut or Hubbard squash

1 cup peeled and cubed turnip

1 cup chopped cauliflower

1 cup chopped green cabbage

1 cup sliced celery

2 tablespoons butter

2 tablespoons unbleached white flour

1 tablespoon minced garlic (4 to 5 large cloves)

1 tablespoon peeled and minced fresh ginger root (1 walnut-sized piece)

1 cup heavy cream

2 cups milk

½ cup minced fresh parsley

1 teaspoon salt

Dash of black pepper

Hubbard Vegetable Bisque

5 cups water or stock

6 cups peeled and cubed Hubbard squash

5 tablespoons butter

1 cup diced onion (2 onions)

2 cups chopped broccoli, stems and florets

4 cloves garlic, minced (1 tablespoon)

1 teaspoon leaf thyme

1 teaspoon basil

1½ cups sliced mushrooms

1 cup chopped kale or spinach

4 tablespoons unbleached white flour

1 cup heavy cream

1 teaspoon salt

Dash of black pepper or to taste

*A*nother wonderful winter soup which can mainly be supplied from a garden's harvest. Hubbard squashes are known for their outlandish sizes, though baby Hubbards are now becoming available. In stores, Hubbards are often found cut up into smaller, more manageable sizes. The extra squash puree freezes well. Hubbard squash can replace pumpkin in a pie quite deliciously.

Bring water or stock to boil in a 4-quart soup pot. Add squash and cook on medium heat, covered, until nice and tender (approximately 20 minutes).

Melt 1 tablespoon butter in a 10-inch fry pan and sauté onions and broccoli with garlic, thyme, and basil over medium heat. When onions begin to brown and become tender, add mushrooms and cook a few minutes more. Set aside.

Puree squash in blender or food processor, leaving just a few chunks. Return to soup pot. Add the sautéed vegetables to pureed soup, along with kale or spinach, and simmer uncovered.

In same fry pan in which you sautéed the vegetables (no need to wash it), add the remaining 4 tablespoons butter and melt on low heat. When melted, add flour and cook on very low heat, stirring occasionally, for a few minutes. Slowly add cream, stirring well with a whisk. Then add the mixture to soup. Continue to simmer for 10 minutes or more. Add salt and pepper and serve.

8 servings

Mushroom Barley Soup

This is a thick and hearty soup, wonderful with or without the sour cream.

Combine barley and boiling water or stock in a 4-quart soup pot. Cover and simmer until tender, about 40 minutes.

In large cast-iron fry pan, heat the oil and sauté the onions, carrots, and dill weed. A few minutes later, add the celery. When browned and cooked nicely, add to soup pot. Sauté mushrooms in same fry pan quickly on high heat until lightly cooked, then add to soup pot. Let simmer 30 minutes covered. Add salt, pepper, tamari, and more water or stock as needed. The barley or rice will continue to absorb water, making the soup thick. Before serving, add parsley.

To add a creamy taste to mushroom barley soup, mix the flour with the sour cream. Stir until thick. Add slowly to soup on low heat and serve.

8 servings

Mushroom Rice Soup. Substitute 1 cup raw brown rice (2 cups cooked) for the barley and proceed with the recipe.

1 cup raw barley (2 cups cooked)

6 cups boiling water or stock (more as needed)

2 tablespoons sunflower oil

2 cups chopped onion

2 cups sliced carrots (2 carrots)

1 tablespoon dried dill weed

1½ cups sliced celery (2 stalks)

4 cups sliced mushrooms

1 teaspoon salt

Black pepper or cayenne pepper to taste

1 tablespoon tamari

½ cup minced fresh parsley

⅓ cup unbleached white flour (optional)

1 cup sour cream (optional)

Mushroom Bisque

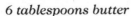

6 tablespoons butter

1 cup chopped onion (2 onions)

2 cups chopped celery (1½ to 2 stalks, with greens)

2 teaspoons dried dill weed or 3 tablespoons minced fresh dill weed

2 cups finely chopped spinach

4 cups sliced mushrooms

5 cups milk

4 tablespoons unbleached white flour

1 cup water

½ teaspoon salt

Dash of black pepper

1 teaspoon tamari

Mushroom soup is always a big seller at the café, and this is quick and easy to prepare, as well as delicious. If fresh dill weed is available, use it for an especially tasty soup.

In a 3-quart soup pot melt 2 tablespoons butter and sauté onions, celery, and dill weed over medium heat. When the onions begin to brown (about 10 minutes), add spinach and mushrooms and sauté until tender (approximately 3 to 5 minutes more). Add 4 cups milk and simmer on low flame, uncovered. Meanwhile, melt the remaining 4 tablespoons butter in small pan. Add flour and stir until smooth. Add remaining 1 cup milk stirring with a whisk, then add to soup along with water. Add salt, pepper, and tamari. Simmer 10 minutes more and serve.

6 servings

Potato Cauliflower Soup

Potato soups are always popular at the café, and
inexpensive to make. The potatoes add a smooth
and creamy consistency when pureed. For those avoid-
ing dairy products, simply omit the cream and flour
step of the recipe.

In a 4-quart soup pot, heat the oil and sauté the onions, dill weed, and thyme until tender and beginning to
brown. Add cauliflower and cook a few minutes more.
Add stock or water and potatoes. Cover and cook on medium heat until tender (approximately 30 minutes). Remove from heat, and in a blender puree approximately
half the soup (or 6 cups), 2 cups at a time. Return puree
to soup pot. Simmer on lowest heat, and add bay leaves,
salt, pepper, and tamari. Cook approximately 20 minutes
more uncovered, stirring occasionally.

Mix cream with flour and stir to smooth out lumps.
Turn off heat and add to soup along with parsley. Check
seasoning. Thin with water or milk if the soup has gotten
too thick after sitting. Reheat if necessary and serve.

8 servings

Potato Mushroom Soup. Substitute 5 cups sliced
mushrooms and 1½ cups celery for the cauliflower.
Sauté the celery with the onions. Sauté the mushrooms
separately and set aside, adding to soup after the other
vegetables have been pureed in blender.

3 tablespoons oil

*2 cups chopped onion (4
onions)*

2 teaspoons dried dill weed

1 teasoon dried leaf thyme

*1 medium head
cauliflower, sliced*

6 cups stock or water

*4 cups diced unpeeled
potatoes (4 medium
potatoes)*

4 bay leaves

1 teaspoon salt

¼ teaspoon black pepper

1 tablespoon tamari

1 cup heavy cream

*4 tablespoons unbleached
white flour*

*½ cup minced fresh
parsley*

Potato Cheddar Soup

4 cups water

4 cups diced unpeeled potatoes (4 medium potatoes)

1 cup chopped onion (2 onions)

1 cup sliced celery

1½ teaspoons salt

¼ cup butter

2 cups grated sharp cheddar cheese

2 tablespoons unbleached white flour

2 cups milk

⅛ teaspoon black pepper

½ teaspoon powdered mustard

¼ cup minced fresh parsley

¼ teaspoon dried dill weed

½ teaspoon celery seed

1 cup chopped tomatoes, canned or fresh

A Vermont tradition for a snowy day. The vegetables are commonly on hand throughout the winter, and the sharp Vermont cheddar cheese zests the soup up nicely.

Bring water to boil in a 3-quart soup pot. Add potatoes, onions, celery, and salt. Cook 15 minutes, covered, over medium heat.

In separate 2-quart saucepan, melt butter over low heat. Slowly add cheese, then stir in flour. Slowly add the milk, spices, and herbs to cheese mix, stirring with a whisk. Add cheese mix to potatoes, then add tomatoes and stir. Simmer on very low heat 15 minutes more, uncovered. This will burn easily, so stir often. It's worth the caution!

6 to 8 servings

Corn and Cheese Chowder

I*made this soup on the Horn of the Moon Café's opening day. It couldn't have been more popular, and it still is. Now on our anniversary we make a huge pot of chowder and sell it at the old opening day price of 50¢ a cup and 90¢ a bowl.*

Combine potatoes, water or stock, and bay leaves in a 3-quart soup pot. Bring to a boil and simmer, covered, until tender. Meanwhile, melt the butter in a fry pan and sauté the onions with cumin until brown. Add to soup, then add corn. Mix flour with cream until smooth, then add slowly to soup. Add grated cheese, about ½ cup at a time, and stir until melted. Keep heat low and watch bottom of pot. When all the cheese is melted in, add chives and parsley, season with salt and pepper, and serve.

6 to 8 servings

4 large unpeeled potatoes, diced

4 cups water or stock

2 to 3 bay leaves

1 tablespoon butter

1 cup chopped onion (2 onions)

1 teaspoon cumin seed

3 cups corn kernels, fresh or frozen

2 tablespoons unbleached white flour

1 cup heavy cream

2 cups grated cheese (combination of Monterey Jack and cheddar, or your favorites)

1 tablespoon chopped fresh chives

½ cup minced fresh parsley

1 teaspoon salt

Dash of black pepper

Potato Leek Soup

6 cups water or stock

6 cups diced potatoes (5 medium to large potatoes)

4 tablespoons butter

2 cups thinly sliced leeks (3 large leeks) (wash well and don't use the very upper tough tops)

1 cup chopped celery

1 teaspoon dried leaf thyme

1½ teaspoons dried dill weed

1 teaspoon salt

Black pepper to taste

2 tablespoons unbleached white flour

1 cup heavy cream

½ cup minced fresh parsley

The first time I made this soup was in springtime after I went gathering wild leeks with my friend's mother, Priscilla. Priscilla knows the woods behind her family farm well and named many of the plants and wild edibles as we walked. The soup that I made later in the day was eaten with relish by all.

Cultivated leeks are much larger than the wild variety and typically contain much grit and sand in their leaves, so wash them well before using.

Bring water or stock to a boil in soup pot. Add potatoes. (Only if you desire white, white soup should you peel the potatoes—I don't bother!) Cover and cook until tender (20 to 25 minutes). Turn off heat and puree ¾ of the potatoes in blender. Pour back into soup pot.

In a 10-inch fry pan, melt 2 tablespoons butter and sauté the leeks, celery, thyme, and dill weed until the leeks are well coated with butter. Cover and cook on low heat until the leeks are tender (10 to 15 minutes). Add to the potatoes along with salt and pepper. In the same pan in which the leeks were sautéed, melt the remaining 2 tablespoons butter, then add the flour. Brown for 1 minute on low heat. Whisk in cream and turn off heat. Add to the soup, then add parsley. Simmer 10 to 15 minutes, uncovered, and serve. If you allow the soup to sit before serving, you will need to thin it with some water or milk.

8 servings

Tomato Corn Chowder

Fresh corn makes for an especially tasty soup.

In a 3-quart soup pot, heat the oil and sauté the onions with the oregano and thyme over medium heat until browned. Add the canned and fresh tomatoes, then the water. Lower the heat and simmer 30 minutes covered, stirring occasionally. Mix flour and cream together in bowl until smooth. Stir a little soup (about a ladle's worth) into the cream. Stir in another ladle of soup, then add the mixture to the soup. Simmer on very low heat, adding corn, parsley, salt, and pepper. Simmer 15 minutes uncovered and serve. Garnish with freshly grated cheddar cheese on top if you like.

6 servings

2 tablespoons sunflower oil

1½ cups chopped onion (3 onions)

1 teaspoon oregano

1 teaspoon dried leaf thyme

One 28-ounce can crushed tomatoes

2 cups diced fresh tomatoes (3 medium tomatoes)

4 cups water

¼ cup unbleached white flour

1 cup heavy cream

2 cups corn kernels, fresh or frozen

¼ cup minced fresh parsley

½ teaspoon salt

White pepper to taste

Freshly grated cheddar cheese

Tomato Barley Soup

6 cups water

1 cup uncooked barley

2 tablespoons sunflower oil

1 cup chopped onion (2 onions)

4 large cloves garlic, minced

¾ cup coarsely chopped carrot

1 teaspoon basil

½ teaspoon tarragon

2 cups chopped broccoli, stems and florets

One 28-ounce can whole tomatoes in tomato juice, chopped

2 cups tomato juice

½ teaspoon salt

Black pepper to taste

In a 4-quart soup pot bring water to a boil. Add barley, lower heat to a simmer, cover, and cook until barley is tender (approximately 1 hour). Add oil to 10-inch fry pan and set over medium heat. When oil is hot, add onions, garlic, carrots, basil, and tarragon. When onions begin to brown, add broccoli and cook until just tender. Add vegetables to cooked barley along with chopped tomatoes in juice plus the additional 2 cups tomato juice. Cook 30 minutes more, covered, stirring occasionally. Add salt and pepper, stir well, and serve.

8 servings

Alphabet Vegetable Soup

Bring water or stock to a boil in a 3-quart soup pot over medium heat. Add potatoes, carrots, and bay leaves and cover. Cook until potatoes are just tender, then lower heat to a simmer.

Set 10-inch fry pan over medium heat; add oil, then onion, celery, and basil. After 2 minutes add green peppers and sauté until tender; do not overcook. Add onion mixture, corn, lima beans and tomatoes to soup.

In separate saucepan bring 2 cups water to a boil. Add alphabet noodles and cook until just tender (approximately 5 minutes). Add to soup along with salt, pepper, and honey. Cook 5 minutes more and serve.

8 servings

4 cups water or soup stock

1 cup chopped unpeeled potatoes (1 potato)

¾ cup diced carrot

2 bay leaves

1 tablespoon sunflower oil

¾ cup diced onion (1 to 2 onions)

¾ cup chopped celery

1 teaspoon basil

½ cup diced green pepper (1 small pepper)

1 cup corn kernels, fresh or frozen

1 cup frozen lima beans

One 15-ounce can whole tomatoes, coarsely chopped, and juice, or 2 cups chopped fresh tomatoes

2 cups water

¾ cup alphabet noodles

½ teaspoon salt

Dash of black pepper

½ teaspoon honey

Russian Tomato Cabbage Soup

1 cup chopped onion (2 onions)

1 teaspoon tarragon

1 teaspoon dried dill weed or 1 tablespoon chopped fresh dill weed

1 teaspoon dill seed

2 tablespoons sunflower oil

4 cups thinly sliced white cabbage

1 cup chopped kale

1 cup water

Two 28-ounce cans whole peeled tomatoes

2 tablespoons minced fresh parsley

Dash of black pepper

1 teaspoon honey

In preheated 3-quart soup pot sauté the onions, tarragon, dried dill weed, and dill seed in oil on medium heat. When onions just begin to brown, add cabbage and continue to cook until cabbage begins to get tender. Add kale and cook for 2 more minutes. Lower heat to a simmer and add the water. Drain the tomato juice from the canned tomatoes into the soup pot. Chop the canned tomatoes slightly (the chopping blade of a food processor does the job quickly) and add to the soup. Simmer 15 minutes covered, add parsley, fresh dill (if using), pepper, and honey. Stir well and serve. (This soup needs no salt if canned tomatoes have salt in them.)

6 servings

Creamy Tomato Soup

Creamy Tomato Soup is our standby for when disaster strikes at the café. If the soup burns, gets dropped, or if someone comes into work 3 hours late, Creamy Tomato comes to the rescue.

Many customers at the café ask for this recipe. I am always embarrassed to tell them just how simple it is.

Heat the butter in a 10-inch fry pan and sauté the onions over medium heat, cooking until golden brown. Combine the onions and tomatoes in a 3-quart soup pot. Add lemon juice and water or stock and simmer on low heat, covered, for 45 minutes, stirring occasionally. Mix cream and flour together until smooth. Add to soup, and return to a simmer, uncovered. Add parsley, salt, and pepper. Serve hot!

6 servings

- *2 tablespoons butter*
- *1½ cups chopped onion (3 onions)*
- *Two 28-ounce cans crushed tomatoes*
- *Juice of 1 lemon*
- *2 cups water or stock*
- *1 cup heavy cream*
- *4 tablespoons unbleached white or pastry flour*
- *⅓ cup minced fresh parsley*
- *½ teaspoon salt*
- *Dash of white pepper*

Creamy Broccoli Soup

In a 4-quart cast-iron Dutch oven or other soup pot, heat butter on medium heat. When hot, add onions, garlic, basil, and thyme. When onions begin to brown, add broccoli. Sauté until tender; don't overcook. Then pull out your blender. Add 3 cups water or stock to pot, then blend approximately half the soup until smooth. If mixture is too liquidy in the blender, it will try to jump out, in which case drain some of the excess liquid back into the soup. Pour pureed broccoli back into soup pot and add remaining cup water or stock.

In a small bowl, mix the cream and flour and stir until smooth and lumps are gone. Begin to heat soup again on low heat and add the cream-flour mixture. Then add salt and pepper. Don't allow to boil. Simmer uncovered 30 minutes more and serve.

6 servings

Cream of Spinach. Substitute 10 cups *packed* raw spinach for broccoli. Follow the instructions above, adding 1 tablespoon lemon juice at the end.

- *2 tablespoons butter*
- *1 cup finely chopped onion (2 onions)*
- *3 cloves garlic, minced*
- *1½ teaspoons basil*
- *2 teaspoons thyme*
- *6 cups chopped broccoli (1 large head, including some leaves, leaving a few broccoli florets whole)*
- *4 cups water or stock*
- *1 cup heavy cream*
- *4 tablespoons unbleached white flour*
- *1 teaspoon salt*
- *Freshly ground black pepper or cayenne pepper*

Creamy Green Bean Soup

5 cups water

1½ pounds green beans, chopped at an angle into 1½-inch pieces (about 6 cups)

5 tablespoons butter

1½ cups finely chopped onion (3 onions)

1 teaspoon dried leaf thyme

1½ teaspoons dried dill weed

2 bay leaves

3 tablespoons unbleached white flour

½ cup heavy cream

1 teaspoon salt

Dash of black pepper to taste

1 cup milk

If your garden is producing green beans abundantly, this soup is for you.

Bring water to a boil in a 4-quart soup pot. Add the green beans, return to a boil, cover, and then simmer 30 minutes.

Melt 2 tablespoons butter in a 10-inch fry pan and sauté the onions with the thyme and dill weed until onions are lightly browned. Add onions to green beans and turn off heat. Let sit a few minutes, then puree approximately ¾ of the green bean mixture in blender. Return the puree to soup pot and add bay leaves.

Melt the remaining 3 tablespoons butter in pan in which you sautéed the onions. Add the flour to butter and stir until lightly browned on low heat. Whisk in cream. Add a ladle of soup to cream mixture, stir in, add another, then pour cream mixture into soup. Add salt, pepper, and milk. Simmer on low heat for 15 minutes uncovered and serve.

6 servings

Asparagus Medley Soup

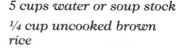

A delicious spring treat. Make a pot to celebrate another winter come and gone.

Bring water or soup stock to a boil in a 4-quart soup pot. Add rice, potatoes, and carrots. Cover and simmer until the potatoes are barely tender (approximately 15 minutes). Meanwhile, melt the butter in a fry pan and sauté the leeks, celery, thyme, and dill weed. When just tender, add to potatoes along with asparagus and spinach. Add milk, salt, and pepper. Simmer 30 minutes more uncovered, stirring occasionally, and serve.

8 servings

5 cups water or soup stock

¼ cup uncooked brown rice

2 cups halved and sliced unpeeled potatoes (2 medium potatoes)

1 cup sliced carrots (1 carrot)

2 tablespoons butter

2 leeks, sliced (wash well; they're always sandy)

1 cup sliced celery

½ teaspoon dried leaf thyme

½ teaspoon dried dill weed

10 stalks fresh asparagus, sliced (remove tough ends)

2 cups chopped fresh spinach

3 cups milk

1½ teaspoons salt

Dash of white pepper

Primavera Soup

5 *cups water*

2 *cups fiddleheads, washed and cleaned*

1 *tablespoon sunflower oil*

¾ *cup onion rings, sliced in half (2 onions)*

1 *cup sliced carrots (1 carrot)*

3 *large cloves garlic, minced*

½ *teaspoon tarragon*

½ *teaspoon dried leaf thyme*

1 *cup zucchini, cut into julienne sticks 2 inches long (1 small zucchini)*

2 *cups sliced mushrooms*

2 *cups chopped red Swiss chard*

4 *cups milk*

1 *teaspoon salt*

Dash of black pepper

1 *tablespoon minced fresh dill weed*

2 *tablespoons minced fresh parsley*

Gathering and eating fiddlehead ferns is a traditional Vermont spring activity. However, you must know which variety to pick. Don't choose the fuzzy, tall fiddleheads. The edible ferns have a paper-dry parchmentlike sheath that sheds off them.

Fiddleheads are best when about 4 inches above the ground, with a 1-inch tightly curled head on them. The scales should be scrubbed off from tip to stalk and washed well. Don't gather ferns that have been growing close to the roadside because they could contain lead from car exhaust fumes.

Fiddleheads are indigenous to New England. Their flavor is somewhere between that of asparagus and spinach.

Boil 2 cups water in a pot, add fiddleheads, and simmer 5 minutes. Drain and rinse under cold water, drain again, and set aside. Meanwhile, set a 4-quart soup pot over medium heat and add oil. When hot, add onions, carrots, garlic, tarragon, and thyme. Cook over medium heat, stirring occasionally. When onions begin to brown, add zucchini. Cook 2 minutes more and add mushrooms and Swiss chard. Cook 3 to 4 minutes more until mushrooms are just tender.

Add remaining 3 cups water and milk to vegetables, along with salt, pepper, dill weed, parsley, and fiddleheads. Simmer on low heat 10 to 15 minutes covered, stirring occasionally, and serve.

6 to 8 servings

Spinach Leek Neufchâtel Soup

Set soup pot over medium heat. When hot, add 2 tablespoons butter, then onions, celery, thyme, and dill weed. After the onions begin to get tender, add leeks. Sauté until onions begin to brown, then add spinach and cook until just tender. Add water and simmer 10 minutes covered.

In 4-quart saucepan, melt remaining 2 tablespoons butter over low heat, add flour, and stir well. Then add cheese, slowly adding milk to this mixture, ½ cup at a time, until 2 cups milk have been added. Stir mixture well with a whisk between each addition of milk. When mixture is smooth, add a ladle of soup to cheese mixture; repeat twice more. Then combine this mixture with that in soup pot. Add remaining milk, salt, and pepper and stir. Simmer until hot and serve.

8 servings

4 tablespoons butter

¾ cup finely chopped onion

¾ cup sliced celery

½ teaspoon dried leaf thyme

1 teaspoon dried dill weed

4 medium-sized leeks, sliced (wash well)

8 slightly packed cups coarsely chopped spinach

4 cups water

3 tablespoons unbleached white flour

1 cup neufchâtel or cream cheese (8-ounce package)

4 cups milk

½ teaspoon salt

Dash of black pepper

Miso Vegetable Soup

8 cups water or stock

¼ cup sunflower oil

1½ cups chopped onion (3 onions)

6 large cloves garlic, minced

One 1-inch piece fresh ginger root, peeled and minced

2 cups thinly sliced carrot (2 carrots)

1 cup sliced mushrooms

2 cups chopped Chinese cabbage, bok choy, or celery (3 to 4 stalks)

1 square tofu, drained, pressed, and cut in small cubes (½ pound)

Cayenne pepper or freshly ground black pepper to taste

1 tablespoon tamari

½ cup miso

½ cup warm water

½ cup minced fresh parsley

4 scallions, sliced

Miso soup is the vegetarian alternative to Mom's chicken soup that many of us were fed as children when we were feeling sick. Miso is said to have special healing properties.

I was part of a large week-long sit-in outside the gates of Vermont's only nuclear power plant some years ago. The March weather was unsympathetic to our antinuclear demonstration as we sat, ate, and slept out in the rain and cold. Every day a group of volunteers would make and donate a large pot of miso soup to the demonstrators. The hot soup was wonderful and welcomed by all. The cooks believed that the miso would help us dispel the low levels of radiation that our bodies were absorbing by being so close to the plant.

Begin heating the water or stock in a 4-quart soup pot.

Heat 2 tablespoons oil in a wok and sauté onions, garlic, and ginger over medium heat. Add carrots a few minutes later. As vegetables begin to brown, add mushrooms and Chinese cabbage, bok choy, or celery. Cook 2 minutes longer and add to hot stock or water in soup pot, and lower to a simmer. Wipe out the wok and heat the remaining 2 tablespoons oil. Sauté tofu. Cook until brown and firm, adding pepper or cayenne as it cooks and stirring occasionally. Just when it looks done, pour the tamari over it and stir in quickly. Cook another minute, then add to soup pot.

Thin miso with warm water, and add to soup just before serving, along with the parsley. Don't allow soup to boil; keep it on very low heat. Taste for seasoning, garnish with scallions, and serve.

8 servings

Oriental Bean Thread Soup

This is an unusual soup, lovely to look at and filling to eat. Add some fresh snow peas in season along with the Chinese cabbage. A bowl of brown rice will complement the soup nicely for a simple meal.

Heat 3 tablespoons oil in a 10-inch cast-iron fry pan and sauté the tofu over medium heat. Do not crowd the tofu or it will crumble. Sauté in 2 batches if the pan is small. Just before removing the tofu from the pan, pour 1 tablespoon tamari over the tofu and gently toss. Cook 1 minute, remove from the pan, and set aside. The tofu should be lightly browned and firm.

In the same fry pan, heat the sesame oil and sauté the garlic, ginger, and carrots over medium heat. After 5 minutes, add zucchini and broccoli and cook 5 minutes more, or until tender.

Meanwhile, heat the water or stock in a 4-quart soup pot. Bring to a boil, then simmer. Add the sautéed vegetables to soup pot and simmer, uncovered. Add bok choy or Chinese cabbage and bean threads. Add the remaining 3 tablespoons tamari, tofu, and cayenne. Simmer 15 minutes uncovered and serve, garnished with fresh scallions.

8 servings

---

3 tablespoons sunflower oil

2 squares tofu, cut in ½-inch cubes (1 pound)

¼ cup tamari

2 tablespoons sesame oil

3 cloves garlic, minced

2 tablespoons minced fresh ginger root

¾ cup carrot, halved lengthwise and sliced into thin sticks (1 small carrot)

¾ cup sliced zucchini (1 small zucchini) or snow peas

1 cup sliced broccoli, stems and florets

7 cups water or vegetable stock

1 cup sliced bok choy or Chinese cabbage, using part of greens

1 cup bean threads or rice noodles, broken in half

Dash of cayenne pepper

4 scallions, sliced

Chili

2 cups uncooked kidney
beans

7 cups water

⅔ cup soy grits

3 cups crushed tomatoes,
canned or fresh

2 to 3 bay leaves

3 tablespoons sunflower oil

2 cups chopped onion (4
onions)

6 cloves garlic, minced

1 cup chopped green
pepper (1 large or 2 small
peppers)

1 cup chopped carrots (2
small carrots)

2 small dried or fresh chili
peppers, chopped fine

1 teaspoon basil

1½ teaspoons oregano

1 teaspoon cumin seed

½ teaspoon ground
coriander

½ teaspoon chili powder

1 teaspoon salt

¼ to ½ teaspoon cayenne
pepper

Minced onion (optional)

Grated cheddar cheese
(optional)

This is a favorite among many café regulars. It is inexpensive to make, filling, and a great treat on a cold winter's day. Carpenters come in from working out in the cold and order a bowl of chili with cheese and onions on the top and some whole-grain bread on the side.

Newcomers to the café invariably eye me suspiciously and ask, "Is there any meat in this chili?"

"No," I answer, "this is true vegetarian fare."

Soak the kidney beans in water 6 to 8 hours. Bring to a boil in a 4-quart soup pot. Cover and simmer until soft (1½ to 2 hours). Add soy grits and canned or fresh tomatoes (in season) along with bay leaves. Continue to simmer 30 minutes more, covered.

Heat the oil in a 10-inch cast-iron fry pan and sauté onions, garlic, green pepper and carrots along with chili peppers, basil, oregano, cumin, coriander, and chili powder until onions brown. Then add to bean mixture, adding more water if necessary. Add salt and cayenne (¼ teaspoon if you like mild chili). Remember, the hotness sneaks up on you, so take more than one taste before adding more! Simmer, stirring occasionally, and cook 20 minutes more uncovered. Serve garnished with minced onion and grated cheddar cheese. This soup freezes well.

6 servings

Black Bean Soup

A wintertime favorite at the café; the flavor is unique and wonderful. The appearance is similar to that of chocolate pudding, and more than once a customer has said, "I'll have some of that!" and pointed to a bowl of black bean soup. Some have been greatly surprised, upon a closer look, to see carrots, onions, and celery floating around in their assumed pudding.

Black beans invariably seem to have a few stones or pebbles mixed in, so sort through them well while rinsing.

Wash the beans. Combine with the water and soak 6 to 8 hours.

Cook the beans in a 3-quart soup pot on medium heat, covered, until soft (approximately 1½ to 2 hours or 30 to 45 minutes in pressure cooker). Pour ⅔ of the beans into a blender and puree. Return to heat, add the bay leaves, and simmer uncovered, stirring occasionally.

Heat the oil in a large skillet and sauté the onions, garlic, celery, carrot, cumin, basil, celery seed, and cayenne until the vegetables are tender (10 to 15 minutes). Add to the beans, along with the parsley, lemon juice, and salt. Add 2 cups or more water to thin the soup to a desirable consistency. Cook another ½ hour, stirring occasionally, and serve topped with a dollop of sour cream.

8 servings

2 cups uncooked black beans

6 cups water

2 bay leaves

2 tablespoons sunflower oil

1 cup chopped onion (2 onions)

4 cloves garlic, minced

2 cups chopped celery (3 stalks, with leaves)

1 cup diced carrot (1 large carrot)

½ teaspoon cumin seed

1 teaspoon basil

¼ teaspoon celery seed

Dash of cayenne pepper

¼ cup minced fresh parsley

Juice of 1 large lemon

1 teaspoon salt

Sour cream

Butternut White Bean Ginger Soup

1 cup uncooked white beans

10 cups water

2 pounds butternut squash, whole (6 cups after it's been peeled, seeded, and diced)

2 tablespoons sunflower oil

1 cup chopped onion (2 onions)

1 cup chopped celery

2 tablespoons minced fresh ginger root

4 cloves garlic, minced (1 tablespoon)

1 teaspoon salt

Black pepper to taste

¼ cup minced fresh parsley

This soup came about in an unusual way. Molly, a baker at the café, was browsing through a cooking magazine on her break. She was reading aloud interesting titles of recipes to the rest of the kitchen crew as they worked.

Judy, the soup cook, heard this name and decided to make the soup the next day. She never bothered to look at the recipe until after she completed her soup. Hers, she discovered, was completely different from the magazine's, but delicious just the same.

In a 4-quart soup pot, bring the white beans to a boil in 7 cups water. Simmer, covered, 1½ hours or until the beans are tender but not mushy. (Beans will cook more quickly if you presoak them in the water a few hours before cooking.)

Meanwhile, prepare vegetables. Peel the squash with a vegetable peeler, then seed and dice. In separate pot, cook squash in remaining 3 cups water, covered. Simmer until tender and drain. Then puree all the squash in a blender. You will have to do this in several batches. Add to the cooked white beans.

In a fry pan, heat the oil and sauté the onion, celery, ginger, and garlic, stirring occasionally. When tender and beginning to brown, add to soup pot along with salt, pepper, and parsley. Simmer 15 minutes uncovered and serve. After it sits it will thicken; thin with a bit of water.

8 servings

Indian Split Pea Soup

Also known as dal, this is often served as a condiment or a first course in an Indian meal. At the café, we often follow it with a vegetable curry along with rice or a homemade chapati.

Wash peas. Add to water or stock in a 3-quart soup pot. Bring to a boil and cook on low heat for 45 minutes, half covered with a lid, stirring occasionally.

Heat the oil in a fry pan and sauté the onions, garlic, and ginger until lightly browned and tender. Add to split peas along with all the remaining ingredients. Lower heat to simmer, cover, and continue to cook 30 minutes more, stirring occasionally.

6 servings

2 cups uncooked yellow split peas

8 cups water or stock

2 tablespoons sunflower oil

1 cup diced onion

1½ tablespoons minced garlic (4 to 5 cloves)

1 tablespoon minced fresh ginger root

1½ cups chopped kale or spinach

¼ teaspoon ground cumin

¼ teaspoon ground coriander

½ teaspoon turmeric

⅛ teaspoon cayenne pepper

1 teaspoon salt

Canadian Split Pea Soup

8 cups water

2 cups uncooked yellow split peas

1 tablespoon sunflower oil

4 large cloves garlic, minced

¾ cup chopped onion (2 onions)

¾ cup sliced carrot (1 carrot)

¾ cup sliced celery

1 teaspoon thyme

1 cup chopped unpeeled potato (1 potato)

1 cup chopped peeled turnip or rutabaga

1 teaspoon salt

1 teaspoon cider vinegar

⅛ teaspoon black pepper

¼ cup chopped fresh parsley

Bring water to boil in a 4-quart soup pot. Add split peas, lower heat to a simmer, and cover loosely. Cook, stirring occasionally, for 1 hour, until split peas are tender.

Meanwhile, set a 10-inch cast-iron fry pan over medium heat. Add oil and when hot add the garlic, onions, carrots, celery, and thyme. Sauté until tender. Add sautéed vegetables, potato, and turnip to the cooked peas; continue to simmer. Add the salt, vinegar, pepper, and parsley. Cook the soup 30 minutes more, covered, stirring occasionally, until the vegetables are tender and the peas have dissolved.

6 servings

Split Pea Vegetable Soup

This is a basic, hearty, and inexpensive soup to make. Don't allow the split peas and barley to stick to the bottom of the pot, for it scorches easily and the burned flavor will ruin the soup.

Bring water to a boil in a 4-quart soup pot. Add split peas, bay leaves, and barley. Simmer, leaving cover slightly ajar, and cook 1 hour, stirring occasionally.

Heat the oil in a 10-inch fry pan and sauté the onions, garlic, carrot, and potato, with the thyme and basil, until onions begin to brown. Add celery and cook a few minutes more. Add vegetables to soup pot. Add salt and tamari, pepper, and caraway seeds (but not miso if you're using it). Cook 45 minutes more on very low heat, covered, or simmer on top of your wood stove, stirring occasionally. If you want to use miso instead of salt and tamari, add just before serving, stir in well, and don't allow soup to boil. This freezes well.

8 servings

8 cups water

1½ cups uncooked green split peas

2 bay leaves

⅓ cup uncooked barley

2 tablespoons sunflower oil

1 cup diced onion (2 onions)

4 large cloves garlic, minced

¾ cup sliced carrot (1 carrot)

1 cup diced unpeeled potato (1 medium potato)

1 teaspoon dried leaf thyme

1 teaspoon basil

1 cup sliced celery (2 stalks, with greens chopped)

1 teaspoon salt + 1 teaspoon tamari (or ½ cup miso for a miso broth)

¼ teaspoon black pepper, or to taste

½ teaspoon caraway seeds

Lentil Vegetable Soup

1½ cups uncooked green lentils

⅓ cup uncooked barley or brown rice

8 cups water

1 tablespoon sunflower oil

1 cup chopped onion (2 onions)

1 cup chopped carrot (2 small carrots)

4 cloves garlic, minced

1 teaspoon dried whole thyme

1 teaspoon basil

½ teaspoon oregano

1½ cups sliced celery (2 to 3 stalks)

½ cup minced fresh parsley

1 teaspoon salt or 1 tablespoon tamari

½ teaspoon black pepper

Sort through lentils to remove any pebbles and rinse. Combine the lentils, barley, and water in a 4-quart soup pot and cook 1 hour, leaving cover slightly ajar; add more water as needed.

Heat the oil in fry pan and sauté the onions, carrots, and garlic with the thyme, basil, and oregano. After the onions begin to brown, add celery. Cook a few minutes more and add to lentils. Simmer for another 45 minutes, covered, stirring occasionally. Check seasoning. Add parsley, salt or tamari, and pepper and serve.

8 servings

Garden Bean Soup

An *old-fashioned, delicious vegetable soup.*

Soak the yellow-eyed beans in water 8 hours. Bring to a boil in a 4-quart soup pot. Simmer and cook, covered, with the lid cracked, for 1 hour.

Preheat a 10-inch fry pan, add oil, and after a minute add onions and tarragon. Sauté for a few minutes, add celery and squash, and continue to cook on medium heat until onions begin to brown. Add to cooked beans along with potato, bay leaf, green beans, and carrots. Simmer 20 minutes covered until vegetables are tender, stirring occasionally. Add peas, salt, lemon juice, and pepper. Cook 5 minutes more and serve.

6 large
servings

1 cup uncooked yellow-eyed beans

6 cups water

1 tablespoon sunflower oil

1 cup chopped onion (2 onions)

1 teaspoon tarragon

1 cup diced celery

1 cup sliced yellow squash

1 cup diced unpeeled potato (1 potato)

1 bay leaf

1 cup sliced green beans

1 cup diced carrot (2 small carrots)

1 cup peas, fresh or frozen

1 teaspoon salt

1 tablespoon lemon juice (½ lemon)

Black pepper to taste

Gypsy Vegetable Stew

5 tablespoons sunflower oil

1½ cups chopped onion (3 onions)

2 tablespoons minced garlic

2 cups cubed unpeeled potatoes (2 potatoes)

1½ cups sliced carrots (2 carrots)

1 teaspoon dried leaf thyme

1½ cups sliced zucchini or yellow squash (1 medium)

1½ cups chopped green beans

2 cups chopped broccoli, stems and florets

1½ cups chopped kale or spinach

1½ cups chopped green cabbage

1 cup lima beans (frozen or fresh) or ½ cup dried, soaked and cooked until tender

4 cups water

2 squares tofu, cubed (1 pound)

2 tablespoons tamari

2 teaspoons paprika

½ teaspoon ground cumin

½ teaspoon cayenne pepper

1 teaspoon salt

½ cup dry red wine

4 tablespoons unbleached white flour

We serve this thick and chunky stew at the café with a green salad and a crusty bread for a simple but hearty meal.

In a 4-quart soup pot, heat 3 tablespoons oil and sauté the onions, garlic, potatoes, carrots, and thyme. When they begin to get tender, add rest of vegetables, except lima beans. Sauté until these vegetables begin to get tender. Add lima beans and water. Simmer, covered, stirring occasionally.

Meanwhile, in 10-inch cast-iron fry pan, heat the remaining 2 tablespoons oil. When hot, add tofu and sauté. When browned on all sides, pour 1 tablespoon tamari over the tofu and stir for 1 minute more. Add to vegetables along with paprika, cumin, cayenne, salt, wine, and remaining 1 tablespoon tamari. In same fry pan in which you sautéed the tofu, brown flour on medium heat. Slowly add some of the soup water to form a paste. Thin to a smooth consistency and add to soup. If you cannot get lumps out, put into blender for 1 minute, then add to soup. Simmer covered until vegetables are tender and stew is bubbly, stirring occasionally. Serve in big, hearty soup bowls with a crusty bread and some good cheese.

6 to 8 servings

Chilled or Hot Potato Zucchini Soup

Every summer zucchini jokes abound in Vermont. Question: Why do Vermonters only lock their cars in August and September?

Answer: Because it's zucchini season!

It seems as if no matter how little zucchini you grow in your garden, you soon have too much. Friends and neighbors try to give it away to one another and baskets of free zucchini are found in Vermont businesses. Here's a recipe to help use up some of the excess crop.

Bring water to a boil in a 4-quart soup pot. Add potatoes and carrots and cook until tender. Meanwhile, in preheated fry pan, sauté the onions, garlic, and basil in oil on medium heat. When the onions just begin to brown, add zucchini and continue to cook until tender. Combine zucchini mixture with potato mixture, and puree in blender. Return to pot, but do not return to heat if a chilled soup is desired. Add cream, milk, parsley, dill, salt, and pepper, stir well, chill 2 hours, and serve with a few sprigs of fresh dill on top. If serving hot, return to heat until hot enough to serve, stirring occasionally.

8 servings

4 cups water

4 cups chopped unpeeled potatoes (4 potatoes)

¾ cup diced carrot (1 medium)

1 cup diced onion (2 onions)

4 large cloves garlic, minced

1 teaspoon basil

1 tablespoon sunflower oil

4 cups chopped zucchini (2 medium zucchini)

½ cup heavy cream

1 cup milk

¼ cup minced fresh parsley

2 tablespoons minced fresh dill weed

1 teaspoon salt

Dash of ground black pepper

Few sprigs fresh dill weed

Chilled Avocado Cucumber Soup

4 cups or 2 medium
cucumbers, chopped
(reserve 1 cup) (peel
cucumbers only if the skins
are waxed)

2 ripe avocados, pitted and
peeled

3 large cloves garlic

½ packed cup fresh
parsley sprigs

2 cups yogurt

1 cup water, or 1 cup ice
cubes to chill soup quickly

½ teaspoon salt

½ cup chopped scallions (2
to 3 scallions)

A quick and easy soup to prepare. It's great for a
hot summer's day when you don't want to turn
the stove on.

In a medium-sized bowl, combine 3 cups chopped cucumbers, avocados, garlic, parsley, yogurt, water or ice
cubes, and salt. In a blender puree this mixture in
batches until smooth, transferring the blended soup into
a 2-quart glass pitcher. When all the mixture has been
blended, stir in the reserved cup of chopped cucumber
and the scallions. Chill 1 hour and serve.

6 to 8 servings

Chilled Spicy Tomato Avocado Soup

Refreshing as well as quick and easy to prepare on a hot, muggy day.

In a blender, puree the garlic, hot pepper, and 1 avocado with 2 cups tomato juice until smooth. Pour into a pitcher, add remaining tomato juice, cilantro, red onion, tomato, lemon juice, and the remaining ½ avocado, which should be chopped. Mix and chill at least 1 hour.

4 servings

3 large cloves garlic

2 tablespoons chopped fresh Jalapeño pepper

1½ avocados, pitted and peeled

4 cups tomato juice

¼ cup finely chopped fresh cilantro (Chinese parsley)

½ cup finely diced red onion

1 medium tomato, coarsely chopped

1 tablespoon lemon juice

Chilled Fruit Soup

Slice cantaloupe in half, discard seeds, and form into melon balls. Put 2 cups in a blender; reserve the remaining balls in a large 2-quart pitcher. Add banana to blender. Remove the pits from the peaches and add peaches to the blender along with 2 cups orange juice. Puree until smooth. Pour into the pitcher. Now puree 1 cup blueberries along with cinnamon, ice cubes, pineapple coconut juice, lemon juice, vanilla, and remaining orange juice. Again run blender until smooth. Pour pureed blueberries into pitcher along with the remaining 1 cup whole blueberries. Stir well, chill at least 1 hour, and serve.

6 to 8 servings

1 ripe cantaloupe (about 3 cups melon balls)

1 ripe banana, peeled

4 large ripe peaches

4 cups orange juice

2 cups fresh blueberries

¼ teaspoon ground cinnamon

1 cup ice cubes

1 cup pineapple coconut juice

2 tablespoons lemon juice

½ teaspoon vanilla extract

Chilled Summer Strawberry Melon Soup

4 cups seeded watermelon
pieces

2 ripe bananas, peeled

1 cup apple cider or juice

½ cup yogurt

½ cup sour cream or heavy
cream

¼ teaspoon cinnamon

2 ice cubes

2 cups sliced fresh
strawberries

¼ cup cold mint tea

Fresh mint sprigs

In a blender, puree the watermelon, bananas, cider or juice, yogurt, cream, cinnamon, and ice cubes. Run until smooth. Pour into a 2-quart pitcher; add sliced strawberries and cold mint tea. Cover and chill 1 hour. Serve garnished with fresh mint sprigs.

6 servings

Chilled Peachy Keen Soup

12 medium-sized peaches

6 cups boiling water

1½ cups cold water

1 tablespoon honey

2 tablespoons lemon juice

1 cup sour cream

½ teaspoon cinnamon

¼ teaspoon nutmeg

1 teaspoon vanilla extract

Set whole peaches in boiling water, 3 or 4 at a time. Cook 2 to 3 minutes. Remove and set in a bowl of cold water. This hot water bath will allow the peel to be easily removed from the peach, and even loosen up the pit. Repeat until all the peaches have been blanched. Peel, pit, and coarsely chop the peaches. You will have approximately 4 cups peaches.

In a blender, combine about 1½ cups peaches with ¾ cup cold water, honey, lemon juice, and ½ cup sour cream. Puree until smooth and pour into 2-quart pitcher. Now, puree 1½ cups more peaches with ¾ cup more water, ½ cup sour cream, and the cinnamon, nutmeg, and vanilla. When smooth, turn off blender and mix second puree together with the first in pitcher. Add the remaining 1 cup chopped peaches. Stir well. Chill at least 2 hours and serve.

6 to 8 servings

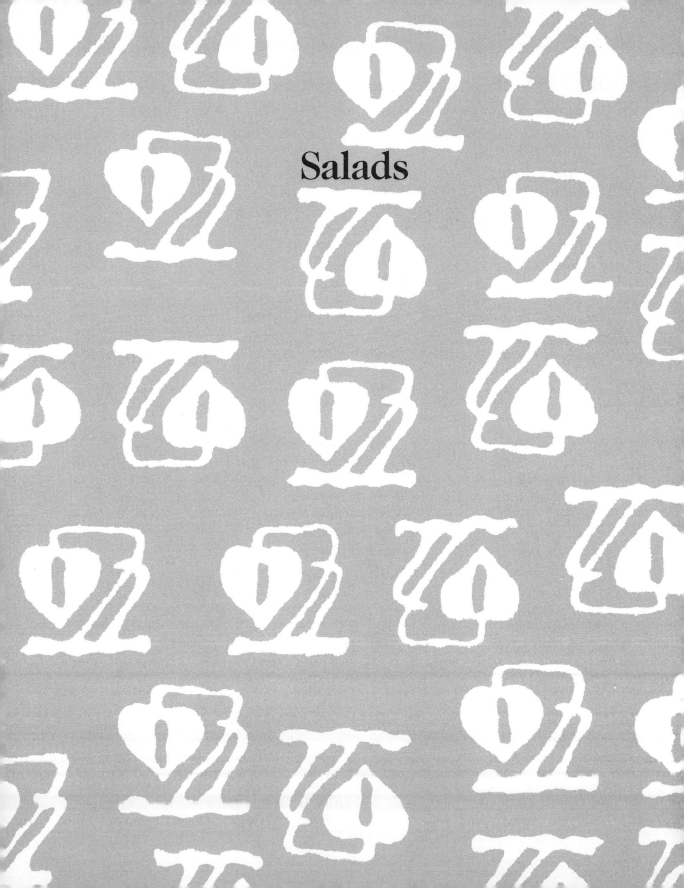

Salads

Lettuce and Beyond (page 111)

Basic Green Salad

Barley and Hazelnut Salad

Tabouli

Garden Pasta Salad

Garbanzo Pasta Salad

Spring Shell Salad

Spiral Pasta Salad with Mushrooms, Broccoli, and Tempeh

Oriental Salad

Marinated Rice Salad

Wild Rice with Pine Nuts

Couscous Salad

Lemon Couscous Salad with Macadamia Nuts

White Bean Salad

Three-Bean Salad

Greek Salad

Triple Pepper Salad

Guacamole

Mushroom Salad

Marinated Potato Salad

Kiwi Lime Fruit Salad

Stuffed Honeydew Melon

Dressings (page 133)

Herb Dressing

Green Vinaigrette Dressing

Dilly Vinaigrette Dressing

Creamy Italian Dressing

Tahini Dressing

Tahini Yogurt Dressing

Parsley, Buttermilk, and Parmesan Dressing

Sour Cream and Garlic Dressing

Cucumber Dill Dressing

Avocado Cream Cheese Dressing

Russian Dressing

Tofu Russian Dressing

Spicy Tomato Dressing

Tofu Dill Dressing

Lettuce and Beyond

The salads at the café are always prepared with fresh, crisp greens and vegetables. We want our salads to be beautiful to look at and delicious to eat. For this reason certain vegetables are chosen for their color as well as taste and nutritional value.

We make special salads during the hot summer months when people want lighter foods. The café cooks combine garden vegetables with couscous, pasta, grains, beans, or fruit in season. These creations are a far cry from the salads of iceberg lettuce and pale tomatoes served in so many restaurants.

When choosing which salad to make at the Horn of the Moon, we first consider cost and availability of vegetable varieties. Every attentive food shopper knows that produce prices can fluctuate widely, so it pays to buy carefully. Using locally grown vegetables will improve the quality of a salad. A farmer's market sets up across the street from the café every Saturday beginning in early spring and continuing late into the fall. If you can locate one, you will find that the produce is reasonably priced as well as freshly picked.

Certain growers raise their produce organically and use no toxic chemicals to control insects, pests, and plant diseases. Practicing organic methods is a difficult challenge for a commercial-scale farm; these farmers are sometimes confronted with deciding whether to spray a crop or lose it. Crop rotation, companion planting, and other biodynamic techniques can solve or reduce these problems.

There are many different kinds of lettuce and greens to choose from to create an attractive salad. Read through the Basic Green Salad recipe for a listing of assorted greens and vegetables. Avoid buying wilted or dried-out-looking produce, which will taste just like it looks.

Salad greens should be washed thoroughly. Break apart each head or bunch of greens and soak them in a large bowl of cold water. If they are particularly dirty, pour out the water and repeat the process. You should run each leaf under running water after first opening up the leaves that are folded or curled.

After bathing your greens, it is important to dry them off well. A salad spinner is a wonderful invention that removes excess water from the leaves. A well-dried salad will prevent your salad dressing from sliding off the greens. If you don't have a salad spinner, set the leaves in a colander to drain and shake them well.

Wrap salads, vegetables, and fruits carefully before refrigerating. This is especially important in frost-free refrigerators. The loveliest ripe tomato will quickly be wrinkled and dried up if left unprotected in these coolers.

Leftovers from a previous meal can be added to and become tomorrow's fresh salad. A bowl of cold brown rice or cooked pasta needs only some sliced vegetables and oil and vinegar to become a new and interesting meal. Or you can try marinating a selection of vegetables for a few hours in an oil and vinegar mixture. Drain them well and save the marinade for another time. Add the marinated vegetables to greens or grains and toss well.

If a salad is planned as the main course of a meal, it should include balanced protein in its ingredients. Salads prepared with nuts, beans, grains, or cheese, such as Garbanzo Pasta, Wild Rice with Pine Nuts, or Oriental, are good choices. Other salads may need a protein or grain alongside to complete the meal. Including a dressing made with tofu, tahini, or cheese will also raise the protein level in your meal. Cooked beans, grated cheeses, sprouts, and other protein sources can be added to a basic green salad to produce a satisfying dinner.

Salad dressings should be coordinated with the meal you are serving. Many salads need only a vinaigrette dressing which will not dominate the flavor of the vegetables or interfere with the main dish. Sometimes a more interesting flavor is needed to dress up a simple meal. In this situation, possible choices include Parsley, Buttermilk, and Parmesan, Sour Cream and Garlic, and Avocado Cream Cheese dressings.

Dress a salad when you are ready to serve it. Pour on just enough to coat the greens lightly, and then toss the salad well. Few remnants of the dressing should be found in the bottom of the bowl. At home I often serve the salad dressing on the side so that leftover salad can be served again. A dressed salad will become wilted and soggy more quickly.

Salads have become increasingly popular at the café and across the country because of their low calorie content, budget price, and delicious flavor. Some restaurants, however, wash their vegetables in a chemical sulfite bath which prevents them from browning and wilting, but which can cause serious allergic reactions. The chemicals are often used at salad bars where vegetables and fruits are left in the warm air for long periods of time. Be aware of this possibility when dining out and ask if sulfites are used. Some states, including Vermont, have issued regulations requiring restaurants to indicate in their menus if they use these chemicals.

A Basic Green Salad

**Greens to Choose From
(pick 1, 2, or 3):**

Green or red leaf lettuce

Romaine or Boston lettuce

*Buttercrunch or summer
Bibb lettuce*

*Iceberg and garden
varieties*

Fresh spinach leaves

Curly or Belgian endive

Watercress

*Mustard greens (just a
few)*

*Fresh chopped herbs
(chives, dill, parsley,
cilantro, basil)*

**Vegetables to Add (pick at
least 3):**

Grated or sliced carrots

*White or red cabbage, cut
into thin strips*

*Cauliflower or broccoli
florets*

Sliced cucumbers

Alfalfa or salad sprouts

*Cherry tomatoes (or sliced
chunks of tomatoes)*

Red onion rings

*Green and red pepper
slices*

Mushroom slices

Avocado slices

Snow peas or green peas

*Quartered or sliced
radishes*

A green salad can be as simple as fresh Bibb lettuce tossed in a vinaigrette dressing, or it can be as complicated as you like. Vegetables can add variety, color, and texture that will dress up an otherwise simple salad. If you always put the same vegetables and greens in your salad and are tired of it, why not try something new—pick a new kind of lettuce and add a different vegetable or dressing to the salad. Salads can be endlessly combined to form interesting meals.

For a main course salad, choose 2 or 3 greens, a minimum of 6 vegetables, and at least 2 items offering protein from the Other Choices column. Choose a light oil and vinegar dressing that will not disguise the assorted vegetable flavors. Serve your salad with a crusty loaf of fresh bread and some sweet butter on the side.

Sliced celery

Green beans

Cut-up cooked potatoes

Grated, peeled fresh beets

*Marinated vegetables, like
artichoke hearts or
cauliflower*

Cooked asparagus

Sliced fennel

Other Choices:

Grated cheeses

Roasted nuts

Tofu or tempeh

*Cooked chick peas and
beans*

Olives

Hard-boiled eggs

Hot peppers

Croutons

Apple slices

Cooked pasta

Barley and Hazelnut Salad

This is a very tasty salad, and it is always a popular special at the café. Though the work is painstakingly slow, we slice in half, rather than chop, each hazelnut, which gives the salad an elegant look. Avoid pearled commercial barley; organic barley is best.

In a 1-quart saucepan, combine the barley, wheat berries, and water. Bring to a boil, then simmer, covered, until all the water is absorbed. Allow to cool.

When the barley is cool, combine in a medium-sized bowl with the lemon juice, olive oil, salt, and black pepper to taste. Add the chopped veggies, parsley, garlic, and nuts. Stir and check seasoning. It's best if it gets to sit a few hours, refrigerated, before serving. Serve on a bed of salad greens and vegetables or in pita bread with sprouts, lettuce, and sliced tomato.

4 servings

1 cup uncooked organic barley

⅓ cup wheat berries

2⅔ cups water

½ cup lemon juice (approximately 3 large lemons)

⅓ cup olive oil

½ teaspoon salt

Freshly ground black pepper to taste

2 stalks celery, finely chopped

1 carrot, very finely chopped

½ cup minced fresh parsley

4 large cloves garlic, minced

½ cup halved or chopped roasted filberts or hazelnuts (they are the same thing; roasted almonds may be substituted)

Tabouli

3½ cups boiling water

2 cups uncooked bulgur

4 stalks celery, finely
chopped

6 scallions, finely chopped

1 carrot, finely chopped

3 large tomatoes, chopped

¼ cup olive oil

⅓ cup lemon juice

1 cup minced fresh parsley

1 tablespoon fresh or dried
mint leaves

4 cloves garlic, minced

1½ teaspoons salt

⅛ teaspoon black pepper
or cayenne pepper

¾ cup cooked chick peas
(optional)

A delicious Middle Eastern salad made with bulgur,
cracked wheat. The salad can be a summertime
meal in itself.

Pour the boiling water over the bulgur in large bowl.
Cover, stir occasionally, and allow bulgur to absorb
water. Uncover and let cool; this will take around 30
minutes. Drain off any excess water. Add the vegetables
to cooled bulgur along with oil, lemon juice, parsley, and
seasonings. (Chick peas are good to add for protein.) Let
sit to marinate for at least 1 hour. Before serving, check
seasoning and the oil-to-lemon-juice ratio. Bulgur will absorb a lot while sitting. Serve as a side dish, on top of a
salad, or in pita bread along with sprouts, lettuce, grated
feta cheese, and Herb Dressing (page 133) on top.

6 to 8 servings

Garden Pasta Salad

A *good choice for a summer potluck supper.*

Bring water to a boil in a 4-quart pot. Add pasta and cook until just tender (approximately 3 minutes for fresh pasta, 5 to 7 minutes for dry pasta). Drain and pour into a medium-sized bowl. Heat 1 tablespoon olive oil in a fry pan and cook the zucchini over medium heat for 3 minutes. Add zucchini and remaining ingredients, except the Parmesan cheese, to pasta. Stir and chill 1 hour. Serve with a small bowl of Parmesan cheese on the side, or garnish the top of the salad with it.

4 to 6 servings

3 quarts water

1 pound spinach spiral or rotini pasta

5 tablespoons olive oil

1 small zucchini, cut lengthwise in half and then sliced

3 tablespoons lemon juice

1/3 cup minced fresh parsley

1 tablespoon chopped fresh basil (or 1 teaspoon dried basil)

3 scallions, sliced

1/2 green pepper, diced

2 medium tomatoes, chopped

3/4 cup snow peas, sliced in half at an angle

Dash of freshly ground black pepper

1/2 teaspoon salt

1/2 cup finely grated Parmesan cheese (optional)

Garbanzo Pasta Salad

*1 cup uncooked garbanzo
beans (chick peas), soaked
overnight in 4 cups water
(or 2 cups cooked)*

3 quarts water

*1 pound spinach pasta
(spirals, shells, elbows)*

⅓ cup olive oil

5 tablespoons lemon juice

*½ pint cherry tomatoes,
sliced in half*

*1 cup diced green pepper
(1 large pepper)*

5 scallions, sliced

*¼ cup minced fresh
parsley*

3 cloves garlic, minced

¼ teaspoon dried dill weed

1 to 2 teaspoons tamari

¼ teaspoon salt

Black pepper to taste

*Garnish with grated
Parmesan or add 1 cup of
your favorite cheese, diced,
to the salad (optional)*

Cook soaked garbanzo beans 2½ to 3 hours (or in pressure cooker 45 minutes to 1 hour) or until tender. Drain well. Bring a 4-quart pot with 3 quarts water to boil. Add pasta and cook until al dente (2 to 3 minutes if fresh pasta, 5 to 7 minutes if not). Drain well. Pour cold water over pasta to cool it and drain again. Pour pasta into medium-sized bowl, add olive oil, lemon juice, and the rest of the ingredients. Chill 1 hour and serve.

6 servings

Spring Shell Salad

In a 4-quart pot cook pasta in 3 quarts boiling water. When al dente (2 to 3 minutes if fresh pasta, 5 to 7 minutes if dry), drain water, reserving some to steam asparagus in. Pour pasta into medium-sized bowl.

Set vegetable steamer in pot and reheat water. Steam asparagus until just tender, slightly crunchy and bright green. Rinse, drain and pour into cooling pasta along with 6 tablespoons olive oil and the vinegar.

In small fry pan heat 2 teaspoons olive oil. Add garlic, zucchini, and dried basil. Sauté until zucchini is just barely tender. Add to pasta along with tomatoes, salt, parsley and fresh basil. Chill 1 hour and serve.

4 to 6 servings

1 pound shell macaroni

3 quarts boiling water

2 cups sliced asparagus (approximately ¾ pound before cutting up)

6 tablespoons plus 2 teaspoons olive oil

4 tablespoons herb vinegar

4 large cloves garlic, minced

1 cup sliced zucchini

2 tablespoons chopped fresh basil (or 2 teaspoons dried basil)

1 pint cherry tomatoes (cut in half if tomatoes are large, leave whole if small)

½ teaspoon salt

2 tablespoons chopped fresh parsley

Spiral Pasta Salad with Mushrooms, Broccoli, and Tempeh

1 package (8 ounces) tempeh

1½ cups sunflower oil

½ cup cider vinegar

5 tablespoons tamari

½ teaspoon ground ginger

¼ cup red wine

3 quarts water

1 pound pasta spirals or rotini, preferably spinach

2 cups broccoli, chopped (leave florets whole)

4 cloves garlic, minced

1 teaspoon dried basil

4 tablespoons olive oil

2 cups sliced mushrooms

2 medium tomatoes, cut in half and then sliced

½ cup minced fresh parsley

2 tablespoons lemon juice

Black pepper to taste

A tasty way to introduce tempeh into the diet of those who haven't had it before. Tempeh is especially delicious when marinated before it's cooked.

Slice the tempeh in half horizontally. You will now have 2 pieces of the original length and width but half as thick (fig. 2). Cut 6 pieces across the width of the tempeh (fig. 3). Cut these pieces in half again across the shorter side (fig. 4). Cut once more at a 45° angle to form small triangles (fig. 5). Combine oil, vinegar, 4 tablespoons tamari, wine, and ginger in a medium-sized bowl. Add tempeh and let sit at least 4 hours. Stir occasionally.

Bring 3 quarts water to a boil in a 4-quart pot for the pasta. Cook pasta until al dente (2 to 3 minutes if fresh pasta, 5 to 7 minutes if not). Drain and pour cold water over pasta. Drain well. Pour into large bowl.

In a 10-inch cast-iron pan, sauté broccoli, garlic, and basil together with 1 tablespoon oil until bright green and tender but not overcooked. Set aside in bowl to cool. Add remaining 3 tablespoons oil to fry pan. When hot, add tempeh after draining the marinade from it (reserve marinade). Cook until it begins to brown, stirring occasionally. Pour 1 teaspoon tamari over it. Cook 1 minute more. Turn off heat and allow to cool.

Toss ⅓ cup of the marinade, remaining 2 teaspoons tamari, and the rest of the ingredients with pasta. Stir well and serve or refrigerate until ready to serve.

Save the rest of the marinade. Store in a jar in the refrigerator or make into a salad dressing, adding some herbs and garlic to it.

6 servings

Oriental Salad

Marinade

¾ cup sunflower oil

¼ cup cider vinegar

1 tablespoon tamari

Salad

1 square tofu, cut into ½-inch cubes (½ pound)

1 teaspoon minced fresh ginger root

1 tablespoon oil

1 tablespoon plus 1 teaspoon tamari

One 5.3-ounce package Chinese-style rice noodles

1½ quarts boiling water

2 tablespoons sesame oil (do not substitute any other oil)

2 tablespoons lemon juice (approximately ½ lemon)

6 scallions, chopped

1 cup snow peas, sliced in half on an angle

¼ cup minced fresh parsley

1 red pepper, sliced in thin strips and cut in half

An unusual and tasty salad that offers protein balance as well.

Combine oil, vinegar, and 1 tablespoon tamari in a medium-sized bowl. Add tofu to marinade mix and refrigerate. This should sit for at least 2 hours, but a day is fine. Then drain (save marinade for other dishes). Sauté the tofu and fresh ginger in 1 tablespoon oil. When tofu is browned and crispy, pour 1 tablespoon tamari over it and stir for 1 minute more. Cook noodles in boiling water for 3 minutes until just done. Do not overcook. Drain quickly and pour into bowl. Add sesame oil and lemon juice immediately. Stir in, tossing with forks. Add remaining 1 teaspoon tamari and rest of ingredients. Toss well and serve.

4 to 6 servings

Marinated Rice Salad

An inexpensive salad option, and a great way to use up leftover rice.

Wash rice and put in a 2-quart pot with water. Bring to a boil, lower heat to a simmer, and cook, covered, until all the water is absorbed (approximately 45 minutes). Pour into medium-sized bowl and allow to cool. Pour lemon juice over rice and stir in.

When rice is cooled to lukewarm, add the vegetables, salt, pepper, and oil. Stir in well and chill at least 1 hour. Garnish with tomato.

6 to 8 servings

1½ cups uncooked medium or long grain brown rice (or 3 cups cooked rice)

3 cups water

Juice of 2 lemons

3 scallions, chopped

1 cup diced red pepper

¼ cup minced fresh parsley

1 cup celery, cut at a very sharp angle

½ cup peas, fresh or frozen

½ teaspoon salt

Freshly ground black pepper to taste

¼ cup olive oil

2 cups cherry tomatoes, sliced in half (or 2 medium tomatoes, halved and cut into quarters)

Wild Rice with Pine Nuts

¾ *cup uncooked wild rice*

2½ *cups water*

¾ *cup uncooked long grain brown rice*

1½ *cups water*

4 *cups water*

¼ *cup olive oil*

¼ *cup lemon juice (2 lemons)*

¾ *cup sunflower oil*

⅓ *cup cider vinegar*

1 *tablespoon tamari*

2 *cups sliced mushrooms*

4 *cloves garlic, minced*

1 *cup finely diced celery*

½ *cup finely diced red pepper*

¼ *cup minced fresh parsley*

½ *cup roasted pine nuts*

½ *teaspoon salt*

The wild rice and pine nuts are costly ingredients for the salad, but a little goes a long way. Buy the ingredients when you're feeling wealthy, and enjoy them!

Wash wild and brown rice separately. Bring 2 separate pots of water to a boil. Add wild rice to 2½ cups boiling water and brown rice to 1½ cups boiling water. Lower heat, simmer, and cook covered, with lid cracked, until water is evaporated and rice is tender but not soggy (50 to 60 minutes). If rice is still too chewy, add ¼ cup more water and cook until evaporated. Combine wild and brown rice in a medium-sized bowl and set aside to cool. As rice cools, add olive oil and lemon juice. This will help to prevent rice from sticking.

In a small bowl combine oil, vinegar, tamari, and mushrooms. Allow to marinate for at least 1 hour. Then drain, saving marinade for another time.

Preheat fry pan over medium heat. Add marinated mushrooms and garlic. Sauté until mushrooms are just tender (2 to 3 minutes). Add to cooling rice. Add remaining ingredients. Stir in well. Allow to finish cooling in refrigerator at least 1 hour. Serve on a bed of lettuce.

6 servings

Couscous Salad

Couscous originates from Morocco. These tiny, rock-hard balls of semolina flour (similar in appearance to millet) need only a hot water bath to turn them into a delightful, fluffy pasta. This is a light and colorful salad that will be a welcome dinner on a sweltering summer night.

In a medium-sized bowl, pour boiling water over couscous. Stir and cover, stirring occasionally, keeping covered until all the water has been absorbed (about 30 minutes). Uncover and allow to cool. Add chick peas.

In a fry pan, melt butter over medium heat. Add mushrooms, thyme, and garlic. Sauté until just tender. Add to couscous along with the rest of the ingredients. Chill 1 hour before serving.

8 servings

3 cups boiling water

2 cups couscous

2 cups cooked chick peas

1 tablespoon butter

2 cups sliced mushrooms

½ teaspoon dried leaf thyme

3 large cloves garlic, minced

1 medium-sized red pepper, chopped

1 cup peas, cooked fresh or frozen

½ cup currants

½ teaspoon salt

½ cup minced fresh parsley

1 teaspoon ground cumin

¼ teaspoon cayenne pepper

6 tablespoons olive oil

6 tablespoons lemon juice

Lemon Couscous Salad with Macadamia Nuts

1½ cups couscous

2 cups boiling water

1 tablespoon sunflower oil

3 cloves garlic, minced

2 cups chopped broccoli, stems and florets

¼ teaspoon dried dill weed

¾ cup chopped celery

1 cup whole macadamia nuts

¼ cup minced fresh parsley

½ pint cherry tomatoes, sliced in half

6 tablespoons lemon juice

6 tablespoons olive oil

½ teaspoon salt

The macadamia nuts make this salad especially nice, but cashew nuts may be substituted.

Put couscous into medium-sized mixing bowl. Pour boiling water over couscous and cover, stirring occasionally until all water is absorbed (about 30 minutes). Allow to cool.

In 1 tablespoon oil in small fry pan, sauté the garlic, broccoli, and dill weed. Cook over low to medium heat until just tender. Add to couscous along with celery, nuts, parsley, tomatoes, lemon juice, olive oil, and salt. Stir gently. Chill, covered, in refrigerator at least 1 hour.

6 to 8 servings

White Bean Salad

Sort and rinse beans, then soak in water 6 to 8 hours. Add bay leaf and bring to a boil. Cook and simmer 1 hour, or until soft but not mushy. Drain well, discarding bay leaf. Allow beans to cool for 20 minutes. Pour beans into medium bowl, add the vegetables, and stir. In blender, blend together the garlic and remaining ingredients, then pour over the vegetable-bean mixture. Stir well and allow to marinate in refrigerator at least 1 hour.

6 servings

2½ cups uncooked white or navy beans

7 cups water

1 bay leaf

1 medium-sized sweet red pepper, chopped

1 medium-sized green bell pepper, chopped

6 scallions, sliced

2 cups cooked peas

4 cloves garlic

½ teaspoon salt

2 teaspoons tamari

2 tablespoons lemon juice

2 teaspoons mustard

¼ cup red wine vinegar

¾ cup olive oil

Dash of black pepper

Three-Bean Salad

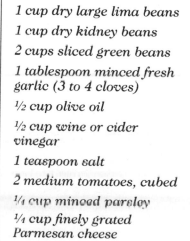

Soak lima and kidney beans in separate 2-quart pots. Cover beans with 1 quart water in each pot. Allow to soak 8 hours or overnight. Cook beans separately; bring to a boil, and simmer until just tender (about 1 hour for lima beans and 1½ hours for kidney beans). Drain well. Pour into medium-sized bowl and stir beans gently so they do not break apart.

Steam green beans until just barely tender. If using frozen green beans, do not cook them but add to cooked beans as is. Add steamed and drained green beans to lima and kidney beans. Add remaining ingredients. Stir gently, chill at least 1 hour, and serve.

6 to 8 servings

1 cup dry large lima beans

1 cup dry kidney beans

2 cups sliced green beans

1 tablespoon minced fresh garlic (3 to 4 cloves)

½ cup olive oil

½ cup wine or cider vinegar

1 teaspoon salt

2 medium tomatoes, cubed

¼ cup minced parsley

¼ cup finely grated Parmesan cheese

Greek Salad

Marinade

1½ cups sunflower oil

*¾ cup herb vinegar
(tarragon or dill is nice)*

¼ cup tamari

Salad

*1 can (14 ounces)
artichoke hearts, drained
and cut in half*

*1 medium-sized red onion,
sliced thinly (1 cup)*

*2 fresh medium tomatoes,
cut in half and sliced into
wedges*

*½ pound tender spinach
leaves, washed*

1 cup grated carrots

*½ cup pitted and chopped
Greek olives*

*3 cups (¾ pound) grated
or crumbled feta cheese*

W*e often serve this at weddings and luncheons
that the café caters. It always disappears fast!*

Mix oil, vinegar, and tamari together in small to medium-sized bowl. Add the artichoke hearts, onions, and
tomatoes. Allow to marinate for at least 2 hours; up to 24
hours is fine. Place spinach, carrots, olives, and feta in
salad bowl and toss. Drain marinated vegetables and top
spinach salad with them, toss, and serve. Use marinade
for a dressing. It also holds well refrigerated in a closed
jar until used again.

6 to 8 servings

Triple Pepper Salad

In a blender, mix ½ cup olive oil, garlic, vinegar, and salt. While blender is still running slowly, pour in remaining olive oil and blend until oil is mixed in.

Roast the peppers by sticking a fork into each pepper and holding it over an open flame until the skin puffs up and lightly browns. The skin should peel off easily, leaving the pepper still intact. Or set all the peppers in a preheated 400° oven and bake about 10 minutes until skins begin to bubble. Run them under cold water, peel, and slice.

In large bowl combine the peppers, onions, and chick peas. Pour the olive oil mixture over the peppers. Cover and refrigerate 3 to 4 hours. Strain vegetables, allowing to drain for 20 minutes. Save marinade. Lay out a few green lettuce leaves on a large platter. Set Triple Pepper Salad on top of lettuce and serve. Garnish with a few sprigs of parsley.

6 servings

1½ cups olive oil

5 large cloves garlic

¾ cup wine vinegar

½ teaspoon salt

2 yellow medium bell peppers

2 red medium bell peppers

2 green medium bell peppers

1 medium-sized red onion, coarsely chopped

1 cup cooked chick peas

A few green leafy lettuce leaves

Parsley

Guacamole

G uacamole goes with almost any Mexican meal at the café. It's served as a dip along with corn chips, or it tops a tossed green salad with tomato wedges, onion rings, and green peppers on the side, or it might be dolloped on top of a burrito, flauta, chimichanga, or enchilada. We occasionally stuff some inside of a bean and cheese burrito to make a guacamole burrito.

Peel and pit avocados. Mash well or puree in food processor. Add rest of ingredients (except corn chips or greens) and stir well. Serve with corn chips or on top of fresh salad greens.

Approximately
2 cups

2 ripe avocados

2 large cloves garlic, minced

½ cup finely chopped onion

Juice of 1 lemon

½ teaspoon ground cumin

1½ cups diced tomatoes

¼ teaspoon dried dill weed

½ teaspoon salt

Dash of cayenne pepper

Corn chips, or fresh salad greens

Mushroom Salad

1 cup heavy cream

¼ cup sour cream

1 tablespoon lemon juice

½ teaspoon Dijon mustard

Dash of black pepper

¼ teaspoon salt

1 pound sliced fresh mushrooms (around 6 packed cups)

¼ cup minced parsley

¼ cup finely diced red onion

1 lightly packed cup fresh spinach leaves

1 lightly packed cup watercress sprigs

A deliciously rich salad chock-full of mushrooms, it is at its best when served the same day it is made.

Set a heavy-gauge small saucepan over medium heat. Add heavy cream and bring to a slight boil. Lower heat to a very small simmer so that cream bubbles but doesn't boil over. Simmer 30 minutes, stirring occasionally. The cream should be thick and slightly yellow in color. Remove from heat.

Add sour cream, lemon juice, mustard, pepper, and salt to cream. Stir well. In a large mixing bowl, combine the mushrooms, parsley, and onions. Pour the cream mixture over the mushrooms and toss well.

Arrange spinach leaves to cover the bottom of a medium-sized salad bowl. Pour mushroom mixture on top of spinach leaves. Garnish the sides of the bowl with watercress sprigs and serve.

6 servings

Marinated Potato Salad

3 pounds potatoes (6 medium potatoes)

½ cup diced carrot (1 small carrot)

1½ cups green pepper sliced thin

6 scallions, sliced

¾ cup peas, fresh or frozen

¼ cup minced parsley

1 teaspoon salt

⅔ cup olive oil

⅔ cup cider vinegar

½ teaspoon dried dill weed

C ertain summer events—outdoor weddings, barbecues, picnics, and potlucks—simply go with potato salad, and it's missed if it's not there!

Wash potatoes well. Cover them with water in a 3-quart pot and bring to a boil. (Don't cut or peel the potatoes.) When just tender, drain and rinse with cold water. Cut into small cubes when cool enough to handle. Put potatoes into medium-sized bowl and add rest of ingredients. Stir well, chill at least 1 hour, and serve.

6 to 8 servings

Kiwi Lime Fruit Salad

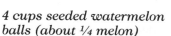

Combine all the fruits in a medium-sized bowl. Pour lime juice over them and gently stir in. Mix sour cream together with maple syrup and vanilla. Pour over salad just before serving.

6 to 8 servings

4 cups seeded watermelon balls (about 1/4 melon)

2 cups cantaloupe melon balls (1 small ripe cantaloupe)

3 kiwi fruit, peeled and sliced lengthwise in half and then crosswise into 1/4-inch slices

2 ripe bananas, peeled and sliced

1 cup seedless green grapes

1 cup sliced fresh strawberries

3 to 4 tablespoons lime juice to taste

1/2 cup sour cream

2 teaspoons maple syrup

1/2 teaspoon vanilla extract

Stuffed Honeydew Melon

1 large ripe honeydew melon, cut lengthwise in half, seeded, and formed into melon balls (reserve melon shells)

2 ripe peaches, pitted and sliced

1 ripe banana, peeled and cut into ¼-inch slices

1 cup red seedless grapes

½ fresh pineapple, peeled, cored, and cut into chunks (about 2 cups)

3 tablespoons lemon juice

½ cup sour cream (optional)

T*his is a beautiful-looking arrangement of fruit and works well at an outdoor buffet or summer potluck. When the café caters weddings we follow the same idea, using a long green watermelon, and increase the variety of fruit to include strawberries, blueberries, nectarines, and more.*

Set honeydew balls into a medium-sized bowl. Gently stir in the remaining fruits. Pour lemon juice (and sour cream if you like) over the fruits and stir. Pour any excess juice out of the melon shells. Pour fruit filling into both halves. It will be heaping but should fit. Serve right away if possible or wrap well in plastic wrap and refrigerate until serving.

For ½ stuffed melon, simply reserve the other ½ melon for slices. Cut back amounts by ½ where applicable (e.g., use the whole banana, but just 1 large peach).

10 to 12
servings

Dressings

Herb Dressing

Customers always request our recipe for this dressing. It's delicious on salads and we also serve it on the side with certain chapatis and sandwiches.

In a blender, combine ¼ cup oil, garlic, parsley, dill weed, chives, pepper, and celery seed. Blend 30 seconds.

Add vinegar, ¼ cup more oil, and salt. Blend again on low speed. After a few seconds, lift lid and slowly add the rest of the oil, running blender at low speed until oil is mixed in.

1½ cups

1 cup sunflower oil

2 large cloves garlic

½ cup fresh parsley sprigs

2 teaspoons dried dill weed

1 teaspoon dried chives

Dash of freshly ground black pepper

¼ teaspoon celery seed

⅓ cup cider vinegar

¼ teaspoon salt

Green Vinaigrette Dressing

In blender, puree garlic, parsley, and ½ cup olive oil. When nice and green, add rest of ingredients and puree once again.

1 cup

3 garlic cloves

¼ packed cup fresh parsley sprigs

¾ cup olive oil

1 tablespoon Dijon mustard

⅓ cup wine or herb vinegar

Freshly ground black pepper to taste

Dilly Vinaigrette Dressing

¾ cup olive oil

⅓ cup cider vinegar

⅓ cup chopped fresh dill weed

½ teaspoon salt

2 teaspoons dried chives (or 4 teaspoons chopped fresh chives)

Dash of freshly ground black pepper

In a blender, combine ¼ cup olive oil and the remaining ingredients. Run blender at low speed, lift lid, and slowly pour in the remaining olive oil. Return lid to blender and run at high speed 1 minute. This will thicken when refrigerated; allow to warm at room temperature 15 minutes before serving.

1 cup

Creamy Italian Dressing

2 cloves garlic

½ ripe medium tomato

3 tablespoons cider vinegar

½ cup yogurt

½ packed cup fresh parsley sprigs

2 teaspoons basil

2 teaspoons oregano

½ teaspoon salt

⅛ teaspoon ground black pepper

1 teaspoon celery seed

1 teaspoon honey

½ cup olive or sunflower oil

Put all ingredients except oil in a blender. Run blender and slowly pour oil into dressing while blender is running.

2 cups

Tahini Dressing

Mix tahini with lemon juice in a bowl, then slowly add water until tahini thins out. Stir in garlic, cumin, parsley, tamari, and cayenne.

2 cups

1 cup tahini
Juice of 1 lemon
¾ cup water
3 cloves garlic, minced
1 teaspoon ground cumin
¼ cup minced fresh parsley
2 teaspoons tamari
Dash of cayenne pepper

Tahini Yogurt Dressing

Mix tahini and yogurt together in a small bowl. Stir in water to thin; mix in parsley and tamari.

1 cup

½ cup tahini
¼ cup yogurt
½ cup water
¼ cup minced fresh parsley
1 teaspoon tamari

Parsley, Buttermilk, and Parmesan Dressing

Place all ingredients except Parmesan in blender. Cover and run 1 minute until smooth and well blended. Add Parmesan and run for 30 seconds more.

1⅓ cups

5 cloves garlic
1 cup buttermilk
1 packed cup fresh parsley sprigs
¼ cup finely grated Parmesan cheese

Sour Cream and Garlic Dressing

2 tablespoons very finely
minced garlic

¼ cup minced fresh
parsley

2 cups sour cream

½ teaspoon salt

⅛ teaspoon black pepper

1 tablespoon very finely
chopped fresh dill weed
(optional)

*T*his dressing is specifically aimed at garlic lovers,
and it is a regular and popular menu option at the
café. Vermonters have been accused by out-of-state
friends of eating more garlic per capita than any other
state in the union. They might be right!

Mix all ingredients together in a bowl. (If you have a
food processor, chop the garlic and parsley together with
a chopping blade and then add to sour cream.) Allow
dressing to sit at least 30 minutes for garlic to spread out
its flavor.

2 cups

Cucumber Dill Dressing

1 cup sour cream

½ cup fresh dill weed
sprigs

½ cup fresh parsley sprigs

1 cucumber, peeled only if
the skin has been waxed,
sliced lengthwise in half,
seeds scooped out, and
then cut up

2 cloves garlic

¼ teaspoon salt

Dash of black pepper

Place all ingredients in blender. Blend until smooth.

2 cups

Avocado Cream Cheese Dressing

Rich and delicious!

Put all ingredients into food processor or blender. Run until smooth. Turn off and stir to get lumps out. Turn on once again and run until smooth. Scrape out dressing with a rubber spatula. Best when served fresh.

1 cup

1 ripe avocado

1 tablespoon lemon juice

½ cup cream cheese, softened to room temperature

¼ teaspoon dried dill weed

1 clove garlic

⅛ teaspoon salt

¼ cup warm water

Russian Dressing

Embarrassingly simple to make, and it goes well with a Tempeh Reuben (page 159).

Mix in bowl until blended.

¾ cup

½ cup mayonnaise

¼ cup ketchup

¼ teaspoon dried dill weed

1 teaspoon chopped fresh chives

Tofu Russian Dressing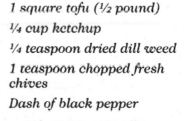

Place tofu in blender and run until smooth. Then combine with the remaining ingredients in a bowl and mix until blended.

¾ oup

1 square tofu (½ pound)

¼ cup ketchup

¼ teaspoon dried dill weed

1 teaspoon chopped fresh chives

Dash of black pepper

Spicy Tomato Dressing

1½ *cups tomato juice*

2 *large cloves garlic,
minced*

1 *tablespoon chopped fresh
cilantro (Chinese parsley)*

1 *tablespoon chopped fresh
chives*

Dash of cayenne pepper

A *tasty low-calorie dressing.*

Mix all ingredients together, stir well, and serve.

1½ cups

Tofu Dill Dressing

2 *cloves garlic*

1 *square tofu (½ pound)*

¼ *packed cup fresh
parsley sprigs*

1 *teaspoon dried dill weed*

¼ *teaspoon salt*

¼ *cup cider vinegar*

¾ *cup sunflower oil*

In a blender, combine the garlic, tofu, parsley, dill weed, salt, vinegar, and ¼ cup oil. Run until smooth. Turn off blender and stir if necessary. Slowly pour in remaining ½ cup oil with blender running on low speed.

Almost 2 cups

Simple Meals

Appetizers (page 142)

Hummus
Spinach Water Chestnut Dip
Onion Dip
Bleu Cheese Dip
Baked Artichoke Dip
Salsa
Roasted Nuts
Cheese-Stuffed Wrappers
Nachos

Sandwiches (page 149)

The Hot Greek Pita
Stuffed Pita Pockets
Melted Medley or Vegetable Medley in a Pita
Falafel and Lemon Tahini Sauce for Falafel
Greek Veggie Pita
Egg Salad
Garden Bagels
Broccoli Mushroom Sandwich with Three Cheeses
Farmer Cheese Melt
Ratatouille Open-Faced Sandwiches
Asparagus Open-Faced Sandwiches with Cream Cheese Sauce
Tempeh Reuben
Your Basic Sandwich
Mushroom Cheese Rolls

Burgers (page 163)

Tofu Burgers
Lentil Burgers
Mushroom Barley Burgers
Marinated Tempeh Burgers
Spicy Mexican Bean Burgers
Veggie Rice Burgers

Chapatis (page 169)

Tofu Chapati or Spread
Sea Vegetable Chapati
Sunshine Chapati
California Chapati
Broccoli and Cheddar Chapati

Stuffed Things (page 173)

Herb Stuffed Eggs
Stuffed Popovers
Baked Stuffed Potatoes
Tofu Stuffed Mushrooms
Florentine Stuffed Mushrooms

Even though Montpelier is the smallest state capital in the country, with a population of approximately 10,000 residents, there is still a large demand for good, simple food. Many working people commute into town daily from the surrounding rural areas. This addition to Montpelier's daytime population tends to make lunch at the café one of the busiest and most hectic parts of the day. "Here they come," Heidi the cook yells as the nearby bell tower clock strikes noon. The café's large wooden door swings open to a wave of entering customers.

Since lunchtime can be so busy, and most people have a limited lunch hour, we offer quick, easy-to-serve menu specials to reduce fuss and preparation. Many of these meals can also be served as a lighter main course for supper as well.

Other simple meals can be packed up in a brown bag lunch for the next day. Hummus makes a wonderful sandwich spread or dip. Many of the burgers are surprisingly delicious cold. Chapatis are a light alternative to a sandwich and are easy to eat while driving, if rolled tightly with one end wrapped in a sandwich bag. Herb Stuffed Eggs can go on a picnic, alongside a salad or as an appetizer. Nachos can be served as hors d'oeuvres, but many customers also order them for a quick lunch or dinner.

Single-person households will find solace in this chapter. The Melted Medley Pita is a fast and filling meal in itself and a favorite of mine when I'm home alone. Many of these dishes such as Falafel, Hummus, and Spicy Mexican Bean, Marinated Tempeh, and Lentil burgers can be frozen in smaller portions.

Every parent knows that children can be difficult and picky eaters. Fortunately, young people find some things more fun to eat than others. Generally, messy foods that get picked up and handled without the aid of utensils fall into this category, including nachos, veggie bagels, and stuffed pita sandwiches. Burgers smeared with mayonnaise and ketchup and topped with melted cheese, sprouts, and tomato result in messy hands and faces, but happy, satisfied kids.

Appetizers

Hummus

2 cups raw chick peas
(also known as garbanzo
beans)

6 cups water

1 tablespoon sunflower oil

1½ cups finely chopped
onion (3 onions)

¾ cup finely diced carrot
(1 medium carrot)

5 large cloves garlic,
minced

1 cup tahini

2 tablespoons tamari

½ cup lemon juice

1 teaspoon ground cumin

¼ teaspoon cayenne
pepper

½ teaspoon salt

*H*ummus is Middle Eastern in origin and traditionally served as a dip, but it also works well as a
spread or sandwich filling. The consistency in this recipe is best for sandwiches. For a dip, simply thin the
mixture with a little cold water.

*Chick peas or garbanzo beans need to cook for
hours before they become tender. It is more efficient to
make a large amount of Hummus since it freezes so
well. This recipe will yield 1½ quarts of Hummus:
freeze 1 or 2 containers of it for another time—you
won't regret it!*

Soak chick peas in water 6 hours or overnight. (In
warm weather refrigerate the peas while soaking or they
might ferment.) Bring chick peas to a boil and simmer,
covered, 2 to 3 hours or until tender (in a pressure
cooker they will take about 45 minutes).

Meanwhile, in a preheated 10-inch fry pan, heat the
oil, then add onions, carrots, and garlic. Sauté until
browned and tender.

Drain chick peas and mash with a bean masher or grating blade of a food processor. When pureed well, add the
remaining ingredients and mix thoroughly.

1½ quarts

Spinach Water Chestnut Dip

This is best when served the day it is made.

In cast-iron 10-inch fry pan, melt butter on medium heat. Add spinach and cook until just tender. Turn off heat, press any excess water out of spinach, and put into small bowl. Add rest of ingredients, mix thoroughly, and serve with chips.

2 cups

1 tablespoon butter

4 lightly packed cups chopped spinach

1 cup sour cream

½ cup yogurt

½ cup chopped watercress

2 large cloves garlic, minced

½ cup chopped water chestnuts

1 tablespoon finely chopped fresh dill weed (or 1 teaspoon dried dill weed)

½ teaspoon salt

Chips for dipping

Onion Dip

This is a natural and improved variation of soup-mix onion dip.

Heat the oil in a small fry pan and sauté onions on high heat until nicely browned (approximately 10 minutes). Stir often. Turn off heat and mix in vegetable concentrate well. Let onions cool a bit, then add them to sour cream in a bowl along with chives. Serve with cut-up veggies and chips.

3 cups

1 tablespoon sunflower oil

1 cup finely chopped onion

1½ tablespoons vegetable concentrate (vegetable base for soup in powder form)

2 cups sour cream

1 tablespoon chopped fresh chives

Cut-up raw vegetables and chips for dipping

Bleu Cheese Dip

1 cup sour cream

1½ cups grated or crumbled bleu cheese

½ cup yogurt

1 tablespoon chopped fresh dill weed (or 1 teaspoon dried dill weed)

⅛ teaspoon salt

Chips and/or raw vegetables for dipping

Mix all ingredients together in a small bowl. Serve with chips and/or vegetable dippers.

2 cups

Baked Artichoke Dip

1 can artichoke hearts (14 ounces), drained

4 large cloves garlic, minced

½ cup plus 2 tablespoons finely grated or Parmesan or Romano cheese

1 tablespoon lemon juice

¼ cup mayonnaise

¼ cup cream cheese, softened

2 tablespoons bread crumbs

Chips, crackers or raw vegetables for dipping

My friend Doug brought this dip to a party. It was quickly surrounded by artichoke lovers. We all sat down on the floor beside the dip and ate until it was all gone.

Finely chop artichoke hearts or run through a food processor along with the garlic using the steel chopping blade. Combine the ½ cup cheese, lemon juice, mayonnaise, and cream cheese. Mix well with the artichoke-garlic mixture. Put mixture into a 1-quart casserole dish. Sprinkle the top with bread crumbs and the remaining cheese. Bake 20 minutes at 375° until bubbly. Serve with chips, vegetable dippers, bread or crackers.

2 cups

Salsa

The café serves Salsa on the side with all our Mexican specials. It is a spicy hot sauce with tiny pieces of raw vegetables mixed into it. Salsa can also be served as a dip along with a bowl of corn chips or used as a sauce on Nachos.

Crush tomatoes; chop or run lightly through food processor. Combine with rest of ingredients. Chill until ready to serve.

3 cups

One 28-ounce can whole tomatoes in tomato juice (In season, 6 finely diced medium-sized fresh garden tomatoes are a wonderful option!)

1 tablespoon minced garlic

¼ teaspoon salt

2 teaspoons cider vinegar

2 teaspoons sunflower oil

2 teaspoons lemon juice

2 teaspoons ground cumin

½ cup very finely chopped onion (1 onion)

¾ cup very finely chopped green pepper (1 large pepper)

4 scallions, thinly sliced

¼ to ½ teaspoon cayenne pepper (to taste)

1 or 2 fresh hot chili peppers, minced (optional)

Roasted Nuts

These are a delicious snack. And it's much more economical to roast your own raw nuts.

In a pan with an edge on it, roast nuts in a 325° oven 10 minutes, stirring after 5 minutes. Pull out of oven and pour the tamari over nuts. Stir, making sure all the nuts get covered with tamari. Return to oven for approximately 5 more minutes, stirring once. They should be crisp, golden, and all the tamari absorbed. (They can burn easily, so don't forget about them!) Cool and store in a jar to keep fresh.

6 cups

6 cups nuts (cashews, almonds, walnuts, sunflower seeds, or a mixture)

3 tablespoons tamari

Cheese-Stuffed Wrappers

3 lightly packed cups grated Jalepeño pepper Jack cheese

3 lightly packed cups grated Monterey Jack or cheddar cheese

1 package egg roll wrappers (available with no additives in natural foods and grocery stores)

2½ cups sunflower oil

A *shortcut of the time-consuming egg roll, these wrappers are delicious and make a great appetizer.*

Mix cheeses together in a bowl. Place 1 wrapper out on a counter with 1 corner pointed toward you. Put ½ cup cheese into center of wrapper (fig. 1). Fold sides in (fig. 2) and moisten around edge with finger dabbed in warm water. Fold one more corner over filling (fig. 3), seal, after moistening edges once again with water, and continue to wrap roll tightly as you would roll up a blintz or as if you were making a snugly fitting envelope (fig. 4). Seal (fig. 5), using water on the edges. Repeat with another wrapper until you use up all the cheese. This will make 12 rolls, which can be stored wrapped in plastic or in a container until you're ready to cook them.

Heat oil in a 2-quart deep saucepan until hot (5 to 10 minutes on medium heat). Test by dipping corner of wrapper into oil: if it sizzles, it's hot enough. Drop 2 rolls gently into oil. Cook a few minutes until golden, then turn over, using slotted spoon or cooking chopsticks. Continue to cook another minute until golden brown, then remove from oil, drain on paper towels 1 to 2 minutes, and serve. Best when served nice and hot so that cheese oozes out. These can be reheated in oven and will store uncooked in refrigerator up to a week.

12 wrappers

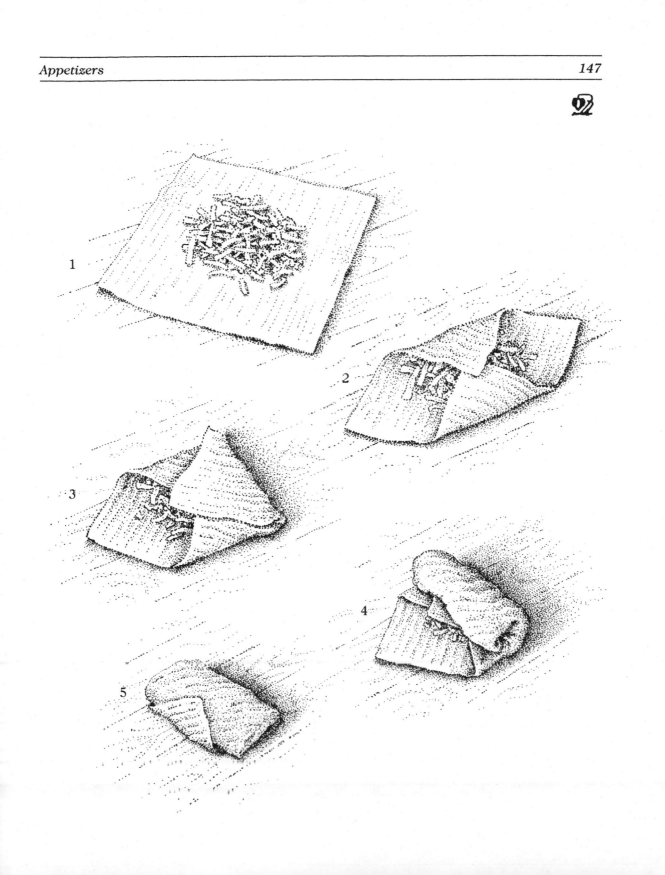

Nachos

Chips

Corn tortillas

4 cups sunflower oil

Salt (optional)

Sauce

*2 cups chopped zucchini
(1 medium-sized zucchini)*

1 cup chopped onion

*1 cup chopped green
pepper*

1 fresh hot chili pepper

5 large cloves garlic

2 teaspoons cumin seed

2 teaspoons chili powder

1½ cups tomato sauce

Cayenne pepper to taste

Cheese

*Grated Jalapeño pepper
Jack cheese (buy a plain
Monterey Jack or cheddar
cheese for those who don't
enjoy spicy foods,
especially children)*

Nachos can be as simple or involved as you feel like getting. You can buy corn chips rather than make them from tortillas, buy salsa or make nacho sauce, and add refried beans or guacamole to them. You can find all the ingredients at natural-food stores, with many chips and salsas now coming in salt-free as well as salted varieties. In any event, they will be a popular and delicious treat.

Cut corn tortillas (approximately 2 tortillas per person) into 6 pie-shaped slices per tortilla. Heat 1 quart sunflower oil in a 2-quart saucepan. When hot add 2 or 3 cut-up tortillas to oil. Tortillas should cook very quickly as long as the oil is hot enough. If chips begin to look soggy and greasy allow the oil to reheat for 1–2 minutes before adding more tortillas. Cook until just crisp, drain, and set on paper towels. Repeat until you have enough chips. A dash of salt over the tortillas is optional. The oil can be reused a few times for deep frying.

In food processor or blender, puree all sauce ingredients except tomato sauce and cayenne until smooth. Simmer this vegetable puree in a saucepan over low heat 15 minutes, then add tomato sauce. Simmer 10 minutes more. Taste for spiciness; add cayenne if you like a hotter sauce.

To assemble nachos, preheat oven to 400°. Lay out chips on cookie sheet. Spread sauce lightly over chips, then cover with grated cheese. Bake 5 to 7 minutes until bubbly and serve.

Options:

1. Before putting on your nacho sauce, spread chips with 1 to 2 cups refried beans.

2. Slice some fresh hot chili peppers and place on top of the cheese.

3. After baking nachos, top with guacamole, or lettuce and tomato and onion rings, or sour cream, or all of the above options for supernachos!

Sandwiches

The Hot Greek Pita

A rich and tasty blend of baked feta and cottage cheese stuffed into a pita with crunchy veggies and topped with Tahini Dressing.

Run cottage cheese through blender or food processor, if possible, to make mix smoother. Combine in medium-sized bowl with the feta cheese, basil, oregano, garlic, tahini, and pepper. Mix well. Put approximately ½ cup of the mixture in each pita half. Heat in 400° oven 5 to 7 minutes. Fill each pocket with spinach leaves, tomatoes, onion rings, and peppers; top with sprouts. Serve Tahini Dressing on the side.

4 servings

1 pound cottage cheese

1 cup crumbled or grated feta cheese

1 teaspoon basil

1 teaspoon oregano

2 cloves garlic, finely minced

1 tablespoon tahini

Dash of black pepper

2 whole pita breads, cut in half

Spinach leaves

2 medium tomatoes, sliced

1 red onion, sliced into rings

1 medium red or green pepper, sliced

Sprouts

Tahini Dressing (page 135)

Stuffed Pita Pockets

1 tablespoon sunflower oil

1½ cups chopped broccoli, stems and florets

½ cup chopped onion (1 onion)

3 large cloves garlic, minced

¼ teaspoon basil

¼ teaspoon dried leaf thyme

1 cup sliced zucchini (1 small zucchini)

2 cups sliced mushrooms

¼ teaspoon salt

Dash of black pepper

2 whole pita breads

Mozzarella cheese

Sharp cheddar cheese

2 medium tomatoes, sliced

Preheat oven to 375°. Set 10-inch fry pan on medium heat. Add oil, then the broccoli, onions, garlic, basil, and thyme. Sauté 2 minutes, then add zucchini and sauté 1 minute. Add mushrooms, salt, and pepper and stir well. Cook 2 minutes more until just tender. Remove from heat, set aside, and drain if juicy.

Cut pita breads in half to form 4 pockets. Put ½ cup sautéed vegetables into each pocket. Filling should be used up. Add 3 thin slices each of mozzarella and cheddar cheese to each pocket. Follow with 2 slices tomato. Bake on a cookie sheet 7 minutes and serve.

4 pockets

Melted Medley or Vegetable Medley in a Pita

These pita sandwiches are on the café's regular menu. They are filled with raw and sautéed vegetables, and melted cheese on the top is a delicious option. They are quite filling and can be a meal in themselves.

Preheat oven to 375°. Set 10-inch fry pan over medium heat. Add oil, then onions and basil. Cook a few minutes, until onions begin to brown. Add broccoli and salt and continue to cook until broccoli is just tender. Remove from heat.

Cut a circle around the edge of each pita bread. Cut all around the outside circumference of the pita and pull the 2 halves apart. You will have 2 full circles from each pita and have split the pita in half, not across.

Lay out the 4 bottoms of pita bread on a baking sheet. Place approximately ½ cup broccoli mixture onto each pita bottom. Set fresh spinach leaves over the broccoli mixture and follow with sliced mushrooms. If you want cheese on your pita, put enough thin slices of cheese over the vegetables to cover pita. If no cheese is going on the pita, cover vegetables with sliced tomatoes. Bake for 7 minutes until vegetables are hot and spinach has wilted. Cheese should be nicely melted.

Pull pita bottoms out of oven and place pita tops in the oven while you prepare the rest of the pita. Place pitas on plates and top with tomato slices (if you have not already) and sprouts. Now take the pita tops out of the oven and top each sandwich with one. Serve with a side of Herb Dressing.

1 tablespoon sunflower oil

½ cup chopped onion (1 onion)

½ teaspoon basil

3 cups chopped broccoli, stems and florets

¼ teaspoon salt

4 whole pita breads

3 slightly packed cups fresh spinach leaves

2 cups sliced mushrooms

Colby or cheddar cheese, sliced thin (optional)

3 medium tomatoes, sliced

2 cups alfalfa sprouts

Herb Dressing (page 133)

4 large servings

Falafel

2 cups dried chick peas

4 cups water

Approximately 4 cups plus 1 tablespoon sunflower oil (save and reuse for other deep frying meals)

½ cup minced onion (1 onion)

8 cloves garlic, minced

½ teaspoon salt

1 teaspoon ground cumin

1 teaspoon turmeric

½ teaspoon ground coriander

½ teaspoon cayenne pepper

½ cup tahini

1 cup bread crumbs

About 1 cup whole wheat pastry flour

8 large pita breads

Lettuce leaves

6 medium tomatoes, sliced

2 onions, sliced into rings

2 cucumbers, sliced (peel only if the skin is waxed)

2 green peppers, sliced

Lemon Tahini Sauce (page 153)

Falafel is a Middle Eastern delight and always a popular lunch special at the café. It is labor intensive to make, but much of the time is involved in cooking the beans and preparing the mix. Consequently, this recipe makes a large amount: freeze half the mix for another meal. The cooked falafel balls also freeze well.

Soak the chick peas overnight in at least 4 cups water. Then cook until very soft, adding more water as needed (2 to 3 hours on top of stove or 45 to 60 minutes in a pressure cooker). You will have 4 cups cooked chick peas.

Heat 1 tablespoon oil in a small frying pan. Sauté onions and garlic over medium heat. As onions begin to brown, add salt and spices and turn heat off.

Drain chick peas well and mash finely (or put through food mill or use chopping or grating blade of food processor). Add onions, garlic, spices, and tahini to beans. Stir, then add bread crumbs and ½ cup whole wheat flour. Mix well (your hands work best for this job). The mixture should be somewhat firm; add more flour if needed.

Heat about 4 cups oil in a deep saucepan—the oil should be about 2 to 3 inches deep. Roll some of the mix into a ball the size of a golf ball (go smaller rather than bigger), and then dip balls in flour. When oil has heated on medium high heat for approximately 7 minutes, put in 1 ball. The oil should boil and foam around it. If it doesn't foam enough, raise the heat. If there's too much foam boiling over the pan, turn down the heat. If the ball falls apart in oil, add more flour to mix. Roll mix into balls once you are certain the mix consistency is good, and dip the remaining balls into flour. You can cook these all up and freeze a portion for another meal.

Slice each pita bread in half to form 2 pockets, then stuff each half with 3 hot falafel balls, lettuce leaves, and tomato, onion, cucumber, and green pepper slices. Serve with lots of Lemon Tahini Sauce.

8 servings (48 golf ball-sized falafel)

Lemon Tahini Sauce for Falafel

It wouldn't be Falafel without it!

Pour tahini into a small to medium-sized mixing bowl. Add lemon juice, spices, and garlic. Stir and add water. Stir well. Add tamari and parsley. If the sauce is too thick, add a bit more water. Serve with Falafel (opposite page), with some sauce on the inside of pita and some on top. This sauce freezes well.

2 cups

1½ cups tahini

⅔ to ¾ cup lemon juice

1½ teaspoons ground cumin

2 teaspoons ground turmeric

½ teaspoon cayenne pepper

6 cloves garlic, minced

1 cup water

2 tablespoons tamari

1 cup minced fresh parsley

Greek Veggie Pita

Cut pita breads in half to form 4 pockets. Stuff each pita with spinach leaves and top with grated carrot. Slip cucumber slices on one side of the spinach leaves, tomato slices and mushrooms on the other. Top with feta cheese and a few onion rings. Serve with Herb Dressing on the side.

4 pockets

2 whole pita breads

4 cups fresh spinach leaves

1 cup grated carrot (1 carrot)

1 small cucumber, sliced (peel only if the skin has been waxed)

2 medium tomatoes, sliced

1½ cups sliced mushrooms

1½ cups grated or crumbled feta cheese

¼ cup raw red onion rings

Herb Dressing (page 133)

Egg Salad

4 large eggs

5 tablespoons mayonnaise

1 cup finely chopped celery
(1 stalk)

¼ cup minced fresh
parsley

1 scallion, minced

Dash of salt and black
pepper

1 tablespoon minced fresh
dill weed

An egg salad sandwich special is a sign of spring at the café. The first warm spring days are often followed by more freezing temperatures and even an occasional heavy snowfall before spring really stays.

Cover eggs with lightly salted water in a pot. Bring to a boil. Boil 12 minutes. Drain out hot water and immerse eggs immediately in cold water, letting it run into pot until eggs are cooled. Peel. (Rapidly cooling the eggs makes them easier to peel. Very fresh eggs are difficult, if not impossible, to peel.)

Chop the eggs finely. Add mayonnaise, vegetables, and seasonings. Cover and cool in refrigerator 1 hour if you like your egg salad cold. I personally like it best when the eggs are still just a little warm. This is wonderful as a sandwich with lettuce and tomato and sprouts on whole wheat or pita bread or on top of a green salad.

Filling for 4
sandwiches

Garden Bagels

1¼ cups cream cheese,
softened

½ cup finely diced carrot
(1 small carrot)

½ cup finely chopped
celery

5 small scallions, chopped

¼ teaspoon celery seed

4 bagels

2 medium tomatoes, sliced

1 cucumber, sliced, (peel
if skin has been waxed)

1 cup alfalfa sprouts

Seasoned vegetable salt

These are a café favorite that I first made and sold while my sandwich business was in operation.

In a small bowl, mix the cream cheese with the carrots, celery, scallions, and celery seed. The easiest way to mix this is with your hand; a spoon will not go easily through this mixture. Now slice your bagels in half lengthwise. Lightly toast them if they are not fresh. Put ¼ cup mixture on each bagel half and spread over the bagel. Top with tomato and cucumber slices, some sprouts, and a dash of vegetable salt.

4 servings

Broccoli Mushroom Sandwich with Three Cheeses

Hot sandwiches are very popular at the café, especially through the cold winter months, and these
are no exception. Open-faced sandwiches are particularly nice for those with smaller appetites. They aren't
quite so filling and allow room for a cup of soup first or
some dessert to follow.

Preheat oven to 375°. Heat a 10-inch fry pan over medium heat. Add oil, then broccoli and thyme. After broccoli cooks 2 to 3 minutes, add mushrooms and salt and
cook until just barely tender. Remove from heat and
drain out any excess juices.

Place bread on cookie sheet. Top each piece of bread
with the broccoli-mushroom mixture. Then spread bleu
cheese over this, followed by slices of mozzarella and
cheddar cheese. Sprinkle walnuts on top and bake 10
minutes.

4 servings

1 tablespoon sunflower oil

2 cups chopped broccoli, stems and florets

½ teaspoon dried leaf thyme

2 cups sliced mushrooms

¼ teaspoon salt

4 slices rye bread

1½ cups grated or crumbled bleu cheese

8 small thin slices mozzarella cheese

8 small thin slices cheddar cheese

¼ cup chopped walnuts

Farmer Cheese Melt

1 cup farmer cheese
(ricotta can be substituted)

4 or 8 slices rye or whole
wheat bread

¼ cup coarsely chopped
mild pickled peppers
(about 6 peppers)

3 medium tomatoes, sliced

1 small onion, sliced thinly

12 thin slices sharp
cheddar cheese

Dash of basil

Butter

The café buys its farmer cheese from Butterworks, a local farm that feeds its herd organic grains. The cheese is exceptional, a creamy, rich, fresh, and wonderful treat.

The pickled hot peppers that I use in these sandwiches are labeled mild on the jar, and a hot pepper lover can certainly eat these like a pickle. The cheese and bread combination cools down these mild peppers to a moderately tasty level of hotness. Those who dislike spicy foods can simply omit the hot pickled peppers.

Preheat oven to 325° if baking and not grilling the sandwiches.

Spread ¼ cup farmer cheese on each of 4 slices bread. Top cheese with pickled peppers. Then spread 3 or 4 slices of tomato over the peppers. Follow this with a few pieces of onion ring. Top each sandwich with 3 slices of cheddar cheese. Sprinkle basil over the cheese.

If baking, set sandwiches on cookie sheets and bake open faced with no tops on the sandwiches. Bake 7 to 10 minutes and serve.

If grilling, preheat thick 10-inch fry pan or griddle over low to medium heat. When hot, butter the bottom of the pan and set 2 sandwiches in along with remaining pieces of bread topping each sandwich. Cover and cook until bread is nicely browned. Lightly butter the top of sandwiches and flip them over. Cover and continue to cook until bread is browned and cheese melts. If cheese is not melting, pour a tablespoon of water into side of pan and quickly cover. The steam will help the cheese to melt quickly. Repeat process for other 2 sandwiches. Cut in half and serve.

4 sandwiches

Ratatouille Open-Faced Sandwiches

I often work at the counter and grill during lunch, and when the café begins to fill up the pace of the staff speeds up dramatically. I start abbreviating everything I say, much to some people's chagrin. A Broccoli and Cheddar Chapati becomes a broc chap, Ellie is El, Caroline, Car, etc.

One particularly busy lunch hour a customer ordered the lunch special from me, which was a Ratatouille Open-Faced Sandwich. I called my order back to the kitchen, "One rat face, please." The laughter rose up around me before I realized what I'd said.

Preheat oven to 375°.

Set a 10-inch fry pan over medium heat; add olive oil, then onion, garlic, basil, oregano, eggplant, zucchini, and pepper. Sauté over medium heat approximately 5 to 7 minutes until vegetables just become tender. Remove from heat. Add tomatoes, salt, and pepper. Drain excess juice out of the vegetables.

Lay out 6 slices of bread. Spread about ⅔ cup ratatouille mixture over each slice. Then cover with thin slices of mozzarella cheese. Follow with a tablespoon of Parmesan cheese. Bake 7 minutes.

6 sandwiches

1 tablespoon olive oil

½ cup chopped onion (1 onion)

5 large cloves garlic, minced

1 teaspoon basil

1 teaspoon oregano

2 cups peeled and diced eggplant

2 cups sliced zucchini (1 medium zucchini)

1 cup sliced red or green pepper (1 large pepper)

2 medium tomatoes, chopped

¼ teaspoon salt

Dash of black pepper

6 slices of your favorite bread

Mozzarella cheese

6 tablespoons grated Parmesan cheese

Asparagus Open-Faced Sandwiches with Cream Cheese Sauce

14 to 16 thin stalks fresh asparagus

1 cup cream cheese

1 teaspoon Dijon-style mustard

1 teaspoon lemon juice

¼ teaspoon dried dill weed

¾ cup milk

4 slices rye bread

Swiss cheese

Preheat oven to 375°.

Cut tough ends off asparagus (1- to 1½-inch pieces at bottom ends of stalks). Steam asparagus until just tender (5 to 7 minutes). Set aside.

Put cream cheese in double boiler on medium flame. When soft, stir in mustard, then lemon juice and dill weed. Slowly pour in milk. Cover and reduce heat to low flame while sandwiches are made and baked.

Spread slices of rye bread on baking sheet. Cover each slice of bread with a thin layer of Swiss cheese. Cut asparagus into bite-sized pieces. Lay across cheese. Bake 7 minutes. Serve with cheese sauce on top of each sandwich.

4 sandwiches

Tempeh Reuben

The vegetarian's Reuben sandwich!

First cut tempeh into thirds, then slice each third in half through the middle to make each piece half as thick as it was. You now have 6 pieces.

Heat oil in 10-inch fry pan. When hot, set 3 pieces of tempeh into oil, turning over when lightly browned. When other side is done, drain on paper towels. Repeat for other 3 pieces. Tempeh can also be baked rather than fried. To bake tempeh, preheat oven to 400°. Brush a cookie sheet and tempeh lightly with oil (and a bit of tamari as well on the tempeh). Bake 10 to 15 minutes until nicely browned.

Lightly toast bread; if using Swiss cheese, toast bread in oven topped with a few slices of Swiss cheese until melted. Make sandwiches with 2 slices tempeh per sandwich. Garnish with sauerkraut, spinach leaves, sprouts, tomatoes, onion rings, and Russian Dressing.

3 sandwiches

One 8-ounce package tempeh

½ cup sunflower oil

Tamari

6 slices rye or pumpernickel bread

6 slices Swiss cheese (optional)

Sauerkraut

Spinach leaves

Sprouts

1 large or 2 small tomatoes, sliced

Onion rings

Russian Dressing (page 137) or Tofu Russian Dressing (page 137)

Your Basic Sandwich

M*any of us fall into ruts in the meals we prepare, especially ones we pull together regularly and quickly. Sandwiches are certainly in this category, and it is especially likely to happen to those who pack a lunch every day. Here are some options that will hopefully give your lunchtime sandwich some style.*

Some Especially Nice Combinations

Avocado deluxe.
Mayo, sprouts, tomato, avocado, and colby cheese on whole wheat

Grilled.
Spinach, tomato, onion rings, mozzarella, cheddar, and Parmesan with Sour Cream and Garlic Dressing (page 136) spread on whole wheat bread

Grilled.
Bleu cheese, Monterey Jack, cheddar, mushrooms, and tomato on 4-grain bread

Baked open-faced.
Havarti cheese with dill, sliced mushrooms, chopped and lightly sautéed broccoli, and topped with roasted walnuts on sourdough rye with mustard

Cold open-faced.
Swiss cheese, cucumber, avocado, red onion slices, and sprouts with Russian Dressing (page 137) on rye

A pocket pita.
Cold with Tofu Spread (page 169), cheddar cheese, sprouts, tomato, avocado, onion, and Herb Dressing (page 133)

Cold or grilled garden cheddar.
Sharp cheddar on whole wheat with cucumber, green pepper, onion, and mayo

Sandwich Fixings and Fillings

Bread Choices

Whole wheat/cracked wheat

Rye/sourdough rye

French/sourdough French

4-grain

Pumpernickel

Rolls

Croissants

Pitas

Bagels

Chapatis

English muffins

Other Options

Walnuts

Olives

Garlic

Pickles

Pickled vegetables

Fresh chopped herbs

Mayonnaise, mustard

Russian Dressing (page 137)

Tahini Dressing (page 135)

Sour Cream and Garlic Dressing (page 136)

Herb Dressing (page 133)

Hard-boiled eggs

Bananas

Tofu

Tempeh

Veggies

Tomato

Red onion

Sprouts

Mushrooms

Spinach

Broccoli

Green and red peppers

Cucumber

Avocado

Zucchini

Hot peppers

Asparagus

Eggplant

Shredded beets

Scallions

Lettuce

Spreads

Hummus (page 142)

Tofu Spread (page 169)

Nut butters

Egg Salad (page 154)

Guacamole (page 129)

Jams

Cheeses

Cheddar

Swiss

Havarti

Havarti with dill

Cream cheese

Gouda

Mozzarella

Bleu cheese

Monterey Jack

Jalapeño pepper Jack

Parmesan

Romano

Feta

Ricotta

Cottage

Farmer

Colby

Provolone

How to Serve It

Cold/closed

Cold/open-faced

Hot/grilled

Open-faced/baked

Toasted (bread only)

Mushroom Cheese Rolls

1 cup warm water

1 tablespoon baker's yeast

1 teaspoon honey

½ teaspoon salt

1 tablespoon sunflower oil

1¼ cups whole wheat flour

1¼ cups unbleached white flour, or as needed

2 tablespoons butter

4 large cloves garlic, minced

¼ teaspoon dried dill weed

4 cups sliced mushrooms

Dash of salt and black pepper

¼ cup finely grated Romano cheese

1 cup grated havarti cheese

½ cup chopped walnuts (optional)

Butter

In a medium-sized bowl, combine the warm water, yeast, honey, and salt. Stir well and allow to sit until mixture is foamy at the top (around 10 minutes). Stir in the oil, whole wheat flour, and 1 cup of the unbleached white flour. Turn out onto floured board and knead for about 10 minutes, using some of the reserved unbleached flour on board as needed. When dough is smooth and elastic, cover and set in a warm place for 1 hour or until doubled.

Preheat oven to 375°. Set a medium fry pan over high heat. Add butter. When melted, add garlic, dill weed, mushrooms, salt and pepper. Sauté 4–5 minutes, or until tender. Drain off any excess liquid and set aside.

Turn the dough out onto floured board and roll into a 12 × 16-inch rectangle. Spread sautéed mushrooms over dough, leaving ½-inch border around the edge. Top with grated cheeses.

Roll up the dough lengthwise, forming a long log, jelly roll fashion. Cut into approximately 1-inch-wide slices. Place rolls cut side down on a buttered cookie sheet 1 inch apart. Sprinkle tops of rolls with walnuts. Bake 20 minutes at 375° until nicely browned on top. Serve topped with a dot of butter.

16 rolls

Burgers

Tofu Burgers

Michelle, a past café worker, created this recipe. She entered it into a tofu recipe contest at our local natural foods store and won. The prize was a tofu cookbook, which she gave to the café.

Tofu burger mix freezes well.

Mash tofu and mix with tahini in medium-sized bowl until smooth. Heat 2 tablespoons oil in a small pan, sauté onion with dill weed until lightly browned, and add to tofu. Mix in sunflower seeds, bread crumbs, tamari, and pepper, adding more bread crumbs as needed until firm. Using ½ cup mixture per patty, form into patties, dipping both sides in whole wheat flour until lightly coated.

In a clean frying pan, heat the remaining 2 tablespoons oil. Fry patties over medium heat until browned on each side. Serve on rolls with tahini, spinach leaves, sprouts, and tomato, with Tahini Dressing or ketchup on the side.

8 to 10
burgers

2 squares tofu, drained and pressed (1 pound)

½ cup tahini

4 tablespoons sunflower oil

¾ cup finely chopped Spanish onion (1 large onion)

1 tablespoon dried dill weed

½ cup finely chopped or ground sunflower seeds

½ cup bread crumbs

2 tablespoons tamari

Black pepper or cayenne pepper to taste

Whole wheat flour

8 to 10 whole wheat rolls

Tahini

Spinach leaves

Alfalfa sprouts

2 medium tomatoes, sliced

Tahini Dressing (page 135)

Ketchup

Lentil Burgers

1½ cups uncooked green lentils

3 cups water

1 cup finely chopped onion (2 onions)

½ teaspoon celery seed

½ teaspoon salt

⅛ teaspoon cayenne pepper

⅓ cup finely chopped fresh parsley

1½ cups bread crumbs

Whole wheat flour

2 to 3 tablespoons sunflower oil

8 slices cheddar cheese (optional)

8 rolls or English muffins

Tomato slices

Onion rings (optional)

Sprouts

Mustard, mayonnaise, or ketchup (optional)

*L*entil Burgers have always been a favorite of mine and were the first vegetarian burger I ever made. They were also a Mother's Best Sandwiches company product and sold well even though they were served cold. The leftovers can become tomorrow's packed lunch. The mix also freezes well.

Wash and pick through lentils. Put into a 2-quart pot with water. Bring to a boil, lower to simmer, and cover pot. Cook until water is evaporated and lentils are tender (30 to 45 minutes). Remove from heat. Add onions and stir. Add celery seed, salt, and cayenne. When the mixture is cool, add parsley and bread crumbs. Mix well, mashing lentils slightly. Taste and adjust seasoning. Form into 8 patties, and dip each side into whole wheat flour to coat lightly.

Heat enough oil to just cover bottom of pan *lightly*. Fry the burgers on medium heat. Flip when brown. Add a slice of cheese to each burger at this point if you like. Lower heat and cover pan until cheese melts. Serve on hot rolls or toasted English muffins with tomato slices, onion rings, sprouts, etc.

8 burgers

Mushroom Barley Burgers

Combine the barley and water in a 2-quart saucepan. Bring to a boil and simmer, covered, until water is evaporated and barley is tender. You will have 2 cups barley. Place 1½ cups barley in a blender and blend until smooth. Put into medium-sized mixing bowl with unblended barley and mix.

Heat 1 tablespoon oil in 10-inch fry pan and sauté the onions and pepper on medium heat with the thyme. When the onions begin to brown, add mushrooms and continue to cook until tender and lightly browned. Remove from heat, drain any liquid, and add to barley along with parsley, nuts, bread crumbs, salt, and cayenne. Mix well. Add more bread crumbs if needed to stiffen mix. Form into 8 patties, and dip into flour on both sides to coat lightly.

Heat fry pan with remaining 2 tablespoons oil and cook burgers until brown. Flip. A slice of cheese can be added; cover pan and let cheese melt. Serve on rolls with lettuce, sprouts, tomato, Tahini Dressing, mayonnaise, or mustard.

8 burgers

1 cup uncooked barley (unhulled organic barley is best)

2 cups water

3 tablespoons sunflower oil

¾ cup minced onion (1 large onion)

¾ cup finely chopped green pepper (1 medium pepper)

1 teaspoon dried leaf thyme

3 firmly packed cups diced mushrooms

¼ cup minced fresh parsley

⅓ cup ground walnuts

¾ cup bread crumbs

1 teaspoon salt

⅛ teaspoon cayenne pepper

Whole wheat flour

8 slices colby or Monterey Jack cheese (optional)

8 whole wheat rolls

Lettuce, sprouts, sliced tomato, Tahini Dressing (page 135), mayonnaise, or mustard

Marinated Tempeh Burgers   92

One 8-ounce package
tempeh

1 cup plus 3 tablespoons
sunflower oil

½ cup cider vinegar

2 tablespoons tamari

4 whole wheat rolls

Tomato slices

Alfalfa sprouts

Onion rings

Tahini, mayonnaise, or
ketchup

Cut tempeh into quarters. Mix 1 cup oil, vinegar, and tamari together in shallow, wide bowl. Put tempeh quarters into bowl and allow to sit, turning over occasionally. Marinate at least 2 hours. You can let it marinate for a day in the refrigerator if you like.

When ready to cook, heat 3 tablespoons oil in a 10-inch fry pan. Lift tempeh from marinade, drain and set it in fry pan on medium heat. Cook until crispy and browned, flip over, and cook other side. Warm rolls in oven. Serve with tomato, sprouts, onion rings, etc.

4 burgers

Spicy Mexican Bean Burgers

Heat 10-inch fry pan over medium heat and add 1 tablespoon oil. When hot, add the onions, garlic, oregano, and hot pepper. Stir occasionally, then when onions just begin to brown, add green pepper and sauté mixture 2 minutes more. Remove from heat.

In medium-sized bowl, mix vegetables with mashed beans. Stir and add bread crumbs, cumin, salt, chili powder, and parsley. Mix well and form into patties, using about ½ cup mix per patty to form 5 patties. Dip into whole wheat flour so burgers are lightly coated with flour.

Set 10-inch fry pan over medium heat and add remaining 4 tablespoons oil. When hot, add burgers. Brown on one side, flip over, and top each patty with a slice of cheese. Lower heat and cover pan. Cook until cheese has melted nicely and burger is browned (approximately 5 minutes). Serve on rolls with lettuce on the bottom, tomato slices, onion rings, and Salsa on the top, and extra Salsa on the side.

5 burgers

5 tablespoons sunflower oil

¾ cup diced onion (1 large onion)

1 tablespoon minced garlic (4 large cloves)

½ teaspoon oregano

1 tablespoon minced hot pepper (1 small hot pepper)

½ cup diced green bell pepper (1 small pepper)

2 cups cooked, drained, and mashed pinto beans

½ cup bread crumbs

½ teaspoon ground cumin

½ teaspoon salt

½ teaspoon chili powder

2 tablespoons minced fresh parsley

Whole wheat flour

5 slices Jalapeño pepper Jack cheese

5 whole wheat rolls or English muffins

Lettuce leaves

1 large tomato, sliced

Onion rings (optional)

Salsa (page 145)

Veggie Rice Burgers

3 tablespoons sunflower oil

½ cup diced carrot (1 small carrot)

½ cup diced onion (1 onion)

½ cup diced zucchini

½ cup chopped celery

2 large cloves garlic, minced

½ teaspoon dried leaf thyme

½ teaspoon dried dill weed

2 cups cooked brown rice, mashed slightly

¼ teaspoon salt

1 teaspoon tamari

1 tablespoon tahini

Whole wheat flour

6 slices cheddar cheese (optional)

6 whole wheat rolls

Lettuce or sprouts

1 large tomato, sliced

Tahini Dressing (page 135)

A *great way to use up leftover brown rice.*

Preheat 10-inch fry pan over medium heat. Add 1 tablespoon oil, then carrots, onions, zucchini, celery, garlic, thyme, and dill weed. Sauté, stirring occasionally until vegetables are tender.

Add vegetables to cooked rice in a medium-sized bowl. Mix well, add salt, tamari, and tahini, and mix again. Form into patties, using approximately ½ cup mix per burger. Dip each patty into whole wheat flour so both sides are lightly coated.

Preheat 10-inch fry pan over medium heat. Add remaining 2 tablespoons oil, then burgers. When brown on one side (3 to 5 minutes), flip, adding a slice of cheese per burger if you like. Cover pan and cook until cheese is melted and burger browned. Serve on warmed whole wheat rolls with lettuce or sprouts, tomato slices, and Tahini Dressing on the side.

6 burgers

Chapatis

Tofu Chapati or Spread

This is a nondairy version of egg salad. It's quite delicious and at its best when freshly made. It can be used as a dip with crackers and vegetables on the side, or as a sandwich filling.

A regular menu item at the café is a tofu chapati. Simply spread a thin line of tahini down the center of a chapati, then top with some fresh spinach leaves. Follow with ½ cup Tofu Spread and spread this over the spinach. Top with alfalfa sprouts and serve it with a side of Tahini Dressing (page 135). For an extra treat, add a few slices of avocado on top.

Put tofu into bowl. Mash and mix with tahini, stirring until smooth. Add veggies, parsley, and tamari. Stir until thick and tasty. Add optional ingredients to taste if you like.

3 cups or 6 chapatis

2 squares tofu, drained and pressed (1 pound)

½ cup tahini

3 stalks celery, finely chopped

1 green pepper, finely chopped

3 scallions, thinly sliced and chopped

½ cup finely chopped fresh parsley

2 tablespoons tamari

Cayenne pepper or black pepper to taste (optional)

Nutritional yeast to taste (optional)

Sea Vegetable Chapati

1½ cups uncooked brown rice

3 cups water

⅓ cup dried hiziki (a Japanese sea vegetable)

1½ cups cold water

2 tablespoons sunflower oil

1 cup chopped onion (2 onions)

2 cups chopped carrots (4 small carrots)

¼ cup tamari

Cayenne pepper to taste

6 chapatis (page 67)

Tahini

Spinach leaves

Alfalfa sprouts

Tahini Dressing (page 135)

This is a delicious combination that, surprisingly, some of our more conservative customers at the café love.

Combine brown rice and water. Bring to a boil in a 2-quart pot, then simmer, covered, until water is evaporated. Don't stir. Meanwhile, break up the hiziki and soak 20 minutes in cold water in a bowl. Drain.

Preheat oven to 325°. Heat oil on medium heat in a 10-inch cast-iron fry pan, add onions and carrots, and sauté. Add hiziki after 2 to 3 minutes and remove from heat while veggies are still slightly crisp and carrots bright orange. Add vegetables to the rice in a medium-sized bowl along with tamari and cayenne to taste. Place chapatis in oven for 3 minutes until hot but still soft and pliable. Spread a line of tahini down the center of each chapati. Top with spinach leaves, 1 cup of rice mixture, and sprouts. Serve with a side of Tahini Dressing.

6 servings

Sea Vegetable Burgers. This spread can be made into a burger. Add ½ cup tahini to the spread to firm it up. Form mix into patties, dip each patty in whole wheat flour, and fry in 3 tablespoons sunflower oil on both sides until lightly browned. Serve on a whole wheat roll with some sprouts and spinach leaves and a side of Tahini Dressing.

Sunshine Chapati

Mix tahini with lemon juice in measuring cup, add tamari, and stir well. Lay chapatis out on a counter. Spread mix down the center of each chapati, using approximately 1 tablespoon mix per chapati. Sprinkle 1 teaspoon sunflower seeds over mix on each chapati. Then lay slices of cheese over the sunflower seeds, 3 slices per chapati. Next lay spinach leaves over cheese, 1 cup on each chapati, and top with alfalfa sprouts. Serve with Herb Dressing.

To eat, roll up the chapati lengthwise until you have a rolled-up log.

4 servings

¼ cup tahini

1 tablespoon lemon juice

½ teaspoon tamari

4 chapatis (page 67)

4 teaspoons sunflower seeds

12 long thin slices colby or cheddar cheese

4 cups raw spinach leaves

1 cup alfalfa sprouts

Herb Dressing (page 133)

California Chapati

Lay chapatis out on a counter. Spread ¼ cup cream cheese down the center of each chapati. Cut the avocado in half, peel, and slice, laying ¼ avocado on each chapati over the cream cheese. Top this with lettuce, tomato slices, onion rings, and sprouts, and serve. Serve Herb Dressing on the side if you wish.

4 servings

4 chapatis (page 67)

1 cup cream cheese, softened

1 ripe avocado

8 leafy lettuce leaves

2 medium tomatoes, sliced

1 small Bermuda onion, sliced in rings

1 cup alfalfa sprouts

Herb Dressing (page 135) (optional)

Broccoli and Cheddar Chapati

4 chapatis (page 67)

¼ cup sesame butter (Don't substitute tahini!)

1 cup chopped raw broccoli, stems and florets

12 long thin slices cheddar cheese

8 big green leafy lettuce leaves

2 medium tomatoes, sliced

Herb Dressing (page 133)

Chapati sandwiches are certainly one of the more unique creations that we serve at the Horn. They have a long-standing popular following, especially in the summer months. Some café regulars are known to be slightly addicted to them.

Chapatis are especially nice to pack up and take outside to eat on a sunny mountaintop. If you choose to do this, pack your dressing in a tight-lidded container on the side or you will end up with a soggy chapati or, worse, a soggy backpack.

Lay chapatis out on a counter. Spread 1 tablespoon sesame butter down the center of each chapati. Then spread chopped broccoli over the sesame butter. Follow this with 3 cheese slices laid over the broccoli, again down the center of the chapati. Now add a few lettuce leaves, and then 3 or 4 slices of tomato on top of the lettuce. Have some Herb Dressing ready to sprinkle on top before eating (most people like a tablespoon or so on their chapatis).

To eat, roll up the chapati lengthwise with the filling until you have a rolled-up log. Pick it up like a hot dog and gobble it up.

Stuffed Things

Herb Stuffed Eggs

4 large eggs

¼ cup mayonnaise

1 tablespoon minced fresh
dill weed or 1 teaspoon
dried dill weed

1 tablespoon minced fresh
parsley or 1 teaspoon dried
parsley

1 tablespoon freshly
snipped chives or 1
scallion, chopped

½ teaspoon Dijon-style
mustard

Paprika

A sure sign of fresh eggs was discovered at the café after hard-boiling a number of eggs. It was nearly impossible to peel off the shell of the egg without having the white of the egg come off with it.

If you have farm fresh eggs, let them age for at least a week before attempting to use them for stuffed eggs. It will prevent an exercise in frustration!

In small pot, cover eggs with cold water. Bring to a boil. Boil for 10 minutes. (Boil extra large or jumbo-sized eggs 1 minute extra.) Drain off water and immerse eggs in cold water until cool. Peel and cut in half lengthwise. Scoop out yolks carefully, put into small bowl, and mash. Add rest of ingredients except paprika. Place egg whites on plate with an edge. Stuff with filling and sprinkle with paprika.

4 servings

Tofu Stuffed Mushrooms

1/4 cup finely chopped walnuts

24 large mushrooms

2 tablespoons olive oil

1 square tofu (1/2 pound)

1/2 cup finely diced onion (1 onion)

4 large cloves garlic, minced

1/2 cup finely diced green pepper (1 small pepper)

1/4 teaspoon basil

1/2 teaspoon tarragon

1 tablespoon tahini

1 tablespoon bread crumbs

1 teaspoon tamari

1 tablespoon minced fresh parsley

1/4 teaspoon salt

Dash of cayenne pepper

Paprika

The nondairy variety of stuffed mushroom caps.

Preheat oven to 375°. Roast chopped walnuts in oven 5 minutes. Wash mushrooms and pull stems out of them. Lay caps on cookie sheet that has been oiled with 1 tablespoon oil. Chop mushroom stems very finely and set aside. Drain and press excess water out of tofu and allow to sit wrapped in a paper towel for 10 minutes.

Meanwhile, preheat a 10-inch fry pan, add remaining tablespoon oil, onions, garlic, green pepper, basil, and tarragon. When onions and garlic begin to brown, add minced mushroom stems and continue to cook over medium heat until tender.

Mash tofu in medium-sized bowl. Mix in tahini well. (Your hand works best for this.) Add bread crumbs and tamari, mix, then add walnuts, parsley, salt, and cayenne. Stir well. Add mushroom mixture and stir in well.

Put a heaping tablespoonful of filling into each mushroom center; repeat until all mushroom caps are filled and mix is used up. Sprinkle each mushroom with paprika. Bake at 375° 20 minutes until tender.

6 servings

Stuffed Popovers

The first time Heidi, a cook at the café, served these they were quickly pegged by Tom, a customer sitting at the counter, as Poor People's Brioche. Heidi didn't approve of the name, but everyone loved her creation.

Preheat oven to 425°. Put melted butter, eggs, milk, salt, honey, and flours in a blender. Run until smooth. Butter a 12-hole muffin tin and fill each cup half full with popover batter. Bake 15 minutes. Lower oven temperature to 350° and bake popovers 10 to 15 minutes more until lightly golden. Do not open oven door during baking process until the popovers are nearly done. Take out of oven immediately and make a 1-inch slit across the top of each popover. Now gently go around the edge of each popover with a wide-edged knife. Gently pry and lift up the sides and bottom of each one until it is free. Tilt onto its side in muffin tin and allow to cool.

On a cookie sheet, roast walnuts 5 minutes in the oven and set aside.

In melted butter, sauté the broccoli, garlic, and herbs in a 10-inch fry pan over medium heat. When broccoli turns bright green and begins to become tender, add mushrooms and salt. Continue to cook over medium heat until mushrooms are just done. Remove from heat. Drain vegetables if they contain liquid. In medium-sized bowl, combine broccoli mixture, walnuts, and cheeses. Mix well.

Now continue your slice across the top of each popover to make an opening across the complete diameter of each popover, and then make another at a right angle to form an X across the popover top. Gently stuff with the broccoli-cheese filling until all popovers are filled and mixture is used up. Bake at 350° 15 minutes.

6 servings

Popovers

2 tablespoons butter, melted

3 eggs

1 cup milk

¼ teaspoon salt

1 teaspoon honey

¼ cup whole wheat pastry flour

¾ cup unbleached white flour

Filling

½ cup chopped walnuts

2 tablespoons butter, melted

3 cups chopped broccoli, stems and florets

3 large cloves garlic, minced

½ teaspoon basil

½ teaspoon dried thyme

2 cups sliced mushrooms

¼ teaspoon salt

2 cups grated mozzarella cheese

½ cup grated cheddar

Baked Stuffed Potatoes

4 medium to large baking potatoes

1 cup chopped broccoli, stems and florets

3 tablespoons butter

1 cup sliced and slightly chopped mushrooms

6 scallions, chopped

1 cup sour cream

1½ cups grated sharp cheddar cheese

¼ cup minced fresh parsley

1 teaspoon salt

⅛ teaspoon black pepper

Paprika

Preheat oven to 425°. Bake potatoes on cookie sheet until tender when pierced with a fork (approximately 1 to 1¼ hours).

In a 10-inch fry pan sauté the broccoli in 1 tablespoon butter over medium heat. When it just begins to get tender, add mushrooms and sauté until lightly done. Drain if needed.

Cut the top off each potato so that the insides can easily be scooped out, cutting off just the skin layer (fig. 1). While holding potato with pot holder, carefully scoop out insides (fig. 2) and put into medium-sized bowl. Mash with remaining 2 tablespoons butter. Lower oven temperature to 400°. Add scallions, sautéed vegetables, sour cream, cheese, parsley, salt, and pepper to mashed potatoes and mix well. Fill potato shells with this mixture. Sprinkle top of each potato with paprika. Yes, they will be overflowing with filling (fig. 3) and delicious. Bake 15 minutes more and serve.

4 servings

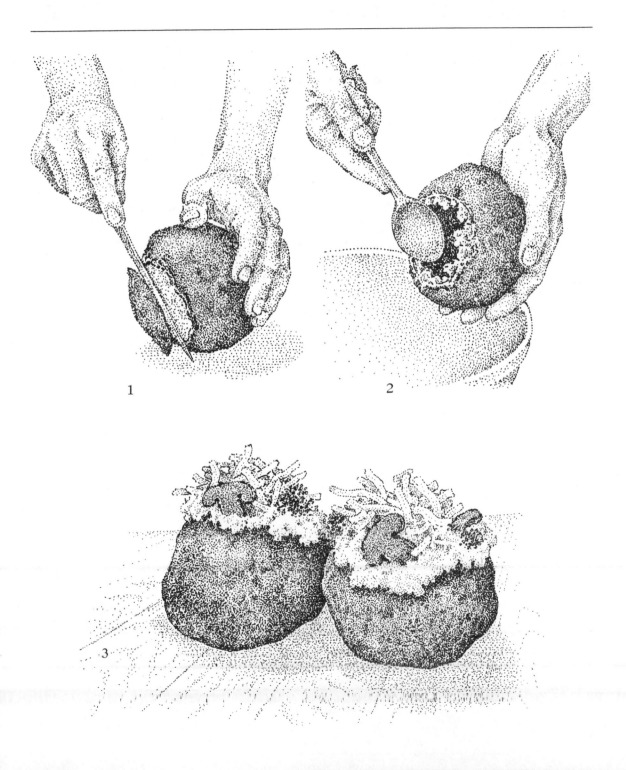

1

2

3

Florentine Stuffed Mushrooms

24 large mushrooms

1 tablespoon plus 2 teaspoons olive oil

2 tablespoons butter

1 cup finely diced onion (2 onions)

¼ teaspoon dried leaf thyme

1½ cups finely chopped fresh spinach

3 tablespoons bread crumbs

½ cup finely grated Parmesan cheese

½ teaspoon salt

Dash of ground black pepper

These are a mushroom lover's delight, and they make a wonderful and very special hors d'oeuvre.

Preheat oven to 375°. Pull stems out of mushrooms and lay caps on cookie sheet that has been oiled with 1 tablespoon oil. Chop the mushroom stems very finely and set aside.

Preheat a 10-inch cast-iron fry pan on medium heat, add butter, and allow to melt. Add onions and thyme. When onions begin to brown, add chopped mushroom stems, spinach, and bread crumbs. Continue to cook on medium to high heat until tender and excess moisture has been absorbed (approximately 5 minutes). Remove from heat. Add Parmesan, salt, and pepper to mixture in fry pan. Stir in well.

Stuff each mushroom cap with filling until it has all been used up. Sprinkle remaining oil over mushroom caps. Bake 15 to 20 minutes.

6 servings

Main Courses

Pasta (page 183)

Stuffed Shells Florentine
French Lasagne
Lasagne Primavera
Mushroom Tofu
    Stroganoff
Tofu "No Meat" Balls
Pasta Primavera
Ricotta Fettuccine
Linguine with
    Mushroom and Garlic
    Sauce
Basil Cream Pasta
Pasta Florentine
Blue Moon Asparagus
    Fettuccine
Three-Herb Pesto
Basic Tomato Garlic
    Sauce

Pizza (page 195)

Spinach Ricotta Deep-
    Dish Pizza
Miso Tofu Pizza
Mexican Pizza
Pizza Alfredo

Pies (page 199)

Luna Pie
Broccoli Feta Pie
Broccoli Mushroom
    Quiche
Spinach Feta Quiche
Avocado Tomato
    Scallion Cheddar
    Quiche
Greek Vegetable Pie
Tofu Mushroom Pie
Shepherd's Pie
Celebration Pot Pie

Mexican (page 208)

Bean and Vegetable
    Burritos
Moon Burritos
Chalupas
Huevos Rancheros
Avocado Tortillas
Garbanzo Chimichangas
Flautas
Baked Mexican
    Vegetable Pie
Black Bean Enchiladas
Layered Enchiladas
Tortitas

Crepes (page 220)

Basic Crepes
Spinach Ricotta Crepes
Broccoli Walnut Crepes
Avocado Cheese Crepes
Pizza Crepes

And More (page 225)

Mushroomkopita
Broccolikopita
Spanikopita
Broccoli Cheese
    Tiropitas
Baked Stuffed Squash
Asparagus, Mushrooms,
    and Rice with a Zesty
    Dijon Cheddar Sauce
Spinach Mushroom
    Strudel with Two
    Cheeses
Mushroom, Spinach,
    and Potato Curry
Tofu Cutlets with
    Mushroom Sauce
Potato Cheese Pierogis
Asparagus Nests
Shish Kebabs
Stir-Fried Vegetables
Szechuan Sauce
Sweet and Sour Sauce
Sesame Lo Mein

How many vegetarians have heard, "Oh, you're a vegetarian, but what do you eat?" Although such questions are becoming less common today, most meat eaters still have a difficult time envisioning what to serve a vegetarian for dinner. They will imagine you at their dining table with a plate full of boiled carrots, peas, and potatoes, or with a fruit salad and cottage cheese. They will wonder how you can live on vegetables alone, and think that it must get boring.

Inviting your traditional carnivore over for dinner can be informative, interesting, and enjoyable for them as well as challenging and fun for you. Dinner is the meal from which meat or fish may be most obviously absent, but this can easily be overridden by a well-planned meal. Vegetarian main courses can be tantalizing to look at as well as delicious and satisfying to eat.

Café dinners combine many ingredients together into one inviting dish. In order to balance amino acids, protein must come from several sources, including cheese, beans, eggs, grains, nuts, or milk products. Combining two or more together in one meal will provide the complementary proteins that are present in meat or fish.

Sometimes we replace the customary meat dish with an alternative, as in Tofu "No Meat" Balls, or Shepherd's Pie. That is not the dish to win over your flesh-eating friends, however. It's more obvious that meat has been replaced in these dishes than in a new creation like Luna Pie, made with a flaky phyllo dough crust filled with mushrooms, cheese, eggs, and tofu. Pasta Florentine is particularly good and combines spinach and Parmesan cheese with garlic, walnuts, and cream. These dishes are popular among vegetarians and meat eaters alike, and will delight anyone who is willing to try them.

The seasons and climate should be considered while you are planning your meal. People tend to eat heavier, starchy, rich foods in cold weather, and choose lighter, simpler foods during the hot summer months.

The café might serve Layered Enchiladas, a pie filled with layers of corn tortillas, beans, cheese, vegetables, and tomato sauce, on a snowy day, while in the summer a Mexican entrée might instead be Chalupas, light, crispy flour tortillas with a layer of beans and cheese in between and topped with fresh salad vegetables and guacamole.

Almost all the entrées need only a tossed salad to accompany them to produce a complete and satisfying meal. When entertaining friends and family, however, you might want to add an appetizer or soup before the main dish along with a dessert to follow.

On days when you will be arriving home just ahead of your guests, it helps to do some advance preparation. Since some dishes are more time-consuming to prepare than others, be sure to read over a recipe ahead of time. Do your beans need to be soaked or even cooked in advance? Should your phyllo dough be defrosted?

You can grate the cheese you will need, chop garlic, and slice vegetables a day ahead of time. A quiche can easily be prepared one or two days in advance. The piecrust can be rolled out and stored in the refrigerator. The filling can be mixed together and refrigerated. Put the quiche together and bake it on the day you want to serve it. Many pasta sauces can be made up ahead of time. Crepes can be cooked in advance and stored in the refrigerator for a few days. Doing some work a day in advance will allow you to spend more time sitting, relaxing, and enjoying your company.

The Horn of the Moon's cooking has grown through the years and has drawn from many different cultures and cuisines to borrow from their best ingredients. These meals cross international borders, mixing oregano into burritos, tofu with pasta, and soy sauce almost everywhere. If only different governments could learn to mix so easily and well!

Pasta

Stuffed Shells Florentine

Put a 4-quart pot of water, covered, on the stove to boil. When water begins to boil, stir in 1 teaspoon salt, and gently add shells. Cook approximately 8 to 10 minutes, stirring occasionally, until just done. Do not overcook! Drain water out and set shells in cold water to cool. This will also prevent sticking.

In a medium-sized bowl, mix ricotta, Parmesan, remaining ½ teaspoon salt, pepper, eggs, spinach, and garlic.

To assemble, have a large casserole dish ready. Put a light layer of tomato sauce on the bottom. Now fill each shell (drain the excess water off of them) with a tablespoon or so of the filling until it has been used up. Place stuffed shells in casserole, spreading a thin layer of tomato sauce between layers of shells. Top with the remaining tomato sauce and the mozzarella cheese. Bake uncovered 30 to 45 minutes at 375° until hot and bubbly.

4 large
servings

3 quarts water

1½ teaspoons salt

1 pound jumbo pasta shells

2 pounds ricotta cheese

1 cup finely grated fresh Parmesan cheese

Black pepper to taste

2 eggs

2 lightly packed cups chopped spinach

1 tablespoon minced fresh garlic

1 quart Basic Tomato Garlic Sauce page 194 (or your favorite recipe)

2 cups grated mozzarella cheese

French Lasagne

Lasagne

1/2 pound lasagne noodles

3 quarts boiling water

2 tablespoons olive oil or butter

1 cup diced onion (2 onions)

4 cloves garlic, minced

1 teaspoon basil

1 teaspoon tarragon

2 cups sliced mushrooms

1 pound ricotta cheese

1 pound small curd cottage cheese

4 eggs, lightly beaten

1 packed cup chopped raw spinach

1/4 teaspoon salt

1/4 teaspoon freshly ground black pepper

1/4 teaspoon nutmeg

1/2 cup finely grated Parmesan cheese

1 1/2 cups grated mozzarella cheese

Béchamel Sauce

1/4 cup butter

1/4 cup unbleached white flour

About 1 3/4 cups milk

1/2 cup finely grated Parmesan cheese

1/8 teaspoon salt

Black pepper to taste

A béchamel sauce replaces the traditional tomato sauce for a rich and delicious lasagne variation.

Cook the noodles in a 4-quart pot with boiling water until al dente. Drain, refill the pot with cold water, and let noodles sit in water.

Heat the oil or butter in a 10-inch fry pan on medium heat and sauté the onions, garlic, basil, and tarragon. When onions begin to brown, add mushrooms and cook until tender.

In a large bowl mix ricotta and cottage cheeses, eggs, sautéed veggies, raw spinach, salt, pepper, nutmeg, Parmesan, and 1/2 cup mozzarella. Preheat oven to 375°.

To make the béchamel sauce, melt butter in a 2-quart saucepan or 10-inch cast-iron fry pan. When melted, add flour and cook a few minutes on low heat. Slowly add milk, stirring constantly; then add Parmesan, salt, and black pepper to taste. Cook until the sauce thickens. Thin with a bit more milk if needed. Remove from heat and set aside.

To assemble the lasagne, brush just a bit of sauce into bottom of 9 × 12-inch pan to cover. Add a layer of noodles, then some of the cheese mixture. Repeat with a layer of noodles, cheese mixture, noodles, and then top with remaining béchamel sauce and remaining 1 cup mozzarella. Bake covered 30 minutes. Remove from oven and allow to set 10 minutes before serving.

6 to 8 servings

Lasagne Primavera

A rich, colorful, and delightfully filling vegetable lasagne that needs no sauce in it. It's always a favorite dinner special at the café.

Preheat oven to 375°. Heat 2 tablespoons oil in 10-inch fry pan over medium heat. Add onions, carrots, garlic, and herbs to hot fry pan. When onions just begin to brown, add broccoli. After 2 to 3 minutes add zucchini. Allow zucchini to cook 2 minutes, then add mushrooms. Cook until just tender. Remove from heat. Drain off any excess liquid.

In medium-sized bowl, mix ricotta, eggs, and Romano cheese. Add cooked vegetables, tomato, parsley, salt, and pepper.

Bring water to a boil in a 4-quart pot. Add noodles and cook until just barely tender. Drain. Oil a 9 × 13-inch pan with the remaining teaspoon oil. Put a layer of noodles over bottom of pan. Pour half the cheese-vegetable mixture over the noodles. Then sprinkle ½ cup mozzarella cheese over this. Top with a layer of noodles, remaining cheese-vegetable mixture, and ½ cup more mozzarella cheese. Top with remaining noodles and remaining 2 cups mozzarella cheese. Sprinkle with paprika. Bake 30 minutes uncovered. Allow to sit 5 to 10 minutes before cutting.

6 servings

2 tablespoons plus 1 teaspoon olive oil

¾ cup chopped onion (1 medium onion)

½ cup diced carrot (1 small carrot)

5 large cloves garlic, minced

1 teaspoon each basil, oregano, and marjoram

2 cups chopped broccoli, stems and florets

1 cup sliced zucchini or yellow squash (1 small squash)

2 cups sliced mushrooms

2 pounds ricotta cheese

2 eggs, beaten

½ cup finely grated Romano cheese

1 medium tomato, chopped

¼ cup minced fresh parsley

¼ teaspoon salt

⅛ teaspoon ground black pepper

3 quarts water

½ pound spinach lasagne noodles

3 cups grated mozzarella cheese

Paprika

Mushroom Tofu Stroganoff

4 tablespoons butter

1½ cups finely chopped onion (3 onions)

4 cloves garlic, minced

1 teaspoon dried dill weed

2 teaspoons basil

3 squares tofu, drained, pressed, and then cut into 1-inch cubes (1½ pounds)

2 tablespoons tamari

4 tightly packed cups sliced mushrooms (about ¼-inch slices)

½ teaspoon salt

¼ teaspoon cayenne pepper

3 quarts water

1 pound curly noodles

Sour cream

½ cup finely chopped fresh parsley

2 teaspoons poppy seeds

This is a delicious and rich stroganoff that we always serve over fresh, curly spinach pasta noodles. It is a favorite of mine and a popular dinner with customers as well.

Melt 2 tablespoons butter in wok or large, deep cast-iron fry pan and sauté the onions, garlic, dill weed, and basil. After 5 minutes, add tofu and continue to cook on medium heat, stirring gently occasionally, until tofu browns nicely. Add tamari and stir. Then add mushrooms, salt, and cayenne. Lower heat, stir, and cook another 5 minutes. Remove from heat.

Bring water to a boil in a 4-quart pot. Cook noodles until tender but not mushy. Drain and return to pot. Toss noodles with 1 tablespoon of butter to prevent sticking.

Add 1 cup sour cream and parsley to mushroom mixture and mix well.

Melt remaining 2 tablespoons butter in saucepan and add poppy seeds. Cook 5 to 10 minutes. Pour onto noodles and toss. Serve noodles with stroganoff on top and dollop of sour cream as garnish.

4 servings

Tofu "No Meat" Balls

The vegetarian alternative to meat balls and spaghetti is always a big hit at the café. Leftover tofu balls are used for a Tofu "No Meat" Ball submarine on French bread, topped with tomato sauce, green peppers, and Parmesan cheese.

Steam eggplant in a 2-quart saucepan over boiling water until tender. In large bowl, mash tofu, and add onions, bread crumbs, eggplant, ½ cup flour, walnuts, salt, pepper, ½ cup Parmesan, parsley, tamari, egg, oregano, marjoram, and thyme. Mix well. The mixture should be somewhat soft and moist but hold together. Add more bread crumbs or flour as needed.

Heat oil in deep 2-quart saucepan. When oil is hot, roll one ball and dip in flour. Test oil for hotness: the ball should cook in 2 to 3 minutes. Roll all the mix into walnut-sized balls and dip in flour. Fry them all up. Drain on paper towels. (The tofu balls can be reheated in a 400° oven 5 to 7 minutes if necessary.)

Put pasta into a 4-quart pot with boiling water. Warm the tomato sauce over medium heat. Cook pasta until al dente (2 to 3 minutes if fresh, 5 to 7 minutes if dry). Drain well. Serve in a large bowl topped with tomato sauce and surrounded by Tofu "No Meat" Balls and garnished with Parmesan cheese.

6 servings (18 balls)

1½ cups diced eggplant, cut into very small cubes (peel eggplant only if the skin is thick and tough looking) (1 small eggplant)

1 square tofu (½ pound)

½ cup minced onion (1 onion)

½ cup bread crumbs

1 cup whole wheat pastry flour

½ cup finely chopped walnuts

¼ teaspoon salt

Dash of black pepper

½ cup finely grated Parmesan cheese

¼ cup minced fresh parsley

1 teaspoon tamari

1 egg, beaten

½ teaspoon each oregano, marjoram, and dried leaf thyme

1½ cups sunflower oil for frying balls

1½ pounds vermicelli or linguine noodles

3 quarts boiling water

4 cups Basic Tomato Garlic Sauce (page 194) (or your favorite recipe)

Grated Parmesan cheese for garnish

Pasta Primavera

2 tablespoons butter

2 tablespoons unbleached white flour

1½ cups heavy cream

Approximately 1½ cups finely grated Parmesan cheese

½ cup milk

2 tablespoons minced fresh parsley

Black pepper to taste

2 tablespoons olive oil

¾ cup diced carrot (1 small carrot)

1½ cups thinly sliced broccoli, stems and florets

4 cloves garlic, minced

1 teaspoon dried leaf thyme

1½ cups zucchini (cut in half lengthwise and then into ¼-inch slices) (1 zucchini)

1 cup snow peas, sliced in thirds at an angle

2 cups sliced mushrooms

½ teaspoon salt

1 pound spinach or plain fettuccine or linguine noodles

3 quarts boiling water

½ pint cherry tomatoes, sliced in half

To make the sauce, melt butter in a heavy-gauge 2-quart saucepan over medium heat. When melted, add flour. Stir 2 minutes on low heat, then slowly pour in cream. Add 1 cup Parmesan, then milk, parsley, and pepper, stirring well. Remove from heat.

Heat the oil and sauté the carrot, broccoli, garlic, and thyme over medium heat. Cover and stir occasionally. After 3 to 4 minutes, add the zucchini and snow peas. After 2 to 3 minutes, add the mushrooms, salt, and pepper. Cook 2 minutes more. Do not overcook the vegetables! Turn off heat and cover.

Cook the pasta in boiling water until just tender and warm up sauce on very low heat. When pasta is done (2 to 3 minutes if fresh, 5 to 7 if not), drain well and pour into medium to large bowl. Stir sauce into pasta well, tossing it. Serve with the vegetables on top of pasta and sauce in the bowl, with tomatoes in the center and remaining Parmesan on the side for garnish.

4 servings

Ricotta Fettuccine

In a 2-quart saucepan, sauté the garlic, onions, and herbs in olive oil over medium heat until lightly browned. Add tomato paste, tomatoes, and pepper. Simmer on very low heat a minimum of 2 hours, stirring occasionally.

Warm the ricotta cheese on very low heat in a saucepan or preferably a double boiler. Bring water to a boil, add pasta, and cook until al dente (2 to 3 minutes if fresh pasta, 5 to 7 if not). Drain. Put into medium-sized bowl along with ricotta cheese, toss quickly but well, and serve right away with sauce on top if you serve the pasta on plates. Or have a bowl of the hot marinara and Parmesan on the side and allow everyone to fix their pasta as they like it.

4 servings

5 large cloves garlic, finely minced (2 tablespoons)

½ cup chopped onion (1 onion)

1 teaspoon basil

1 teaspoon oregano

1 tablespoon olive oil

One 6-ounce can tomato paste

One 28-ounce can whole peeled tomatoes

Dash of black pepper

1 pound ricotta cheese

3 quarts water

1 pound fettuccine, preferably basil or spinach

Freshly grated Parmesan cheese

Linguine with Mushroom and Garlic Sauce

3 quarts water

6 tablespoons butter

8 to 10 large cloves garlic, minced

6 cups sliced mushrooms

1 teaspoon basil

¼ teaspoon salt

Dash of freshly ground black pepper

2 tablespoons olive oil

1 pound linguine

2 tablespoons minced fresh parsley

Grated Parmesan cheese

A *pasta dish for garlic lovers that can be put together quickly. It's great for those times when
you're too hungry to wait for a lengthy prepared meal.*

In large pot, boil water for pasta. Melt 2 tablespoons
butter in saucepan. Add garlic, allow to brown for a minute, then add mushrooms, basil, and salt and cook until
mushrooms are just tender. Add remaining 4 tablespoons
butter, pepper, and oil. Stir and remove from heat. Cook
linguine until al dente. When pasta is done, reheat sauce
and add parsley. Drain pasta, pour into medium-sized
bowl along with sauce, and toss. Serve with Parmesan on
the side.

4 servings

Basil Cream Pasta

½ cup olive oil

4 large cloves garlic

3 packed cups fresh basil leaves

2 cups heavy cream

1¼ cups finely grated Parmesan cheese

¼ teaspoon salt

Dash of freshly ground black pepper

3 quarts water

1 pound fresh fettuccine

M *y father-in-law is strictly a meat-and-potatoes
eater, but even he raved about this pasta dish.*

Put ¼ cup oil and garlic in a blender. Run on low
speed, slowly adding the basil leaves and oil alternately
until you have a fine green paste and have used up all the
oil and basil leaves.

Set a small saucepan over low heat. Add cream, basil
paste, and ¾ cup Parmesan cheese along with salt and
pepper. Heat until sauce is just hot.

Bring water to a boil in large pot, add pasta, and cook
until al dente. Drain well and pour sauce over pasta. Toss
well and serve garnished with remaining Parmesan
cheese.

4 servings

Pasta Florentine

*S*ince fresh basil is difficult and expensive to obtain in winter, we came up with a tasty alternative, spinach pesto!

To roast walnuts, preheat oven to 400°. Set walnuts on a cookie sheet. Bake until lightly golden (approximately 5 minutes). Stir a few times or shake pan. They burn easily!

To make the sauce, you will need a blender or food processor. Put in blender 2 cups spinach, ½ cup Parmesan, ¼ cup walnuts, half the Gruyère, ½ cup oil, 2 cloves garlic, half the salt, pepper, and herbs, and ¼ cup cream. Run until smooth. Repeat with remaining quantities of these ingredients, setting aside ½ cup walnuts for garnish. Keep sauce warm in double boiler.

Bring water to a boil in a 4-quart pot, add pasta, and cook until al dente. Drain, pour into large bowl, toss with the spinach mixture, garnish with walnuts, and serve.

6 servings

1 cup chopped walnuts

4 packed cups chopped raw spinach

1 cup finely grated Parmesan cheese

¾ cup grated Gruyère cheese

1 cup olive oil

4 large cloves garlic

½ teaspoon salt

Dash of black pepper

1 teaspoon basil

1 teaspoon oregano

½ cup heavy cream

3 quarts water

1½ pounds spinach fettuccine

Blue Moon Asparagus Fettuccine

1 pound fresh asparagus

3 quarts water

1 cup heavy cream (½ pint)

¾ cup grated Roquefort cheese tossed with 1 tablespoon unbleached white flour

1½ cups finely grated Parmesan cheese

4 tablespoons butter

1 pound fettuccine noodles

Grownups love this strange-looking, smelly stuff called bleu cheese. I remember as a child watching my mother slice into some and eat it raw! I didn't dare taste it until I was well into my 20s, but when I did I loved it. Beware of quickly moving spoons and pieces of bread darting around and in your sauce as you make this, or it will be consumed well before it gets onto the pasta.

Cut off last 2 inches of asparagus ends. Then cut asparagus at an angle in pieces approximately ¾ to 1 inch long. Lightly steam until just tender. Drain and set aside (if you have a pasta pot where a strainer fits inside, steam asparagus in this, then add more water). In a 4-quart pot set water on to boil for pasta.

In a 10-inch cast-iron fry pan or a 2-quart saucepan, heat the cream on low heat. Slowly add the Roquefort cheese combined with the flour and ¾ cup Parmesan cheese, setting aside the rest for garnish. Stir until this blends in well. Now add the butter and asparagus. Continue to simmer until sauce is smooth and hot.

When water boils, add the pasta and cook until tender (2 to 3 minutes if fresh pasta, 5 to 7 minutes if not). Drain and toss in medium-sized bowl with the sauce. Mix well and serve immediately, along with the remaining Parmesan as a garnish for those who wish more cheese, and a big green salad.

4 servings

Three-Herb Pesto

This version of pesto combines the flavors of fresh thyme, parsley, and basil. Pesto freezes well, so while fresh herbs are prolific, make up some extra and freeze it for a winter delicacy.

In a blender, combine ¼ cup oil, garlic, and ½ cup basil leaves. Blend, stirring occasionally if necessary. Add more fresh basil and blend again. If basil does not turn into a paste, add more oil. Gradually blend in the remaining basil and the parsley and thyme. When all the basil, parsley, and thyme have been blended, add the walnuts, salt, pepper, remaining oil, and ½ cup Parmesan and blend until smooth (reserve ½ cup for topping pasta).

Cook pasta in boiling water in a 4-quart pot until just tender. Drain. For 4 servings, mix half the pesto into hot pasta. (Freeze the rest for another meal.) If serving 8, use all the pesto. Toss well and serve.

8 servings

¾ cup olive oil

6 large cloves garlic

2 packed cups fresh basil leaves

1 packed cup fresh parsley sprigs

½ packed cup fresh thyme leaves (not stems: pull leaves off in the upward direction with fingers, stripping the stems quickly)

½ cup walnuts or pine nuts

¼ teaspoon salt

Dash of black pepper

1 cup grated Parmesan cheese

3 quarts water

1 pound linguine to serve 4 or 2 pounds to serve 8

Basic Tomato Garlic Sauce

2 tablespoons olive oil

6 large cloves garlic, minced

1 cup chopped onion (2 onions)

½ cup diced green pepper (1 small pepper)

1 teaspoon oregano

1 teaspoon basil

½ teaspoon marjoram

2 cups sliced mushrooms

One 15-ounce can tomato sauce

One 12-ounce can tomato paste

One 15-ounce can whole tomatoes, coarsely chopped, plus the liquid, or 2 cups coarsely chopped fresh tomatoes

¼ cup dry red wine

Put the olive oil in a 10-inch fry pan over medium heat and add the garlic, onions, green pepper, oregano, basil, and marjoram. As onions begin to brown, add mushrooms and cook until tender. In 2-quart saucepan, put tomato sauce, tomato paste, and tomatoes and liquid. Add sautéed onion mixture and red wine to tomatoes. Stir. Simmer, covered, 2 hours over low heat, stirring occasionally.

1 quart

Pizza

Spinach Ricotta Deep-Dish Pizza

In medium-sized bowl, place yeast, warm water, and honey. Let sit 5 minutes. Blend whole wheat and 2½ cups unbleached white flour together. When yeast begins to bubble, add oil and salt and slowly stir in flour, reserving ½ cup white flour for kneading. When 3½ cups flour have been mixed in, turn onto lightly floured board. Knead dough 6 minutes. Wash bowl, lightly oil, and put dough back into it. Set in warm spot (not hot!) and cover with damp towel until dough doubles in size (about 1 hour). Then knead dough 3 minutes more. Roll into circle to fit a 14-inch deep-dish pan and set into pan. Press dough out to sides of pan. Let it rise another 45 minutes, covered. Preheat oven to 450°.

Now prepare ricotta filling in a separate bowl by combining ricotta and Parmesan cheeses, salt, pepper, spinach, and garlic. Mix well.

Prick bottom of crust all over with a fork. Press crust sides flat to make a thin edge. Bake 4 to 5 minutes. Pull out and brush oil over crust, then spread with ricotta filling. Top with sliced mushrooms and sprinkle with mozzarella and tomatoes. Bake 15 minutes, until cheese is melted. Cut and serve!

4 to 5 servings

Dough

2 tablespoons dry baker's yeast (2 packages)

1½ cups warm water

1 tablespoon honey

1 cup whole wheat flour

3 cups unbleached white flour

4 tablespoons sunflower oil

2 teaspoons salt

Ricotta Filling

2 cups ricotta cheese

1 cup freshly grated Parmesan cheese

¼ teaspoon salt

Dash of black pepper

2 cups finely chopped fresh spinach

1 tablespoon minced garlic

Have Ready

2 teaspoons olive oil

2 cups sliced mushrooms

1 cup grated mozzarella cheese

One 28-ounce can whole tomatoes, drained and mixed with 1 teaspoon each basil and oregano

Miso Tofu Pizza

Dough

1 cup warm water

1 tablespoon dry baker's yeast (1 package)

1 teaspoon honey

1 tablespoon sunflower oil

½ teaspoon salt

2½ to 3 cups flour (½ whole wheat and ½ unbleached white mixed together)

Cornmeal

Sauce

½ cup miso

Hot water

2 tablespoons sunflower oil

¼ cup whole wheat pastry flour

1¼ cups water

1 cup tahini

2 tablespoons tamari

½ cup finely diced onion

5 cloves garlic, minced

1 teaspoon each basil and oregano

⅛ teaspoon cayenne pepper

½ cup minced fresh parsley

*T*uesday *is Pizza Night at the café and we serve this option as well as the traditional tomato sauce and mozzarella cheese pizza. Everyone loves our "white" pizza once they give it a try, and its popularity increases continually.*

Mix water, yeast, honey, oil, and salt, and let sit until bubbly. Add 2½ cups flour and knead until smooth and even, adding more flour to dough if needed. Place in medium-sized bowl, cover, and allow to rise 1 hour in warm place until doubled in size. Preheat oven to 450°. Sprinkle cornmeal on bottom of pan (12 × 14-inch or 15-inch round). Roll out dough on floured board and stretch dough to corners of pan, folding over edges for a rim. Bake 5 minutes at 450°. Pull out of oven when crust gets a bit firm and is just beginning to turn a little brown on the edges.

Combine the miso and enough hot water to make a thin spreading consistency. Spread onto the baked dough using a rubber spatula. Set aside.

Heat 1 tablespoon oil in saucepan and add flour, stirring and browning in oil. Add the water, then the tahini and tamari, and mix. Lower heat to simmer.

Heat remaining tablespoon oil in a small fry pan and sauté onion and garlic with basil, oregano, and cayenne until onions are browned and liquid is evaporated. Add to tahini mixture with more water as needed to keep smooth. Stir in parsley. Check seasoning and spread over miso on the baked crust.

Choose your favorite toppings. Any combination is fine. Crumbled tofu should go on first, followed by vegetables. Bake another 10 to 15 minutes until hot and golden brown on edges.

4 servings

Toppings

2 squares tofu, crumbled (1 pound)

Sliced mushrooms

Pitted and chopped olives

Sliced green peppers

Sliced onions

Chopped and sautéed broccoli (keep florets whole but chop stems)

Minced garlic

Mexican Pizza

We have served this pizza at the café both with and without the refried beans. No consensus could be reached among staff and customers as to which they liked better. Some folks thought beans on pizza was "just going too far!" while others loved it. In any event, it's a popular pizza. Try it both ways.

Follow basic pizza dough directions for Miso Tofu Pizza on opposite page.

Drain Salsa of any excess liquid. Spread over baked crust (if using refried beans, spread them over crust first). Spread the Jalapeño cheese and 1 cup mozzarella over the Salsa, reserving ½ cup mozzarella. Then lay out the vegetables on top and sprinkle with remaining mozzarella. Bake 10 to 12 minutes more, until bubbly.

4 servings

Have Ready

1½ cups Salsa (page 145)

2 cups refried beans (optional) (page 208)

1 cup grated Jalapeño pepper Jack cheese

1½ cups grated mozzarella cheese

1 green pepper, sliced

1 small onion, sliced

½ cup chopped olives

Pizza Alfredo

Dough

1 cup warm water

1 tablespoon dry baker's yeast (1 package)

1 teaspoon honey

1 tablespoon sunflower oil

½ teaspoon salt

1½ cups whole wheat flour

1½ cups unbleached white flour

1 cup chopped fresh raw spinach

About 2 teaspoons cornmeal

Sauce

2 tablespoons butter

2 tablespoons unbleached white flour

1½ cups heavy cream

1 cup finely grated Parmesan cheese

½ cup milk

2 tablespoons minced fresh parsley

Topping

½ cup finely grated Parmesan cheese

1½ cups sliced mushrooms

1 cup sliced artichoke hearts

1 cup grated mozzarella cheese

Every Tuesday is pizza night at the café and we always serve a special pizza. On holidays like the Fourth of July, Election Day, and Christmas, the crew becomes quite creative with its pizza special. On the Fourth of July, a red, white, and blue pizza was served with red peppers, mozzarella, and bleu cheese on top of a tomato sauce pie. On Election Day, a "Green Party" pizza was the special with fresh spinach in the dough and a zucchini-cheese topping. During the Christmas holidays, the pizza had red and green peppers on top.

This pizza has no theme to it, but the delicious rich sauce makes it a favorite special at the café.

Mix together all dough ingredients except flour, spinach, and cornmeal, and let sit 5 minutes until bubbly. Add flours, first combining them, reserving ¼ cup white flour for rolling out dough. Knead in spinach on floured board. Place in a bowl, covered, and allow to sit in a warm place 1 hour, until doubled in size. Preheat oven to 450°. Knead again on floured board until dough is smooth. Roll out to desired size for a 15-inch round or a 12 × 14-inch rectangular pan. Roll dough just slightly larger than pan to allow for an edge to be tucked over around perimeter of pan. Place dough onto oiled pan, first sprinkling bottom of pan with cornmeal. Bake 5 to 7 minutes, until crust is firm and just barely begins to brown.

Prepare sauce. Melt butter in saucepan on low heat. When melted, add flour, stir and cook 1 minute, then slowly pour in cream. Stir in Parmesan cheese, then milk and parsley. Remove from heat after cheese has melted.

Pour sauce into center of pizza and spread to edges. Sprinkle Parmesan over the sauce, then mushrooms and artichoke hearts. Spread mozzarella over vegetables. Bake 10 minutes more until pizza is bubbly and cheese is just beginning to brown.

4 servings

Pies

Luna Pie

The winter night sky in Vermont can be perfectly clear, and sparkle and shine on very cold nights. The first time I made this pie a sliver of a new moon was rising. I sat by the wood stove while my pie baked and watched the moon through my kitchen window slowly rise. Both the pie and the celestial show were wonderful.

Heat 2 tablespoons oil in a 10-inch fry pan and sauté the onions, basil, thyme, oregano, and celery until onions begin to brown. Drain if needed and set aside.

Heat the remaining 2 tablespoons oil in saucepan and sauté the mushrooms on medium to high heat until all their moisture has evaporated.

In a bowl, mash the tofu with a fork. Using an electric mixer, beat in the eggs. Add cheese, salt, cayenne, and mustard; mix well. Stir in the sautéed vegetables

Preheat oven to 375°. Cut the phyllo sheets into 12-inch squares. Using a pastry brush, brush a sheet of phyllo dough with melted butter. Drape the dough over a 10-inch pie plate. Repeat, laying each sheet on top of the other until 7 are stacked on one another. Gently push dough into bottom of pan. Pour in filling. Butter 3 more sheets of phyllo dough and lay on top of filling. Roll overhanging phyllo dough up to form a piecrust edge. Brush the top of the pie with the remaining melted butter and sprinkle with poppy seeds. Slash top carefully once or twice in center. Bake 30 to 35 minutes, until browned. Let set 10 minutes after removing from oven before cutting.

6 servings

4 tablespoons sunflower oil

1 cup finely chopped onion (2 onions)

1 teaspoon basil

1 teaspoon dried leaf thyme

½ teaspoon oregano

1½ cups finely chopped celery

1 pound mushrooms, chopped very fine

1 square tofu (½ pound)

3 eggs

1½ cups grated cheddar cheese or 1 cup finely grated Parmesan cheese

¾ teaspoon salt

¼ teaspoon cayenne pepper

1 teaspoon mustard, dry or wet

½ box phyllo dough (10 sheets)

¼ cup butter, melted

1 teaspoon poppy seeds

Broccoli Feta Pie

2 tablespoons butter

1 cup finely chopped onion
(2 onions)

4 cloves garlic, minced

2 teaspoons dried dill weed

1 teaspoon marjoram

6 cups chopped fresh
broccoli, stems and florets

½ teaspoon salt

⅛ teaspoon cayenne
pepper or black pepper to
taste

4 eggs

2 cups crumbled or grated
feta cheese

½ cup minced fresh
parsley

10 phyllo leaves (½
package)

5 tablespoons butter,
melted

1 tablespoon sesame seeds

 *quiche variation which looks much more compli-
cated and intricate to make than it really is.*

Melt 2 tablespoons butter in a 10-inch fry pan over medium heat and sauté the onions, garlic, dill weed, and
marjoram. When onions begin to soften and brown, add
broccoli, salt, and pepper. Sauté a few minutes more. Remove from heat when broccoli is still bright green and
slightly crunchy but cooked.

Beat eggs in a large bowl. Add feta, parsley, and onion-
broccoli sauté.

Preheat oven to 350°. Take phyllo out of the refrigerator. Unfold dough and lay flat on table. Brush a sheet
lightly with melted butter. Gently lift dough and fit into a
10-inch buttered springform pan. Fit the phyllo along the
bottom and sides and let the extra dough overhang edges.
Repeat with 5 more sheets, overlapping them. Pour in
the filling. Brush 4 more leaves with butter one at a time
and lay one on top of the other over the filling. Trim
edges of phyllo dough to form a 2-inch overhang. Roll
edges of dough up to form a crust around the pie's edge.
Brush remaining butter on top and sprinkle with the sesame seeds. Bake 40 to 45 minutes until top is golden
brown. Allow to set 10 minutes before serving. Remove
sides of springform pan before serving.

6 servings

Broccoli Mushroom Quiche

A *good introduction for guests not accustomed to vegetarian meals.*

Preheat oven to 375°.

Heat the oil in a 10-inch fry pan and sauté the onions, thyme, basil, and broccoli over medium heat. After 5 minutes, add mushrooms and salt. Sauté until just tender. Remove from heat and drain any excess juices from vegetables.

Roll out piecrust and fit into 10-inch pan. Flute edges. In a bowl, beat eggs. Add sour cream, then cheeses, salt, and pepper. Mix well.

Put vegetables into pie shell and pour the cheese mixture on top, or mix vegetables with cheese and place this mixture into pie shell. Bake 40 to 45 minutes, until golden and puffy. Let set 10 minutes before cutting.

6 servings

2 tablespoons sunflower oil

1 cup chopped onion

1 teaspoon dried leaf thyme

1 teaspoon basil

2 cups chopped broccoli, stems and florets

2 cups sliced mushrooms

1/4 teaspoon salt

1 unbaked pie shell (page 247)

3 eggs

3/4 cup sour cream

2 1/2 cups grated cheddar cheese

1/2 cup grated Monterey Jack cheese

1/4 teaspoon salt

Dash of black pepper

Spinach Feta Quiche

6 packed cups fresh
spinach leaves

1 unbaked 10-inch pie
shell (page 247)

¼ teaspoon basil

1 cup grated or crumbled
feta cheese

1½ cups grated cheddar
cheese

1 tablespoon unbleached
white flour

4 eggs

1½ cups light cream

Dash of paprika

The combination of feta and cheddar cheeses and
fresh spinach makes this quiche extra good.

Preheat oven to 400°. Steam spinach, press excess
water out, and chop. Spread spinach on bottom of pie
shell and sprinkle basil over it. Mix together feta and
cheddar cheeses in medium-sized bowl. Toss flour into
cheeses and spread over spinach in pie shell. Beat eggs
well, add cream, and pour over cheese. Sprinkle with a
dash of paprika.

Bake 15 minutes. Lower heat to 325° and bake 25 to
30 minutes longer, until golden and puffy. Allow to set
10 minutes before cutting.

6 servings

Avocado Tomato Scallion Cheddar Quiche

1 cup sour cream

3 eggs, beaten

3 cups grated sharp
cheddar cheese

Dash of salt

Dash of black pepper

6 scallions, chopped

2 ripe medium tomatoes,
chopped

1 ripe avocado, peeled,
pitted, and sliced into
strips

1 unbaked 10-inch pie
shell (page 247)

A tasty and rich quiche which is always a popular
menu item at the café. A Mexican quiche can be
made by using 1½ cups Jalapeño pepper Jack cheese
and 1½ cups cheddar for a spicy variation which goes
well with the avocado and tomato flavors.

Preheat oven to 375°. Mix together sour cream, eggs,
and cheese in mixing bowl. Stir in salt, pepper, scallions,
and tomatoes. Set aside. Lay out avocado slices on bottom of pie shell. Pour cheese mixture over avocado slices
and spread out evenly. Bake 40 to 45 minutes, until
golden and puffy. Let set 10 minutes before serving.

6 servings

Greek Vegetable Pie

This phyllo crust pie is baked open-faced with the fresh assorted vegetables peeking through the melted cheeses on top. It's always a popular dinner item at the café and quite often sells out.

Heat 1 tablespoon oil in fry pan. Sauté chopped onions, onion rings, and garlic with herbs and spices on medium heat until they begin to soften (approximately 3 to 4 minutes). Add broccoli, cook 3 minutes more, and remove from pan. Heat another tablespoon oil, add zucchini and mushrooms, and sauté 3 minutes. Combine with onion mixture. Drain in colander if mixture is juicy.

Preheat oven to 375°. Butter a 12 × 18-inch pan. Brush each sheet of phyllo dough with melted butter and lay into pan, leaving a 2-inch border on sides to roll into crust later. Use approximately 15 sheets. Spread broccoli-onion-veggie mix over bottom. Then add celery, followed by tomatoes and cheeses. Roll overhanging dough into a piecrust edge around the pan. Sprinkle with a bit of basil and oregano, pepper, and salt. Bake approximately 25 minutes, until golden.

6 to 8 servings

2 tablespoons olive oil

1 cup chopped onion (2 onions)

1 cup onion rings (2 onions)

6 large cloves garlic, minced

2 teaspoons basil

1 teaspoon dried leaf thyme

1 tablespoon oregano

Cayenne pepper or black pepper to taste

½ teaspoon salt

2 cups broccoli (whole florets and chopped stems)

2 cups very thinly sliced zucchini (1 medium zucchini)

2 cups sliced mushrooms

1 package phyllo dough

½ cup butter, melted

2 cups sliced celery

3 chopped fresh medium tomatoes or ½ pint cherry tomatoes, halved

1½ cups grated or crumbled feta cheese

1½ cups grated Swiss, cheddar, or Monterey Jack cheese, or a combination

Basil

Oregano

Freshly ground black pepper

Salt

Tofu Mushroom Pie

2 tablespoons sunflower oil

1½ cups chopped onion (3 small onions)

6 cloves garlic, minced

2 teaspoons dried dill weed

2 teaspoons oregano

2 teaspoons tarragon

5 cups sliced mushrooms

2 squares tofu (1 pound)

¼ cup tahini

4 eggs

¼ teaspoon black pepper or dash of cayenne pepper

1 tablespoon tamari

1 cup grated Parmesan cheese

2 cups grated sharp cheddar cheese

3 fresh medium tomatoes, diced

½ teaspoon salt

½ cup minced fresh parsley

One 1-pound package phyllo dough

1 stick butter, melted

1 tablespoon sesame or poppy seeds

The phyllo dough crust gives this pie a beautiful appearance, and it will taste as good as it looks!

Heat oil in a 10-inch fry pan and sauté the onions, garlic, dill weed, oregano, and tarragon over medium heat. When onions begin to brown, add mushrooms and continue to cook until moisture evaporates, or drain vegetables if needed.

In medium-sized bowl, mash tofu, add tahini, then beat in eggs with electric mixer until light and fluffy. Mix in sautéed vegetables and rest of ingredients except phyllo dough, butter, and seeds. Preheat oven to 350°.

Using a pastry brush, coat each sheet of phyllo dough with melted butter, and lay into 11 × 15-inch pan, leaving overhanging edge of 2 to 3 inches of dough around sides of pan. When approximately half the phyllo dough is used up, gently pour filling into pan and spread to sides and edges of pan. Fold the overhanging dough over the filling. Continue to layer sheets of phyllo on top of filling, folding phyllo to fit pan if necessary. Brush the top layer with butter and sprinkle with sesame or poppy seeds. Bake 30 to 40 minutes, until golden. Allow to cool 10 to 15 minutes before cutting.

8 servings

Shepherd's Pie

*O*ur vegetarian version of Shepherd's Pie was always good at the café, but it reached its optimum in flavor when one of the café cooks added tofu to the recipe. The missing link provided more texture, taste, and protein to the pie.

In a large bowl, combine the mashed potatoes, 2 tablespoons butter, ½ teaspoon salt, ¼ teaspoon pepper, parsley, and cream cheese and set aside.

In a 10-inch skillet, heat the oil over medium heat and sauté the onions, basil, and 1 teaspoon tarragon, along with broccoli or zucchini. A few minutes later, add green pepper, ¼ teaspoon salt, and ⅛ teaspoon pepper. When vegetables are tender but not overcooked, set aside. Add tofu or chick peas to vegetable mix. (If you are using tofu, cut into ½-inch cubes, sauté in oil until firm, and then add to vegetables.) Mix well. Pour into 9 × 13-inch pan or casserole dish.

Heat 1 tablespoon butter in skillet. Sauté the mushrooms and remaining ½ teaspoon tarragon. Remove from heat and stir in corn and sour cream. Layer on top of the vegetables. Then layer on potatoes, then grated cheese. Sprinkle with paprika. Bake covered 30 minutes at 350° and uncovered 10 to 15 minutes, until browned a bit on top. Let sit 10 minutes before cutting.

6 servings

5 cups mashed potatoes (about 4 medium-sized unpeeled potatoes)

3 tablespoons butter

¾ teaspoon salt

¼ plus ⅛ teaspoon black pepper

¼ cup minced fresh parsley

½ cup cream cheese, softened

2 tablespoons sunflower oil

1½ cups chopped onion (3 small onions)

2 teaspoons basil

1½ teaspoons tarragon

2 cups chopped broccoli, stems and florets, or sliced zucchini

1 cup chopped green pepper (1 large pepper)

1 square tofu (½ pound) plus 2 tablespoons oil or 1 cup cooked chick peas

2 cups sliced mushrooms

2 cups corn kernels, fresh or frozen

1¼ cups sour cream

1½ cups grated cheddar cheese

Paprika

Celebration Pot Pie

Filling

2 tablespoons butter

¾ cup chopped onions (1 medium onion)

2 cups chopped unpeeled red potatoes

4 to 5 large cloves garlic, minced

1 teaspoon dried leaf thyme

1 cup cubed butternut squash, peeled and seeded

¾ cup sliced celery

1 cup sliced carrots (1 large carrot)

2 cups chopped broccoli, stems and florets

1 cup water

½ teaspoon salt

⅛ teaspoon nutmeg

⅛ teaspoon cayenne pepper

1 cup peas, fresh or frozen

2 tablespoons sunflower oil

2 squares tofu, cubed (1 pound)

2 teaspoons tamari

*T*he day I heard the news that the cookbook was going to be published we celebrated at the café. Champagne was opened before 11:00 A.M. Eventually I made my way home and created this recipe. It takes a while to make, but provides a full meal in itself that is quite satisfying. All we needed was a glass of champagne on the side for a wonderful celebration.

Set a 4-quart soup pot over medium heat and add butter. When melted, add onions, potatoes, garlic, thyme, and squash. When onions become translucent, add celery, carrots, and broccoli and cook until vegetables are just tender. Lower heat to simmer, add water, salt, nutmeg, cayenne, and peas, and stir well. Simmer 1 to 2 minutes more and turn off heat.

Preheat oven to 450°. In a 10-inch fry pan, add oil and set over medium heat. When hot, add tofu and cook until browned on all sides, stirring occasionally. When browned, pour tamari over it, stir quickly, remove from heat, and add to vegetables.

Prepare sauce. In the same fry pan, add butter. When melted, add flour and cook over low heat until browned. Slowly add the water, stirring constantly with a whisk. Stir in nutritional yeast and tamari. Remove from heat and add to vegetables along with red wine and parsley. Set aside.

Mix flours, baking powder, soda, and salt in medium-sized bowl or food processor bowl. Cut in butter or run through processor with cutting blade. When mixture resembles cornmeal, add the cheese and stir. Mix the egg and buttermilk together and mix into flour-cheese mixture. Knead dough on floured board just enough to hold together and cut into 8 pieces. Butter 4 individual oven-proof bowls or baking dishes that will hold 2 cups vegetables each. Roll 4 pieces of dough out on floured board. Place 1 piece into the bottom of each dish. This should come up the edges of the bowl. Pour vegetable filling into crust. Now roll out the remaining 4 pieces of dough somewhat smaller to fit over the top of each baking dish and crimp edges of dough together. Beat the egg yolk and milk together and brush over each pie top. Prick each top generously with a fork. Bake 15 minutes.

4 servings

Sauce

2 tablespoons butter

2 tablespoons unbleached white flour

1½ cups water

1 tablespoon nutritional yeast

1 tablespoon tamari

½ cup dry red wine

¼ cup minced fresh parsley

Crust

1 cup unbleached white flour

1 cup whole wheat pastry flour

2 teaspoons baking powder

¾ teaspoon baking soda

¾ teaspoon salt

6 tablespoons butter

½ cup grated sharp cheddar cheese

1 egg, beaten

½ cup buttermilk

1 egg yolk, beaten

1 tablespoon milk

Mexican

Bean and Vegetable Burritos

Refried Beans

2 cups uncooked pinto beans

6 cups water

3 large cloves garlic, minced

½ teaspoon salt

1 tablespoon sunflower oil

⅛ teaspoon cayenne pepper

1 teaspoon ground cumin

Vegetable Filling

2 tablespoons sunflower oil

1 cup finely chopped onion (2 onions)

3 large cloves garlic, minced

1 teaspoon oregano

1 cup chopped green pepper

1 cup chopped zucchini (1 small zucchini)

1 cup grated carrot (1 large carrot)

2 small fresh or dried chili peppers, finely chopped

1 teaspoon ground cumin

½ teaspoon salt

Ten 10-inch white flour tortillas

1½ cups grated cheddar cheese

1½ cups grated Jalapeño pepper Jack cheese

Salsa (page 145)

Sour cream

*A*t noontime customers call the café to see if we have burritos on the menu. They are many people's lunchtime favorite.

Soak beans in water 8 hours or overnight. The next day, bring to a boil in a covered 3-quart saucepan and simmer 1½ to 2 hours until tender. Stir occasionally and add more water if needed. Drain out excess water and mash beans. Add minced garlic, salt, oil, cayenne, and cumin. Mix well and set aside. Preheat oven to 400°.

For the filling, heat 2 tablespoons oil in a 10-inch fry pan over medium heat. Sauté onion, minced garlic, and oregano a few minutes on medium heat. Add the green pepper, zucchini, carrot, and chili peppers. Sauté 5 minutes or until tender but not overcooked. Remove from heat. Add cumin and salt and mix in.

Spread approximately ½ cup beans in center of each tortilla. Then cover with the veggies and a mix of both cheeses on each. Distribute the ingredients so that everything is used up. Fold 2 sides of tortilla over bean mix and then fold both remaining sides to form a rectangle. Place folded side down in a large baking pan. Brush with Salsa. Bake approximately 10 to 15 minutes. Serve topped with sour cream and Salsa on the side.

5 large
servings

Moon Burritos

These untraditional burritos are filled with tofu and lots of vegetables. When we called them Tofu, Veggie, and Cheese Burritos they were a slow seller at the café. One night when we planned to serve them as a special I decided to change their name to Moon Burritos to see if they would sell better. We sold out! They are still ever popular.

Soak pinto beans in water for 8 hours or overnight. Bring to a boil in a 2-quart saucepan and simmer, covered, until tender (approximately 2 hours). Drain out excess water, mash beans, and add ½ teaspoon salt, tomatoes, cayenne, and 2 cloves minced garlic. Stir.

Preheat oven to 400°.

Set 10-inch fry pan over medium heat and add 2 tablespoons oil. When oil is hot, add tofu. Cook until browned on all sides. Pour tamari over tofu, cook 1 minute more, and remove from heat. Set tofu aside.

Again set fry pan over medium heat, add remaining oil, then onions, 3 cloves minced garlic, and carrot. When onions begin to brown, add broccoli, zucchini, and green and hot peppers. Cook until just tender. Drain any excess liquid out of mixture. Add ½ teaspoon salt and cumin to mixture and stir well.

Lay out tortillas on counter. Spread ⅓ cup beans in center of each tortilla. Top with vegetables, then a bit of tofu, followed by cheeses that have been mixed together. Fold edges of tortillas in and roll tortillas up. Set on baking sheet. Brush each tortilla with some Salsa and bake 10 minutes. Top with sour cream and a side of Salsa.

4 servings

1½ cups uncooked pinto beans

5 cups water

1 teaspoon salt

¾ cup canned crushed tomatoes

¼ teaspoon cayenne pepper

5 cloves garlic, minced

3 tablespoons sunflower oil

1 square tofu, cut into ½-inch cubes (½ pound)

1 teaspoon tamari

¾ cup chopped onion (1 medium onion)

¾ cup diced carrot (1 carrot)

¾ cup chopped broccoli, stems and florets

¾ cup sliced zucchini (1 small zucchini)

¾ cup chopped green pepper (1 medium pepper)

2 chopped dried chili peppers or 1 finely chopped fresh chili pepper

2 teaspoons ground cumin

Eight 10-inch white flour tortillas

1 cup grated cheddar cheese

2 cups grated Jalapeño pepper Jack cheese

Salsa (page 145)

Sour cream

Chalupas

Twelve 8-inch whole wheat
or white flour tortillas (2
per person needed)

Sunflower oil for frying
tortillas

Soak 2 cups pinto beans in
6 cups water and follow
directions in Bean and
Vegetable Burritos for
refried beans (page 208)

1½ cups grated cheddar
cheese

1½ cups grated Jalapeño
pepper Jack cheese

Have Ready

A preheated 375° oven

Shredded lettuce

Green and red pepper
rings

Onion rings

Diced tomatoes

Guacamole (page 129)

Sour cream

Minced olives

Salsa (page 145)

Chalupas are the café's most popular Mexican dinner special. Traditionally, tortillas are called chalupas in Mexico when they are filled and rolled up into a canoe-shaped roll. Our chalupas are served open-faced so that we can fit more into them.

They involve stacking 2 flour tortillas that have been fried to a crisp golden color on top of one another. In between is a layer of refried beans and melted cheese. The whole tortilla is topped with salad veggies, Guacamole, sour cream, and Salsa. The result is beautiful, delicious, impressive to look at, and a meal in itself.

1. Fry tortillas individually in a 10-inch fry pan in hot oil, enough to generously cover the bottom of pan. The tortilla should sizzle in the oil and quickly bubble up and brown. When tortilla turns lightly golden, flip over and cook the other side. It will cook quickly. Drain and set on paper towels. Cook all 12 tortillas this way.

2. Make your refried beans.

3. Make Guacamole.

4. Make Salsa.

5. Grate cheeses.

6. Lay out your tortillas on 2 large cookie sheets and gently spread all the beans over 6 tortillas. Then spread the cheeses over the beans. These are ready to go in the oven and take only about 7 minutes, just enough time to melt the cheese and get the beans warm, so don't put them in until you're just about ready to eat. Put the extra 6 tortillas in the oven 5 minutes after the bottoms and bake just enough to heat through, about 2 minutes. Prepare all your garnishes. When chalupas come out of the oven, top each with one of the warmed extra tortillas and serve 1 to a plate. They should be generously dressed first with lettuce, then peppers, onions, tomatoes, a big dollop of Guacamole and sour cream, and around this olives and chopped eggs. Serve with a side of Salsa. A hearty appetite is needed to eat a whole chalupa!

6 servings

Huevos Rancheros. For Huevos Rancheros, use 1 tortilla per person. Fry as you would for chalupas. Make the Salsa, refried beans, Guacamole. Have the cheeses and the sliced vegetables ready. Bake tortillas with beans and cheese 5 to 7 minutes. Have 2 fried eggs (over easy) ready to top each tortilla with, then top with vegetables and Guacamole, chalupa style.

Avocado Tortillas

2 firm ripe avocados,
peeled, pitted, and sliced
about ⅛ inch thick

1 tablespoon lemon juice

2 tablespoons sunflower oil

1½ cups finely chopped
onion (3 onions)

5 cloves garlic, minced

3 small dried Jalepeño
chili peppers, crumbled, or
1 finely chopped fresh hot
pepper

1 teaspoon basil

2 teaspoons oregano

1 green pepper, finely
chopped

2 cups thinly sliced
zucchini (cut in half or
quarters lengthwise if
zucchinis are large, then
slice) (1 medium zucchini)

½ teaspoon ground cumin

¼ teaspoon ground
coriander

¾ teaspoon salt

12 8-inch whole wheat
flour tortillas (1 package)

3 medium-sized tomatoes,
diced

2 cups grated Jalepeño
pepper Jack cheese

Sour cream

Salsa (page 145)

The rich flavor of avocados is combined here with chili peppers, Jack cheese, and spicy vegetables and then rolled into flour tortillas and baked. We often serve these with a side of refried beans and salad for a very satisfying meal.

Sprinkle the avocados with lemon juice to prevent browning.

Heat the oil in a 10-inch cast-iron fry pan. Add onions, garlic, chili peppers, basil, and oregano and sauté on medium heat. As onions begin to brown, add green pepper, zucchini, cumin, coriander, and salt. Cook until tender but firm. Remove from heat.

Lay out tortillas on your counter. Preheat oven to 375°. Spoon about 1 tablespoon vegetables onto each tortilla and spread through the middle in about a 1-inch-wide line. Next add 1 tablespoon chopped tomato, then avocado slices, about 5 slices per tortilla. Top with the grated cheese. Use up all the ingredients. Roll up and place in an oiled 12 × 14-inch pan. Brush tortillas lightly with salsa. Cover with aluminum foil and bake 10 to 15 minutes, until cheese is melted and tortillas are a little brown but still soft. Serve with a spoonful of sour cream on each tortilla and Salsa on the side.

6 servings

Garbanzo Chimichangas

No one knew quite what these were when I served them at a buffet dinner, but everyone loved them just the same. *Garbanzo chimichangas combine the taste of falafel from the Middle East with a Mexican burrito and the result is delicious.*

Soak chick peas in water at least 8 hours. Then bring to a boil in a 2-quart saucepan and simmer, covered, until tender (2½ to 3 hours). Drain and mash the beans well or puree in food processor with chopping blade and put into a medium-sized bowl.

Add 2 tablespoons oil to a 10-inch fry pan and set over medium heat. When hot, add onions, oregano, garlic, and carrots. Sauté until onions begin to brown, then add green and hot peppers and cook 2 minutes more. Remove from heat and add vegetables to beans. Add the tomato paste, cumin, salt, and turmeric to mixture. Mix in well.

Lay out tortillas on a counter. Spread ⅓ cup mix across the center of each tortilla, leaving a 2-inch border on each end and 3 inches on each side. Top the bean mixture with the grated cheese, using ⅓ cup per tortilla. Top these with the chopped tomatoes. Now fold the ends in on the tortillas over the bean mixture and roll up the tortilla into a long log. Pin closed with a toothpick.

Preheat oven to 375°. Heat 2 cups oil in a 2-quart saucepan. When hot, add a tortilla to the oil. Cook until bubbly and brown, flip over, and cook the other side until browned. Set on paper towels to drain. Repeat until all the tortillas have been cooked.

Set on cookie sheet and bake 10 minutes. Serve topped with sour cream and a side of Salsa.

5 servings

1½ cups uncooked chick peas

6 cups water

Sunflower oil

¾ cup chopped onion (1 medium onion)

½ teaspoon oregano

4 large cloves garlic, minced

½ cup chopped carrot (1 small carrot)

¾ cup chopped green pepper (1 medium pepper)

2 fresh hot peppers, minced

One 6-ounce can tomato paste

1 teaspoon ground cumin

1 teaspoon salt

½ teaspoon turmeric

Ten 10-inch white flour tortillas

3⅓ cups grated Jalapeño pepper Jack cheese

2 medium tomatoes, chopped

Sour cream

Salsa (page 145)

Flautas

Sunflower oil

¾ cup chopped celery (1 stalk)

1 cup finely chopped onion (1 large onion)

1 cup cream cheese, softened

1 square tofu, cut into small cubes (½ pound)

2 teaspoons tamari

¾ cup grated cheddar cheese

⅛ cup chopped pitted olives

¼ cup minced fresh parsley

1 teaspoon ground cumin

1 teaspoon chili powder

Dash of cayenne pepper

Eight 10-inch white flour tortillas

Sour cream

Salsa (page 145)

I *used to teach an occasional cooking class through a local learning exchange. The Mexican class was always a well-attended one. After cooking a number of different Mexican meals, the whole class would sit down to taste everything.*

Flautas were everyone's favorite. They are similar to a burrito but are deep fried to produce a crisp, bubbly, golden outside and a hot, spicy, cheesy, and delicious inside.

Heat 1 tablespoon oil in a 10-inch fry pan and sauté the celery and onion until lightly browned. Combine with cream cheese in medium-sized bowl. Heat another tablespoon oil and sauté the tofu until brown on all sides. Then pour tamari over it. Cook 1 minute more, stirring. Then add to cream cheese mixture. Add rest of the ingredients except the tortillas, sour cream, and Salsa. Mix well.

Put approximately ⅓ cup mixture on the center of 1 tortilla. Fold both sides toward the center, allowing an inch or so to overlap mix. Then, starting at bottom, roll up jelly roll fashion into a log shape. Roll gently so as to not crack the tortilla. Secure by inserting a toothpick through folded ends. Repeat until all 8 tortillas are folded and rolled up.

Heat approximately 2 cups oil in a small, deep saucepan over medium heat. (Oil can be strained and reused for deep frying.) When hot, add 1 flauta (unless 2 will fit at a time). Cook until lightly golden on each side. Drain and lay out on a paper towel to absorb oil. Serve these right away, or they can be reheated (and will still be delicious!) in the oven at approximately 400° 7 to 10 minutes. Top with sour cream and serve with a side of Salsa.

4 servings

Baked Mexican Vegetable Pie

A delicious and spicy mixture of vegetables layered with two cheeses and covered with a baked custard topping.

Beat together the eggs, sour cream, and parsley in medium-sized bowl and set aside.

Heat the oil in a 10-inch fry pan and sauté the onions and garlic with spices. When the onions begin to brown, add peppers. Add mushrooms a few minutes later. If there is liquid left in the pan, drain well. Put into large bowl. Add fresh tomatoes and corn (don't precook frozen corn), then add flour and salt. Stir well and taste for seasoning. Spread half the sauté into an oiled pan (9 × 12- or 13-inch is fine) and top with half the 2 cheeses that have first been mixed together. Layer the remaining vegetables on top and sprinkle with the remaining cheese mixture. Pour the egg mixture over all and sprinkle generously with paprika. Bake covered 30 minutes at 375°, then uncover and bake 10 to 15 minutes more until golden and set. Allow to cool a few minutes before cutting. Serve topped with a dollop of sour cream and a side of Salsa.

6 to 8 servings

4 large eggs

1½ cups sour cream

½ cup minced fresh parsley

2 tablespoons sunflower oil

1½ cups diced onion (3 onions)

6 cloves garlic, minced

1 teaspoon basil

1 teaspoon oregano

1 teaspoon cumin seed

1 teaspoon ground coriander

½ teaspoon dry mustard

¼ teaspoon cayenne pepper (or to taste) or 1 teaspoon crushed dried chili peppers (or 1 finely diced fresh hot chili)

1 cup diced green pepper (1 large pepper)

2 cups sliced mushrooms or 2 cups thinly sliced zucchini

3 medium tomatoes, diced

2 cups corn kernels, fresh or frozen

2 tablespoons whole wheat flour

1 teaspoon salt

1 cup grated Jalapeño pepper Jack cheese

1 cup grated cheddar cheese

Paprika

Sour cream for garnish

Salsa (page 145)

Black Bean Enchiladas

1½ cups uncooked black beans

6 cups water

2 tablespoons sunflower oil

¾ cup finely chopped onion (1 large onion)

¾ cup finely diced carrot (1 carrot)

1 teaspoon basil

1 teaspoon oregano

1 tablespoon minced garlic (approximately 5 to 6 cloves)

¾ cup finely chopped green pepper (1 medium pepper)

½ teaspoon ground cumin

¼ teaspoon ground coriander

1 crumbled dried chili pepper or 1 minced fresh Jalapeño pepper

1½ teaspoons salt

12 corn tortillas (1 package)

1½ cups Salsa (page 145)

2½ cups grated Jalapeño pepper Jack cheese

Sour cream

Many Mexican households cook with black beans as often if not more than with pinto beans. They offer a nice change and are equally savory as pinto beans.

Soak beans in water in a 2-quart saucepan for 8 hours. Bring to a boil and simmer, covered, 1¼ hours or more, until tender. Drain excess water.

Heat 1 tablespoon oil in a 10-inch fry pan and sauté the onions, carrots, basil, oregano, and garlic. After a few minutes, add peppers, spices, chili pepper, and salt. Continue to cook until vegetables are tender but not overcooked. Add vegetables to beans.

Preheat oven to 375°. Brush each tortilla with oil and Salsa lightly on both sides. Set aside remaining Salsa. Spread out on a cookie sheet. Bake just a few minutes until tender and soft, not crisp.

Put ⅓ cup bean mixture down middle of each tortilla, then a line of cheese. You should have enough beans and cheese to fill all 12 tortillas. Roll up and lay face down on a cookie sheet or in individual baking dishes. Brush with Salsa and bake approximately 7 to 10 minutes, until tender and cheese is melted. Serve with sour cream on top and remaining Salsa, if desired.

6 servings

Layered Enchiladas

Soak beans in water overnight. Cook, covered, approximately 2 hours in a 3-quart saucepan until soft. Drain and mash.

Heat 2 tablespoons oil in a 10-inch fry pan and sauté the onions, garlic, basil, oregano, and chili peppers over medium heat. When they begin to soften, add zucchini and green pepper and sauté another few minutes until tender but still firm. Mix the veggies with the beans. Add tomato, corn, salt, cayenne, and parsley. Stir and set aside.

Set another fry pan over medium heat and add remaining 2 tablespoons oil. When hot, lightly fry up the corn tortillas, 1 or 2 at a time, brushing with a little of the Tomato Garlic Sauce or Salsa, until they are lightly cooked but not crisp. Add more oil to pan if needed. Set tortillas on paper towels to drain.

Put some tomato sauce or Salsa in bottom of 9 × 13-inch pan to lightly cover. Next arrange 6 tortillas to cover the sauce. Cover with half the bean-veggie mix, then half of each of the grated cheeses, more sauce, tortillas, beans, tortillas again, more sauce, ending with cheese. Sprinkle this with a bit more basil and oregano. Bake 40 minutes at 350°. Allow pie to set for 10 minutes before cutting. Serve with Salsa and sour cream on the side.

6 to 8 servings

2 cups uncooked pinto or kidney beans

6 cups water

4 tablespoons sunflower oil

¾ cup finely chopped onion (1 large onion)

5 large cloves garlic, minced

1 teaspoon basil

3 teaspoons oregano

4 crumbled dried chili peppers or 2 minced fresh Jalapeño peppers

1½ cups diced zucchini (1 small zucchini)

1 large green pepper, chopped

1 fresh medium tomato, chopped

1 cup corn kernels, fresh or frozen

1 teaspoon salt

½ teaspoon cayenne pepper (use none if you like your food only mildly spicy)

½ cup minced fresh parsley

18 corn tortillas

4 cups Basic Tomato Garlic Sauce (page 194) or Salsa (page 145)

2 cups grated cheddar cheese

2 cups grated Jack cheese

Salsa

Sour cream

Tortitas

2 cups uncooked pinto
beans

6 cups water

3 large cloves garlic,
minced

½ teaspoon salt

2 teaspoons ground cumin

2 cups plus 2 tablespoons
sunflower oil

⅛ teaspoon cayenne
pepper

10 corn tortillas

2 ripe avocados, cut in
half, peeled, pitted, and
sliced into ⅛-inch-wide
slices

2 cups grated Jalapeño
pepper Jack cheese

1 cup coarsely chopped
green pepper (1 large
pepper)

½ cup coarsely chopped
red onion (1 onion)

2 medium tomatoes,
coarsely chopped

¼ cup chopped fresh
Jalapeño peppers
(optional)

Salsa (page 145) and sour
cream for garnish

*T**o make tortitas you will need a little gadget called
a tortilla basket fryer. One steel basket sits inside
the other (fig. 1) with a corn tortilla scrunched in between. It is then deep fried to produce a crisp corn tortilla shell that can be stuffed with delicious fillings. The
baskets can be ordered through mail-order kitchen
supply houses and are reasonably priced.*

Soak pinto beans in water in a 3-quart pot for 6 to 8
hours. Bring to a boil, cover, and simmer for 1½ to 2
hours until tender. Drain and mash beans, reserving a
small amount of bean juice. Add the garlic, salt, cumin, 2
tablespoons oil, and cayenne to the beans. If beans seem
too stiff and dry, pour a small amount of bean juice into
them and stir in well.

Heat 2 cups oil in a deep saucepan. (First check to
make sure the tortilla basket fryer will fit in the pan.)
When oil is hot, set 1 tortilla on top of the larger basket.
Gently push down into the basket by setting the smaller
basket into the larger (fig. 2). Fry until the tortilla is
crisp but not browned. Repeat until all 10 tortillas have
been cooked. Set them on paper towels to drain.

Preheat oven to 400°. Set the tortitas out on a large
cookie sheet. Spread ¼ cup beans carefully into the bottom of each shell. On top of the beans add avocado slices
to cover the beans. Top with a small amount of grated
Jalapeño cheese. Now cover with ¼ cup more beans, avocado slices, and grated cheese to cover the top of each
tortita. Bake 10 minutes.

Remove from oven and top with green peppers, onions,
tomatoes, and chopped Jalapeño peppers. Serve Salsa
and sour cream on the side for garnish.

5 servings

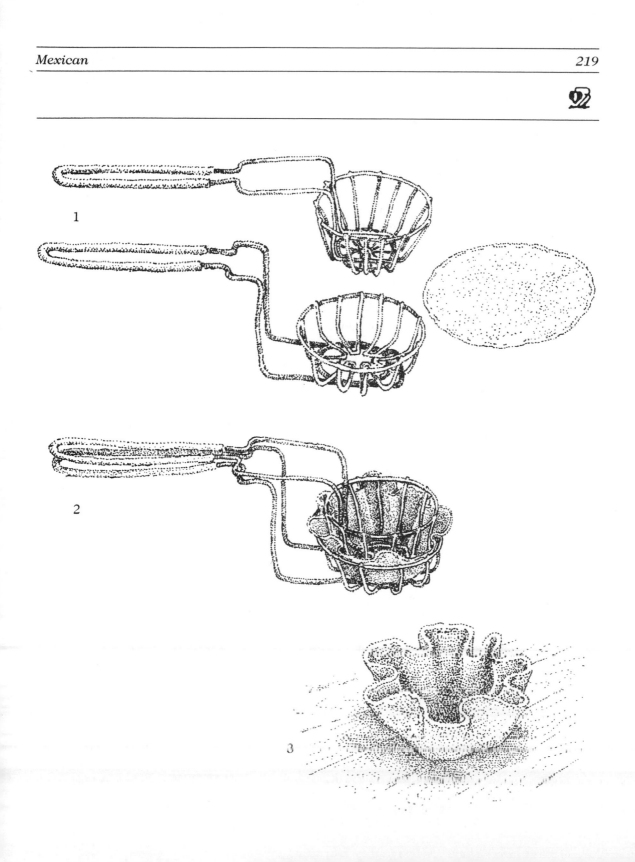

1

2

3

Crepes

Basic Crepes

3 eggs

1 teaspoon honey

⅛ teaspoon salt

1 cup unbleached white flour

½ cup whole wheat pastry flour

1¾ cups milk

2 tablespoons butter, melted

3 to 4 tablespoons butter

In medium-sized bowl, whip eggs until light, then add honey, salt, and flours. Stir in well. Slowly add milk, ¼ cup at a time. When well mixed, add melted butter. Allow batter to sit at room temperature 2 hours if possible. If it sits overnight, refrigerate it and add a bit more milk to thin the batter. The next day allow to sit at room temperature for an hour before using.

To cook, preheat a 10-inch skillet over medium heat. Add ½ tablespoon butter and swirl it around in the pan. Add a bit less than ¼ cup of batter to pan, then quickly swirl pan around so that batter covers the bottom of pan thinly. If too much batter is poured in, try to pour excess batter back into larger bowl. Cook 1 to 2 minutes, until lightly golden in color, then flip crepe over with a spatula, cook 1 minute more, and remove from heat. Add a bit more butter to pan and repeat process until all batter is used up. Stack cooked crepes on top of one another and allow to cool. Be sure to use a small amount of batter or crepes will be too thick.

11 to 12
crepes

Spinach Ricotta Crepes

These are a close relative to spinach manicotti, with a crepe being used instead of pasta. Joy, a past dinner cook at the café of Italian descent, said this is the real Italian style of making manicotti.

In medium-sized bowl, combine the ricotta and Parmesan cheeses, nutmeg, salt, and pepper.

Heat the oil in a skillet and sauté the spinach and garlic with the thyme until tender but not overcooked. Press any excess water out of spinach and add to ricotta mixture. Stir.

Preheat oven to 350°. Fill each crepe with approximately ½ cup spinach-cheese mixture. Then put 2 tablespoons mozzarella in each crepe and roll up tightly. Place seam side down in an oiled shallow baking dish. Lay crepes close together. Top with tomato sauce and the remaining mozzarella. Bake 30 minutes.

5 servings

2 pounds ricotta cheese

¾ cup very finely grated Parmesan cheese

¼ teaspoon nutmeg

½ teaspoon salt

Freshly ground black pepper to taste

2 tablespoons olive oil

4 cups finely chopped fresh spinach

4 cloves garlic, minced

1 teaspoon dried leaf thyme

10 crepes (page 220)

2 cups grated mozzarella cheese

2 cups Basic Tomato Garlic Sauce (page 194)

Broccoli Walnut Crepes

2 tablespoons sunflower oil

1 cup chopped onion (2 small onions)

2 teaspoons basil

2 teaspoons dried leaf thyme

7 cups chopped broccoli (chop stems; leave florets whole)

1 teaspoon salt

⅛ teaspoon black pepper

¾ cup chopped roasted walnuts (to roast nuts, bake on cookie sheet 5 minutes at 375°)

¼ cup finely chopped fresh parsley

10 crepes (page 220)

1½ cups grated cheddar cheese

1½ cups grated Monterey Jack cheese

1 cup sour cream

Roasted walnuts for garnish

Set a 10-inch fry pan over medium heat. Add oil, then onions, basil, and thyme. As onions just become translucent and/or begin to brown, add broccoli to mixture. Continue to cook until just tender, mixing ingredients together. Pour into medium-sized bowl. Add salt and pepper. Add ½ cup roasted walnuts and parsley. Stir well. Preheat oven to 375°.

Lay crepes out on counter. Spread ⅓ cup broccoli mixture down the center of each crepe. Combine cheeses and top each crepe with about 3 tablespoons cheese. Roll up crepes and set seam side down onto lightly oiled shallow baking pan. Bake 10 minutes, until cheese is thoroughly melted. Serve each crepe with a dollop of sour cream topped with a few roasted walnuts.

5 servings

Avocado Cheese Crepes

Heat the oil in a 10-inch skillet and sauté onions, garlic, eggplant, thyme, and basil over medium heat until tender and browned. Don't overcook.

Dice the tomatoes and combine with the sliced water chestnuts in a medium-sized bowl. Add sautéed veggies, salt, and pepper. Stir.

Preheat oven to 375°. Lay out crepes and put ½ cup vegetable mixture in a line down the center of each crepe. Then peel and slice avocados, squeeze lemon over them, and spread 4 to 6 avocado slices over the veggies on each crepe. Add ¼ cup cheese per crepe. Roll up the crepes and place seam side down in a shallow oiled baking pan. Bake 10 minutes. Serve with a dollop of sour cream on top.

4 servings

2 tablespoons olive oil

1 cup finely diced onion (2 small onions)

4 medium-large cloves garlic, minced

3 cups finely diced eggplant (1 small) (peel eggplant only if skin is thick and tough)

1 teaspoon leaf thyme

1 teaspoon basil

2 ripe medium tomatoes

½ cup sliced water chestnuts (one-half 8-ounce can)

¼ teaspoon salt

Freshly ground black pepper to taste

8 crepes (page 220)

2 ripe avocados (the black bumpy ones are tastiest)

½ lemon

2 cups grated cheddar cheese

1 cup sour cream

Pizza Crepes

4 cups Basic Tomato
Garlic Sauce (page 194)

10 crepes (page 220)

2 medium-sized green
peppers, sliced

1 cup sliced onion (2 small
onions)

2 cups sliced mushrooms

3 cups grated mozzarella
cheese

½ cup grated Parmesan
cheese

Lay out crepes on counter. Preheat oven to 375°. Put 2
tablespoons tomato sauce on each crepe, then mix the
peppers, onions, and mushrooms together and place approximately ½ cup vegetables down the center of each
crepe. Cover with 2 tablespoons mozzarella and a sprinkle of Parmesan.

Roll up the crepes, place seam side down in shallow
oiled casserole dish, and top with remaining sauce and
cheese. Bake covered 20 minutes.

5 servings

And More

Mushroomkopita

Preheat oven to 375°. Sauté mushrooms in a 10-inch fry pan in 1 tablespoon butter with thyme. In separate fry pan, sauté onions, garlic, and tarragon in 1 tablespoon butter. Drain both well. (Save juices and use for a soup stock!) Pour into a bowl with the feta cheese and mix well. Beat the eggs and add to mushroom mixture along with bread crumbs, parsley, salt, and pepper.

Heat the remaining butter on low heat until completely melted. Open phyllo dough. Butter the top of a sheet and lay inside a 9 × 13-inch pan with the edge of phyllo overhanging the pan's edge by about 2 inches. Continue this process so that the pan is continually recovered with phyllo dough (gently press it into pan), leaving a border hanging over the edge of the dish. After approximately half the box of phyllo is used up (10 sheets), pour filling into dish. Fold edges of phyllo over to cover the edges of filling and press into sides of pan. Now continue to brush phyllo dough with butter and lay into pan over filling. Fold phyllo in half to fit into pan. Use up the rest of the dough. Brush top sheet of phyllo with butter, and sprinkle on poppy seeds and a dash of thyme and tarragon. Cut a slash across the top of the pie to allow steam to escape. Bake 30 minutes at 375°, until golden brown. Allow to set 10 minutes before cutting.

6 to 8
servings

Broccolikopita. Replace mushrooms with 2 heads broccoli.

Spanikopita. Replace mushrooms with 2 pounds fresh spinach. Wash well and place spinach in a large bowl. Sprinkle spinach generously with salt and tear spinach apart. It will shrink down to less than half a bowlful. Wash well and drain. Press excess water out.

Follow basic recipe, replacing the thyme and tarragon with 1 teaspoon basil and 2 teaspoons oregano. Sauté these herbs with the onion and garlic in butter.

Mix the feta cheese and eggs together but exclude the bread crumbs and parsley. Combine spinach with feta cheese mix. Assemble and bake.

2 pounds sliced mushrooms

1 stick butter (¼ pound)

2 teaspoons leaf thyme

1½ cups chopped onion (3 medium onions)

4 cloves garlic, minced

1½ teaspoons tarragon

2 cups grated or crumbled feta cheese

4 eggs

⅓ cup bread crumbs

¼ cup minced fresh parsley

½ teaspoon salt (less if salted butter is used)

Black pepper to taste

1 pound phyllo dough

1 teaspoon poppy seeds

Broccoli Cheese Tiropitas

8 tablespoons butter

½ cup finely chopped onion (1 onion)

4 large cloves garlic, minced

4 cups chopped broccoli, stems and florets

1 teaspoon oregano

½ teaspoon leaf thyme

2 cups grated or crumbled feta cheese (½ pound)

Dash of black pepper

16 sheets phyllo dough

The café makes these into bite-sized appetizers for parties, where remnants of the delicious, flaky crust will be visible on the floor after everyone leaves. For dinners we make the tiropitas larger and serve each person two. They are wonderful served hot or at room temperature.

Preheat oven to 350°. Heat 10-inch fry pan over medium heat. When hot, add 1 tablespoon butter. When melted, add onions, garlic, broccoli, oregano, and thyme. Cook over medium heat until onions begin to brown and broccoli turns bright green. Remove from heat and pour broccoli mixture into medium-sized bowl. Add feta cheese and pepper; mix well.

Melt remaining 7 tablespoons butter in small saucepan. Using a pastry brush, brush some butter onto a large baking sheet. Spread out a sheet of phyllo dough on a counter and lightly butter the dough. Lay another sheet of dough directly over the first sheet. Fold over lengthwise to cut the size of the sheet in half. Put ½ cup broccoli-cheese mixture onto dough (fig. 1). Fold the first triangle over the mixture (fig. 2). Then gently pick up and turn the triangle into the next fold position (fig. 3). Fold again (fig. 4), then once more (fig. 5), folding the last flap of dough over the triangle (fig. 6). Lay onto buttered cookie sheet. Repeat the process to end up with 8 triangles. Brush remaining melted butter over the triangles on baking sheet and sprinkle with oregano. Bake 20 minutes, until golden brown.

4 servings

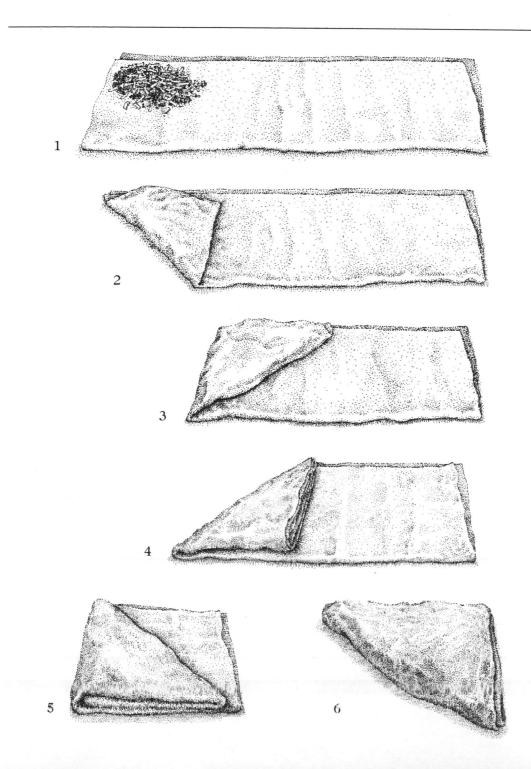

1

2

3

4

5 6

Baked Stuffed Squash

1 medium-sized butternut squash

2 tablespoons sunflower oil

1 cup chopped onions (2 medium onions)

One 1-inch piece ginger root, chopped finely

5 cloves garlic, minced

1 teaspoon dried dill weed

1 teaspoon basil

1 medium sweet red pepper, chopped

1 square tofu, mashed (½ pound)

¾ cup tahini

1½ cups water

1 tablespoon flour

1 tablespoon tamari or more to taste

Ground black pepper to taste

½ cup minced fresh parsley

In 1816 it snowed in Vermont every month of the year. Few crops were harvested, and settlers sustained themselves on pumpkins, turnips, winter squash, and the like. To this day, many Vermonters grow a large winter squash crop which stores well through most of the long cold winter.

The tofu-tahini sauce served over butternut squash adds protein and delicious flavor to a simple meal.

Cut squash in half, scoop out seeds, and bake face down in pan at 400° until tender (approximately 45 minutes).

In a 10-inch fry pan, heat the oil and sauté onions, ginger root, garlic, dill weed, and basil over medium heat until they begin to brown. Add chopped pepper. Continue to cook approximately 2 minutes more.

Meanwhile, put tofu in medium-sized saucepan. Add tahini and mix well. Then slowly add water and cook over low heat, stirring with a whisk, until the sauce is thoroughly combined.

Add flour to sautéed vegetables, then combine vegetables with tofu-tahini sauce. Continue to simmer on very low heat. Add tamari and ground pepper to taste and more water if sauce becomes too thick. Mix in the parsley and serve over squash.

2 large main dish or 4 side dish servings

Asparagus, Mushrooms, and Rice with a Zesty Dijon Cheddar Sauce

Bring rice and water to a boil in a 2-quart saucepan. Lower heat to simmer. Cover and cook until rice is tender and water has been absorbed (approximately 40 minutes).

Cut the last inch off the bottom of asparagus stalks. Then lightly peel off the outermost skin of the next 2 inches of stalk and cut the asparagus at an angle into ½-inch pieces. Steam asparagus until just tender.

Preheat oven to 375°. In a 10-inch skillet, put 1 tablespoon butter. When melted, sauté over medium heat onions, garlic, dill weed, and thyme. When onions just begin to brown, add mushrooms. When mushrooms are barely tender, remove from heat. Add this mixture to cooked rice in medium-sized bowl. Add remaining tablespoon butter, steamed asparagus, lemon juice, salt, and tamari. Stir well. Place into 4 individual baking dishes and bake 15 minutes.

Pour milk into double boiler. When it begins to get hot, add the cheese, stir until melted, then add mustard and dill weed. Keep hot in double boiler.

Top each dish with the mustard-cheese sauce and serve.

4 servings

1½ cups uncooked brown rice

3 cups water

1 pound fresh asparagus

2 tablespoons butter

½ cup chopped onion (1 onion)

3 large cloves garlic, minced

½ teaspoon dried dill weed

1 teaspoon leaf thyme

4 cups sliced mushrooms

2 tablespoons lemon juice

½ teaspoon salt

1 teaspoon tamari

Sauce

1 cup milk

2½ cups grated sharp cheddar cheese

2 teaspoons Dijon-style mustard

⅛ teaspoon dried dill weed

Spinach Mushroom Strudel with Two Cheeses

2 cups farmer cheese
(ricotta may be
substituted)

1 cup finely grated
Parmesan cheese

2 eggs, beaten

6 scallions, chopped

1 tablespoon butter

4 cups sliced mushrooms

½ cup chopped water
chestnuts

1 teaspoon dried dill weed

½ teaspoon leaf thyme

8 lightly packed cups
coarsely chopped fresh
spinach

½ teaspoon salt

Dash of freshly ground
black pepper

1 tablespoon lemon juice

10 sheets phyllo dough

4 tablespoons butter,
melted

1 tablespoon wheat germ

Preheat oven to 350°. In medium-sized mixing bowl, combine farmer and Parmesan cheeses, eggs, and scallions. Set a 10-inch fry pan over medium heat and add butter. When melted, add mushrooms, water chestnuts if fresh (if canned, do not sauté), dill weed, and thyme. Sauté until just tender. Drain excess juice from mushrooms and add to cheese mixture, combining thoroughly.

Steam spinach until tender but not overcooked. Press excess water out of spinach and add to cheese mixture along with canned water chestnuts, salt, pepper, and lemon juice.

Spread a sheet of phyllo dough out on a counter. Brush it lightly with melted butter, then stack another sheet of phyllo directly on top of the first. Butter this sheet of phyllo and repeat 3 more times until a total of 5 sheets are layered one on top of another. Have sheets spread lengthwise in front of you. Pour half the filling mix (about 3 cups) ⅓ down into the center of the dough lengthwise, leaving a 2-inch border on either end (fig. 1). Spread filling to make a 4-inch-wide line down the length of the dough. Fold 2-inch edges over the filling along the length (fig. 2) and on each end (fig. 3). Then gently roll the dough up until it is a snugly rolled log (fig. 4). Repeat the same process so that 2 logs have been made.

Set the strudels seam side down on an 11 × 16-inch buttered cookie sheet. Brush remaining butter over dough and sprinkle with wheat germ. Bake 25 minutes. Allow to sit 5 minutes before cutting. Cut each log at an angle into thirds and serve.

6 servings

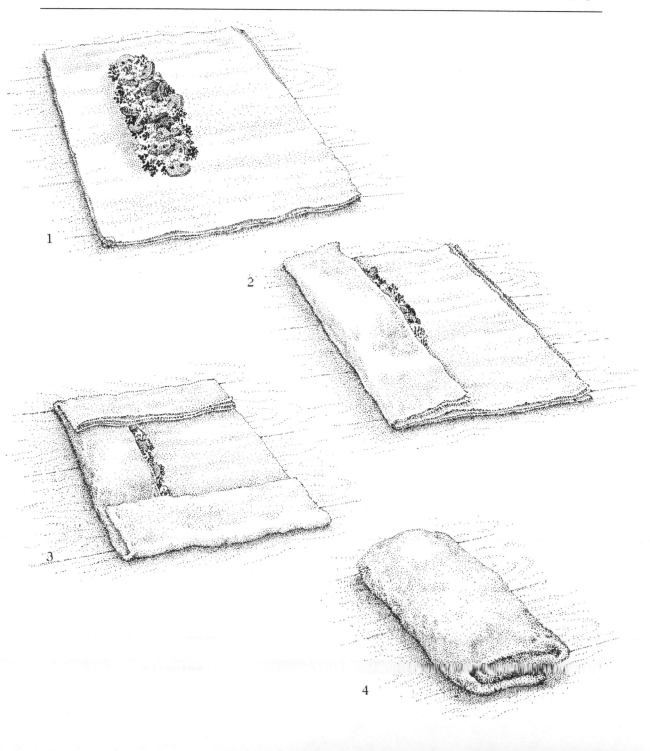

Mushroom, Spinach, and Potato Curry

3 tablespoons sunflower oil

1 tablespoon mustard seed

2 teaspoons turmeric

2 teaspoons cumin seed

½ teaspoon cayenne
pepper, or to taste

½ teaspoon ground
coriander

1 teaspoon salt

4 medium unpeeled
potatoes, sliced and diced
(mixture of both)
(approximately 6 cups)

¾ cup chopped onion (1
medium onion)

1 cup water

¾ pound spinach, washed
and chopped coarsely

¾ pound sliced
mushrooms

About 1½ cups yogurt

We always serve this curry with a chapati on the side and begin the meal with Indian Split Pea Soup (page 99).

Heat oil in wok or 4-quart, deep cast-iron Dutch oven on low to medium heat. Add mustard seed, turmeric, cumin seed, cayenne, coriander, and salt. Cover and let seeds pop. Raise heat a bit higher if needed for them to snap. As they begin to dance, lower heat. When popping stops, add potatoes and onions. Stir well until they are coated with spices.

Add the water, cover, and let simmer until tender, stirring occasionally (about 20 minutes or so). Add additional water as needed. Then add spinach and stir until cooked. Add mushrooms and stir. A few minutes later, add 1 cup yogurt. (Add sooner if moisture is needed!)

Cook 15 to 20 minutes more, stirring occasionally. Check seasoning. Serve with a spoonful of yogurt on top.

6 servings

Tofu Cutlets with Mushroom Sauce

Both children and older non-tofu eaters have been won over by these cutlets. Their crisp, breaded outsides and tender insides are savory on their own, and the mushroom sauce is the pièce de résistance!

Set a 10-inch fry pan over medium heat. When hot, add oil, then add carrots, celery, onions, and thyme. Sauté until tender and lightly browned (around 10 minutes). Add water. Pour the mixture into a blender, puree, and set aside.

Set fry pan over medium heat again and add ½ tablespoon butter. When hot, add mushrooms and cook until just tender. Add blended stock to mushrooms and remove from heat.

Add 2 tablespoons butter to a 2-quart saucepan and set over medium heat. When melted, add the pastry flour. Lower heat to simmer, and cook until flour is browned. Slowly add spoonfuls of mushroom-blended stock mixture to flour and butter until all has been combined. Stir in tamari and parsley. Simmer 10 minutes. Turn off heat. Reheat sauce when cutlets are ready to serve. Thin with a little water if needed.

Blot each tofu square with paper towels. Slice each tofu block into 4 long slices. Set 4 shallow dishes in this order on a counter: first have the tamari mixed with the water, next the pastry flour, then the eggs, and finally a combined mixture of the parsley, sesame seeds, wheat germ, and bread crumbs. Mix the last one well.

Preheat the oil in a fry pan over medium heat. Dip each piece of tofu on both sides into first the tamari, then flour, egg, and lastly the bread crumbs. When the oil is hot, set as many breaded cutlets into pan as will fit. Fry the cutlets until golden brown on each side.

Reheat the sauce on simmer. When all the cutlets are fried, set on a serving plate with the mushroom sauce in a pitcher on the side. The cutlets may be made ahead of time and reheated 10 minutes at 375°.

4 servings

Sauce

1 tablespoon sunflower oil

½ cup each chopped carrot, celery, and onion

½ teaspoon leaf thyme

¾ cup water

2½ tablespoons butter

3 cups sliced mushrooms

2 tablespoons whole wheat pastry flour

2 tablespoons tamari

¼ cup minced fresh parsley

Cutlets

3 squares tofu, drained and pressed (1½ pounds)

2 tablespoons tamari

2 tablespoons water

½ cup whole wheat pastry flour

2 eggs, well beaten

2 tablespoons dried parsley

¼ cup sesame seeds

2 tablespoons wheat germ

1¼ cups bread crumbs

1 cup sunflower oil

Potato Cheese Pierogis

3½ quarts water

2 cups chopped unpeeled potatoes

1 cup farmer cheese

¾ cup grated sharp cheddar cheese

1 tablespoon lemon juice

1 teaspoon Dijon mustard

1 teaspoon dried dill weed

Dash of black pepper

1½ cups unbleached white flour

½ teaspoon salt

⅛ teaspoon nutmeg

4 tablespoons butter

2 eggs, beaten

Butter

1 cup sour cream

Paprika

Pierogis are a small turnover that can be baked or boiled like a dumpling. We have always baked our pierogis at the café. Then I ate at a Polish restaurant in Montreal and ordered pierogis. They boiled theirs, using a dumpling type of dough, and smothered them in butter and dollops of sour cream when they were served. They were delicious.

So I went home and experimented, trying to duplicate what I had eaten. Here is a wonderful, if not exact, replica.

Bring 2 cups water to a boil in a saucepan, add potatoes, and cook until tender. Drain and mash well in a medium-sized bowl. Add the farmer and cheddar cheeses, lemon juice, mustard, dill weed, and pepper. Mix well and set aside.

Combine the flour, salt, and nutmeg in a mixing bowl. Or, if you have a food processor, use the chopping blade attachment and add the flour to the bowl. Cut the butter into the flour mixture until well blended. Add eggs and knead until smooth. This can all be done with the food processor or by hand. Dough should be smooth, moist, and elastic. Divide dough evenly into 16 balls.

Bring 3 quarts water to boil in a 4-quart pot over medium heat. (Set a lid on the pot and the water will boil more quickly.)

Roll out each piece of dough into a 4½-inch-diameter circle. (It doesn't have to be perfectly round.) Put approximately 1½ tablespoons filling onto ½ the circle, leaving a ¼-inch border to the edge of the dough. Now fold the half circle with no filling over the half with filling. Dip a fork in water and press down the edges of the circle to seal it. Repeat this process until all your circles have been rolled out and the filling is all used up.

Place 3 to 4 pierogis into the boiling water, whatever fits in the pot comfortably. When they rise to the top they should then boil 5 minutes. Remove with a slotted spoon when done. Repeat until all the pierogis are cooked. Serve with pats of butter over the pierogis and garnish with dollops of sour cream and a generous sprinkle of paprika.

If you don't plan to eat all the pierogis at once, freeze the uncooked extras for another meal. They can go from their frozen state into boiling water. Just increase the cooking time in the boiling water by 3 minutes.

4 generous servings (16 pierogis)

Asparagus Nests

1 pound fresh asparagus

1 tablespoon butter

1 tablespoon minced garlic (4 large cloves)

1 cup finely grated Parmesan cheese

¼ teaspoon salt

1 tablespoon lemon juice

16 phyllo dough leaves, defrosted

5 tablespoons butter, melted

1½ cups grated havarti dill cheese

One wooden spoon with a long handle on it (minimum 14 inches long)

If you have never worked with phyllo dough before, start with something a bit simpler than this recipe. However, once you are comfortable working with the dough you'll manage these nests with little trouble and impress yourself with the results.

Preheat oven to 375°. Cut the tough ends (the last inch or two) off the asparagus. If the asparagus skin seems thick, use a paring knife or vegetable peeler to peel off the next 2 to 3 inches of tough outermost asparagus skin. Then cut asparagus spears at an angle into 1-inch pieces. Melt the butter in a fry pan and sauté the asparagus and garlic on low heat, covered. Stir every few minutes. Cook until just tender (approximately 10 minutes or more, depending on the thickness of the asparagus). Pour asparagus into medium-sized bowl, add ½ cup Parmesan, salt, and lemon juice, and stir well. Set aside.

Lay out a sheet of phyllo dough lengthwise on a counter and lightly brush with melted butter. Lay another sheet of dough directly on top of first one. Lightly brush it with butter. Sprinkle 1 teaspoon Parmesan cheese lengthwise across the first 3 inches of phyllo dough that is closest to you. Now lay your long wooden spoon handle on the lengthwise end of phyllo dough closest to you. Roll up the dough (fig. 1), slowly wrapping it around the handle; stop rolling when you have a 3-inch border at the end of the dough.

Now gently push the phyllo dough up along the spoon handle (fig. 2), scrunching it up to form a tight coil. Slide this off the spoon (fig. 3) and then coil the dough around until ends meet (fig. 4). The 3-inch border of dough should also circle around, forming a nest. Push edges of coil together (fig. 5), set on buttered cookie sheet, and brush the coil lightly with butter. Repeat this procedure 7 more times, to make a total of 8 nests. Don't worry about the first nest you make. Your second nest will be better and your last perfect. With a pound of phyllo dough you'll have enough extra to make a few mistakes.

Put ¼ cup asparagus mixture into each nest, using up all the mixture. Top with havarti and bake at 375° for 15 minutes.

To make appetizer-size Asparagus Nests, simply use 1
piece of phyllo dough for each tiny nest. Lay the dough
out vertically in relation to you on a counter. Brush the
first half of dough with melted butter. Fold the second
half of dough that is unbuttered over the buttered half.
Now lightly butter this half. Sprinkle ½ teaspoon Parmesan over the first 3 inches of dough, roll up with a
wooden spoon handle, and curve into a nest shape. You
will have enough filling to make 16 tiny Asparagus Nests.
Fill, bake, and serve.

4 servings

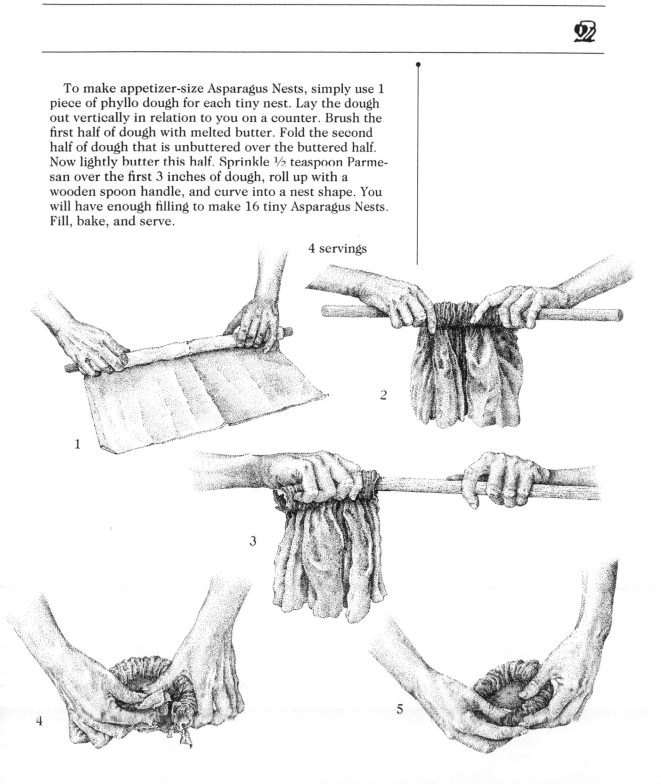

Shish Kebabs

2½ cups sunflower oil

1¼ cups cider vinegar

4 tablespoons tamari

4 tablespoons red wine

2 squares tofu (1 pound)
(cut tofu into ½-inch
squares) or one 8-ounce
package tempeh (cut into 8
slices in both directions)

1 large green pepper
(approximately 1½ cups
chopped into large pieces)

1 cup zucchini, cut into ¼-
inch slices (1 small)

1 cup yellow squash, cut
into ¼-inch slices (1 small)

2 cups halved mushrooms

½ cup onion, cut into large
pieces (1 small onion)

1 pint cherry tomatoes

12 skewers (I use wooden
ones which are used once
and thrown away or you
can invest in the stainless
steel ones which can be
reused)

3 cups water

2 cups couscous

½ cup minced fresh
parsley

½ teaspoon salt

*T*hese are great to serve at an outdoor barbecue to compete with the traditional hot dogs and hamburgers. They make a wonderful summertime meal.

Combine the oil, vinegar, tamari, and red wine in a medium-sized bowl. Add the tofu or tempeh and vegetables to the marinade and allow to soak at least 4 hours; overnight is best. Leave the marinated vegetables in a covered container in the refrigerator until ready to use. Drain off marinade and save. (This can be reused.) Arrange the vegetables and tofu or tempeh on the skewers, rotating the colors, using 3 cubes of tofu per skewer and using all the ingredients up.

Bring water to a boil in a saucepan. Pour over couscous in medium-sized bowl. Cover and stir occasionally. Add parsley and salt and stir. The water will be absorbed in 20 minutes and couscous will stay hot if covered.

Broil the shish kebabs under or over a medium flame, turning occasionally until tomatoes begin to split. Serve over couscous.

6 servings

Stir-Fried Vegetables

Slice tempeh into 6 pieces across widthwise, then cut each piece into 10 pieces. Marinate tempeh in oil, vinegar, and tamari for at least 2 hours. Meanwhile, make your Sweet and Sour or Szechuan Sauce unless you choose to use fresh garlic and ginger in the stir-fry instead of sauce.

Within a half hour before you plan to eat, start the rice, bringing water to a boil and simmering, covered, with the lid cracked until tender.

Drain tempeh, saving the marinade for another time or to use in making a salad dressing. Heat 2 tablespoons sesame oil on medium heat in a wok. Add the drained tempeh, tossing occasionally and cooking until browned and crisp. Set aside on paper towels.

Add remaining tablespoon sesame oil to wok. On medium heat, add the onions, broccoli, and carrots (also add garlic and ginger at this time if you're not making a sauce). After these vegetables cook 2 minutes, add the zucchini, mushrooms, bok choy, and red peppers. Cook another 2 minutes and add the tempeh, snow peas, and water chestnuts or bamboo shoots, along with all the Sweet and Sour Sauce or ½ cup of the Szechuan Sauce. Cook 2 minutes more and serve along with the rice and extra Szechuan Sauce on the side.

6 servings

1 package tempeh (8 ounces)

1 cup sunflower oil

½ cup cider vinegar

2 tablespoons tamari

Szechuan or Sweet and Sour Sauce (pages 240, 241) (optional)

2 cups uncooked brown rice

4 cups water

3 tablespoons sesame oil

½ cup sliced onion (1 small onion)

1 cup chopped broccoli, stems and florets

½ cup sliced carrots (1 small carrot)

2 tablespoons minced garlic

2 tablespoons minced ginger root

1 cup zucchini, sliced into 2-inch sticks (1 small zucchini)

1 cup sliced mushrooms

1 cup sliced bok choy or Chinese cabbage

1 cup thinly sliced red pepper (1 medium pepper)

1 cup snow peas, cut in half at a sharp angle

½ cup sliced water chestnuts or bamboo shoots

Szechuan Sauce

3 tablespoons sunflower oil

1 tablespoon minced fresh ginger root

4 large cloves garlic, minced

1 tablespoon mustard seed

3 tablespoons tamari

1 cup tomato juice

1 teaspoon turmeric

2 teaspoons paprika

2 teaspoons ground cumin

1/4 teaspoon cayenne pepper

1/2 teaspoon crushed dried red chili pepper

1 tablespoon arrowroot

1 tablespoon water

Szechuan Sauce is typically very hot and spicy. This is a milder version which can be made hotter by increasing the amounts of cayenne and red chili pepper. Be sure to taste the sauce a few times before adding any additional cayenne. Hot spices take a moment or two to release their full impact on the palate.

Heidi, a cook at the café, found a jar of unlabeled red powder on the spice shelf. We all looked it over but could not determine if it was paprika or cayenne. Heidi volunteered to do the taste test. She put the tiniest amount of powder into her mouth. "It's paprika," she said. A moment later her eyes popped open wide and she ran to the sink. "Cayenne!" we all said at once.

We serve this sauce with Stir-Fried Vegetables (page 239), mixing some with the stir-fry and having additional sauce on the side for those who like it hot.

In saucepan, heat oil on medium heat. When oil is hot, add the ginger root, garlic, and mustard seed. Cover pot, stirring occasionally. When mustard seeds begin to pop, lower heat. Don't allow seeds to burn, but allow them to pop: the popping cracks the seeds, allowing the flavor of the mustard into the sauce. When popping is over, add tamari, stir quickly, and continue to cook on low heat. Add tomato juice, turmeric, paprika, cumin, cayenne, and chili pepper. Mix arrowroot with water in a small cup. Add to the sauce. When it begins to thicken, remove from heat.

1 cup

Sweet and Sour Sauce

This sauce is very concentrated, and a little goes a long way. We serve it on Stir-Fried Vegetables (page 239), using 2 teaspoons for each serving of stir-fry.

Heat oil in a small saucepan, then add garlic, ginger, and mustard and cumin seed. Continue to cook over medium heat, covered, until seeds begin to snap and pop. Lower heat and allow seeds to finish popping. Lift lid, add rest of ingredients, and stir well. Remove from heat.

³⁄₄ cup

2 tablespoons sunflower oil

4 large cloves garlic, minced

1 tablespoon minced fresh ginger root

2 teaspoons mustard seed

1 teaspoon cumin seed

1 teaspoon turmeric

¹⁄₂ teaspoon ground cinnamon

¹⁄₄ cup honey

¹⁄₄ cup lemon juice

¹⁄₄ cup orange juice

1 tablespoon tamari

Sesame Lo Mein

3 quarts water

¼ cup sunflower oil

2 squares tofu, cut into small cubes (1 pound)

2 tablespoons tamari

½ cup carrot, cut into 2-inch-long thin sticks

2 tablespoons minced garlic

2 tablespoon minced fresh ginger root

1 cup sliced bok choy or celery

1 medium-sized red pepper, sliced into 2-inch-long sticks

1 cup snow peas, cut in half at an angle

One 8-ounce can water chestnuts, sliced

¼ cup sesame seeds

1 pound linguine noodles

2 tablespoons sesame oil

6 scallions

1 cup tahini

Set water on to boil for linguine in 4-quart pot.

In a wok, heat the oil over medium heat. Add tofu and sauté until all sides are lightly browned. Pour 1 tablespoon tamari over tofu and quickly toss in. Drain tofu on paper towels and set aside, but leave wok heat on. Add carrots, garlic, ginger root, and bok choy or celery to wok. After carrots cook 2 minutes, add red pepper, snow peas, water chestnuts, and sesame seeds. Cook 3 minutes more. Add tofu to wok and cook 2 minutes more.

Add linguine to boiling water and stir well. Cook pasta until just al dente and drain. Set into large bowl. Quickly toss with sesame oil, scallions, and remaining tablespoon tamari. Pour wok vegetables onto linguine, then pour tahini over vegetables. Toss well and serve.

6 servings

Desserts

Pies (page 247)

Pie Shell
Graham Cracker Crust
Orange Walnut Crust
Yogurt Cheese Pie
Strawberry Cheese Pie
Strawberry Rhubarb Pie
Blueberry Pie
Raspberry Pie
Apple Pie
Pumpkin Pie
Greek Walnut Pie
Peach Pie
Cranberry Raisin Pie

Cakes (page 259)

Apricot Chocolate
*   Almond Cake*
Poppy Seed Cake
Maple Walnut Cake
Orange Coffee Cake
Mocha Tea Cake
Black Forest Cake
Mandarin Orange
*   Carrot Cake*
Carrot Cake
Chocolate Cheesecake
Maple Tofu Cheesecake

Icings and Frosting (page 267)

Cream Cheese Icing
Maple Icing
Mocha Icing
Orange Walnut Frosting

Brownies, Strudels, and Crisp (page 269)

Chocolate Cream Cheese
*   Brownies*
Chocolate Walnut
*   Brownies*
Blueberry Strudel
Apricot Strudel
Peach Berry Crisp

Cookies (page 274)

Moon Cookies
Carob Chip Cookies
Chocolate Chip Cookies
Oatmeal Raisin Walnut
*   Cookies*
Peanut Butter Cookies
Chocolate Peanut Butter
*   Cookies*
Chocolate Currant
*   Cookies*
Poppy Seed Cookies
Butter Pecan Cookies
Hermit Cookies

One of the first things to catch the eye of a customer entering the café is a glass display case filled with a delicious offering of freshly baked desserts. As you walk by this case, you might be tempted by Chocolate Cream Cheese Brownies, frosted Poppy Seed Cake, Apricot Strudel, or a slice of fresh Carrot Cake. The aroma of apple, pumpkin, or blueberry pies baking is enough to drive many of our customers to select a dessert.

The café baked goods blend lightness, flavor, and an attractive appearance with healthy ingredients to produce a naturally delicious treat. To achieve these qualities, we primarily use a combination of whole wheat pastry and unbleached white flour. The sweetness for the desserts comes from honey and pure maple syrup, which have not been refined and bleached like white sugar. We choose to buy the darker-colored and more flavorful amber maple syrup over the lighter varieties. (Dark amber syrup is also less expensive.) The imitation brands that frequent so many grocery stores contain only traces of the real product and should not be considered worthy to bake with.

The clover honey we use is light in color and flavor. Darker honey harbors a stronger taste which can dominate a dessert. Raw sugar, also known as turbinado sugar, is less refined than white sugar and is available in natural foods stores. It is, however, more expensive than honey. To convert honey or maple syrup to sugar in the following recipes, you will have to increase the amount of liquid in the recipe. Adding one quarter to one half cup liquid for every cup of substituted sweetener will make up for the dryness of the sugar.

Dessert selections, along with the recipes in previous chapters, follow the seasons. In fall and winter the café makes pumpkin and walnut pies and fruit crisps made from dried dates, apricots, and raisins. Poppy Seed, Apricot Chocolate Almond, and Carrot Cakes are also popular wintertime treats. During the warm sunny weather of spring and summer, we bake desserts from a large selection of fresh fruits. Strawberry Rhubarb Pie, and Peach Berry Crisp are lightly sweetened. These treats are delightful and delicious and will not increase dental costs like sugary confections.

When you are trying to decide what dessert to make, consider the nature of the meal that it will follow. If the dinner was a rich and filling one, such as Ricotta Fettucine Alfredo or French Lasagne, choose a light sweet like Blueberry Strudel, Peach Pie, or Orange Coffee Cake. A meal low on protein could include a cheesecake or Yogurt Cheese Pie. During hot muggy weather, serve slices of fresh melon, a bowl of cherries, or a fresh fruit salad.

Allow your guests to rest and digest their food after a particularly long and special dinner. Let conversation flow for a half hour or more before serving tea or coffee and your special treat. It will be more fully appreciated and savored.

Pies

Pie Shell

M aking a crust for a pie or quiche used to be my least favorite thing to do. My pie shell always seemed to crack, fall apart, and stick to the counter. Here's what I've learned. Butter should be well chilled; a cold pie dough rolls out the easiest. Handling the dough too much will warm it up, so roll it out as quickly as you can. If it's too warm, return it to the refrigerator for a quick chill. Food processors will make a piecrust mix in about 10 seconds. Pie dough mix minus the water will store in a plastic bag, refrigerated, for a good week, so make up enough to last and you will have one less thing to do. Pie dough will also freeze. If you need only a bottom, freeze the extra dough and thaw in the refrigerator the night before you plan to use it. The dough will be a bit stiffer to work with, but manageable.

In a small bowl, combine the flours. With a pastry cutter, 2 knives, or using the steel blade in a food processor, cut butter and salt into the flours. When the butter is broken up, continue the process with your fingers (unless you are using a food processor). However, the trick to a good piecrust is not to overhandle the dough, so mix just enough to break butter into small pieces. The mix will hold well in this stage for a week, refrigerated.

Then add the required tablespoons water and mix in well, working dough quickly with your hands. If making a double crust, divide dough in half and form into 2 moist but not sticky flattened balls. If it is a warm day you'll need to chill the dough 30 minutes to an hour before rolling it out.

Wrap the dough in plastic to retain moisture before refrigerating. If you're pinched for time, put the dough into the freezer 10 minutes to chill.

To roll out the shell, lightly flour your work surface. With a rolling pin, roll out your first ball of dough and

One 10-inch top and one 10-inch bottom or two 10-inch bottoms

1 cup unbleached white flour

1 cup whole wheat pastry flour

2/3 cup chilled butter

Dash of salt

5 to 6 tablespoons very cold water

One 10-inch bottom

1/2 cup unbleached white flour

1/2 cup whole wheat pastry flour

1/3 cup chilled butter

Tiny dash of salt

2 to 3 tablespoons very cold water

lightly flour it (keep remaining dough chilled). Occasionally turn dough around while rolling to maintain a round and even shape (see fig. 1). When dough is an inch larger than your pie plate, lay it into the buttered dish (fig. 2). Gently fit the dough into the plate (fig. 3).

If the pie needs no top (such as for a quiche), fold over excess dough around edges of plate to form a thick edge (fig. 4). With your thumb and index finger give the dough a gentle twist and work your way around the edge of the pie until all the edges have been fluted (fig. 5).

If the pie will have a top (such as for a blueberry pie), don't flute the edges yet. Repeat rolling process on floured board with remaining dough, and when crust is not quite as large as your first shell, stop rolling and trim edges to form a circle. Pour your filling in, lay shell on top of filling, and pinch edges together and flute. If you have too fat an edge, trim your shell or pinch some of the excess dough off. Now your pie is ready to be baked.

For a prebaked pie shell, follow directions for rolling out a shell. When edges have been fluted and the oven is preheated, pour 4 cups washed dry beans (kidney, pinto, or black beans work well) into the shell. Bake the required time, usually 10 to 15 minutes at 400°. Pour beans out and set aside in jar for your next prebaked shell.

For a lattice piecrust, follow bottom crust directions but do not flute the edge. Roll out your top pie shell. Cut the shell into half-inch-wide long thin strips. Pour pie filling into shell. Set down one strip on edge of pie; leave a half-inch space. Then set the next strip down. Repeat process until pie has a line of strips across it. Now lay additional strips across at right angles to the original strips of pie dough and weave them under and over with a half-inch space between each line. Repeat until the pie is crisscrossed with a woven top. Trim strips to allow enough length to pinch into overhanging crust, flute the edges together, and bake.

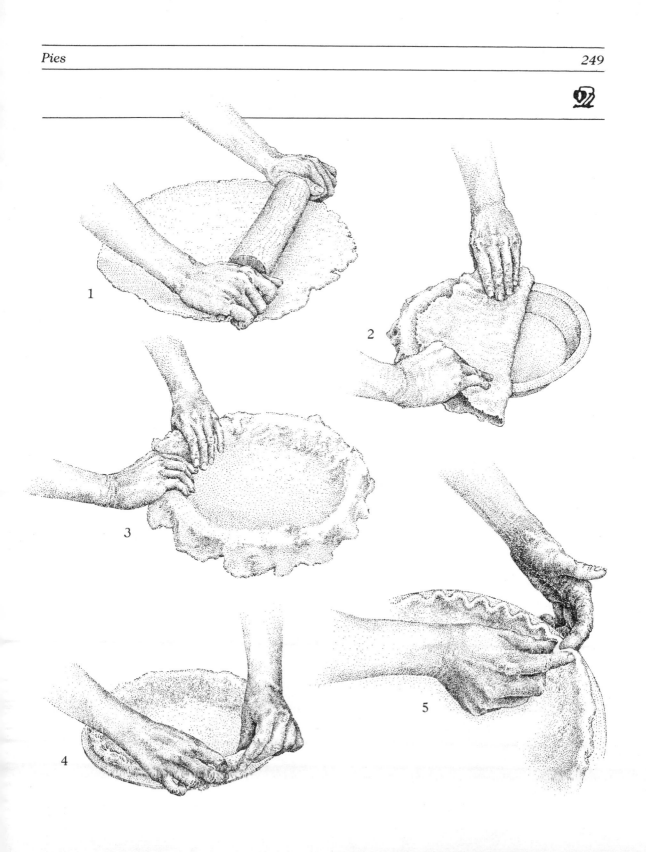

Graham Cracker Crust

1½ cups graham cracker
crumbs

¼ cup chopped almonds
(reduce graham cracker
crumbs to 1¼ cups)
(optional)

¼ cup butter, melted

Mix graham cracker crumbs (and almonds) with butter. Press into buttered 10-inch pie plate. Bake 10 minutes at 325°, until golden brown. Cool.

One 10-inch
pie shell

Orange Walnut Crust

¾ cup unbleached white
flour

½ cup whole wheat pastry
flour

½ cup chopped walnuts

1 teaspoon grated orange
rind

4 tablespoons chilled
butter

2 to 3 tablespoons very
cold orange juice

In a medium-sized bowl, combine the flours. Add the walnuts and orange rind, and mix well. Cut the butter into the flour mixture until it is well blended. A food processor equipped with a chopping blade works well. Add just enough orange juice to form a moist but not wet dough. Form the dough into a ball, wrap in plastic, and chill 1 hour. Roll out the dough to fit into a 10-inch pie plate.

One 10-inch
pie shell

Yogurt Cheese Pie

This is a quick and wonderful pie to prepare, but you have to wait at least 4 hours before you get to eat it!

Bake Graham Cracker Crust 10 minutes at 325°. Cool.

Mix cream cheese, yogurt, honey, and vanilla with electric mixer until smooth. Pour into cooled crust. Bake 10 minutes at 325° until somewhat set; it will set more when cooled. Let set 4 to 6 hours in refrigerator before serving. Garnish with sliced almonds or fruit slices (strawberries, kiwi fruit, cherries, peaches, or blueberries) if desired.

8 servings

1 Graham Cracker Crust (page 250)

1½ cups cream cheese, softened

1½ cups plain yogurt

½ cup honey

2 teaspoons vanilla extract

Sliced almonds, fresh berries, peaches, or other fruit for garnish (optional)

Strawberry Cheese Pie

This was my mother Mary's recipe, handed down to me. It's a rich summer delight of a pie, and is especially wonderful with fresh strawberries.

With an electric mixer, mix the cream cheese with 3 tablespoons honey and vanilla until smooth. Then gently spread on bottom of prebaked and cooled Graham Cracker Crust. Heat the arrowroot with the remaining ¼ cup honey in a saucepan, and stir until smooth. Add 3 cups strawberries and cook until thickened (approximately 10 to 15 minutes). Pour into crust and chill at least 2 hours.

Just before serving, whip cream with vanilla. When the cream begins to thicken, whip in the honey. Continue whipping until peaks form. Spread the whipped cream on top of the pie and garnish with fresh berries.

8 to 10 servings

1 cup cream cheese, softened

¼ cup plus 3 tablespoons honey

1 teaspoon vanilla extract

1 prebaked Graham Cracker Crust (page 250)

4 tablespoons arrowroot

3 cups unsweetened whole strawberries, fresh or frozen

2 cups fresh strawberries for garnish

Whipped Cream

1 cup heavy cream

½ teaspoon vanilla extract

1 tablespoon honey

Strawberry Rhubarb Pie

1 double pie shell (page 247)

4 cups sliced fresh rhubarb (¾-inch to 1-inch pieces)

1 cup honey

6 tablespoons arrowroot

2 cups thickly sliced fresh strawberries

½ teaspoon cinnamon

2 tablespoons unbleached white flour

A *salute to the month of June!*

Prepare the pie dough according to the recipe directions. Roll out the bottom crust and fit into a 10-inch pie plate. Refrigerate the dough and rolled-out crust.

Preheat oven to 350°.

Put sliced rhubarb into a colander with a bowl underneath. Pour honey over rhubarb and allow to drain 1 hour. Mix arrowroot with half of drained honey in saucepan. Heat until thickened on low heat. Add rest of honey to mixture. Mix rhubarb and strawberries together in bowl; add arrowroot-honey mixture along with cinnamon and flour. Gently toss. Pour into 10-inch pie shell. Roll out top crust and top pie with it. Join 2 crusts, curling the upper around the lower's top on edge of pie plate, and flute edges. Pierce top for steam.

Bake 1 hour. Cool and refrigerate a few hours to set.

8 to 10
servings

Blueberry Pie

*W*e always look forward to blueberry season at the café after a long winter of apple and walnut pies. Blueberry Pie is a favorite among staff and customers alike, and usually a scoop of honey-vanilla ice cream is had on the side. The immediate side effect of eating this pie is having a blue smile, but don't worry —it quickly wears off.

Roll out the bottom crust and fit into a 10-inch pie plate. Set aside. Refrigerate the remaining dough.

Mix honey and arrowroot in saucepan. Add salt. Add berries and simmer *gently* until mixture becomes thick and clear. Don't overstir. Stir in butter, lemon juice, and flour. Pour into unbaked pie shell. Roll out remaining dough for piecrust top. (Latticework is optional.) Place top crust over filling and join crusts, fluting edges. If not making a lattice crust, cut a slash in the center of the top crust to allow steam to escape.

Bake 10 minutes at 425°. Then lower oven temperature to 350° and continue to bake 30 minutes more, until golden. Allow to cool at least 1 hour before serving.

8 to 10
servings

1 double pie shell (page 247)

½ cup honey

4 tablespoons arrowroot

¼ teaspoon salt

5 cups fresh blueberries (1½ pints) (or frozen if fresh are not available)

1 tablespoon butter

1 tablespoon lemon juice

2 tablespoons unbleached white or whole wheat pastry flour

Raspberry Pie

Preheat oven to 375°.

Put the honey, flour, and cream in a medium-sized bowl. Beat this mixture with a whisk until it is smooth and there are no lumps. Gently stir the raspberries into this mixture. Pour the filling into the walnut crust. Bake 40 minutes until set. Cool and refrigerate 2 hours before serving.

8 to 10
servings

½ cup honey

½ cup unbleached white flour

¾ cup heavy cream

4 cups fresh raspberries

One 10-inch Orange Walnut Crust (page 250)

Apple Pie

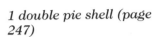

1 double pie shell (page 247)

6 cups sliced unpeeled apples

½ cup honey

2 tablespoons butter, cut into slices

1 teaspoon cinnamon

1 tablespoon lemon juice

2 tablespoons whole wheat pastry flour

The old saying "An apple a day keeps the doctor away" is not appropriate at the café. In fact, just the opposite happens. A busy Montpelier doctor has his lunch picked up for him. He predictably orders a Sunshine Chapati and Apple Pie almost every day.

Only when we don't have apple pie are we likely to keep the doctor and his staff away.

Roll out the bottom crust and fit into a 10-inch pie plate. Set aside. Refrigerate the remaining half of pie dough.

Preheat oven to 425°.

Mix all ingredients together in a medium-sized bowl. Add flour if mixture seems watery. Pour into unbaked pie shell. Roll out second half of pie dough. Place on top and twist pie edges together with thumb and index fingers to flute the edges. Slice a breathing hole in top of pie about 1 inch across.

Bake 10 minutes. Lower oven temperature to 350° and bake 30 minutes more, until golden.

8 to 10
servings

Peach Pie. Use 6 cups sliced unpeeled peaches. Omit the sliced butter and reduce cinnamon to ½ teaspoon.

Pumpkin Pie

Fall foliage travelers eat up our Pumpkin Pies almost as quickly as we can bake them at the café. The pies are made from scratch, beginning with a locally grown, organic pumpkin. Using a fresh pumpkin is economical and will produce a tastier pie with a richer deep golden color. Canned pumpkin puree is an okay, but not first choice, substitute. Butternut and hubbard squashes also make delicious pies.

A pie pumpkin is relatively small in size, round, and orange in color. A jack-o'-lantern pumpkin can also be used for a pie, but it will produce a larger amount of puree. Pumpkin puree freezes well.

Preheat oven to 375°.

Pick a deep orange thick-skinned pumpkin. A 3-pound pumpkin yields 1 quart (4 cups) puree. Cut the pumpkin in half, turn face down on a baking sheet, and bake about 45 minutes, until tender when pierced with a fork. If you are baking a large pumpkin, cut it into chunks or quarter it. The skin will peel off easily after it's been baked and the seeds are easily scooped out. Measure out 1¾ cups pumpkin pulp. (If you want to roast the seeds, put them back in the oven and bake at 325°. Check these often, stirring every few minutes in oven. They burn easily and will roast quickly!)

Preheat oven to 425°. Put the pumpkin pulp, honey, salt, cinnamon, ginger, cloves, cream, sour cream, and egg yolks into blender and puree. Beat whites separately until stiff, then fold into blended puree. Pour into 10-inch pie shell.

Bake 15 minutes at 425°. Reduce heat to 350° and bake 45 minutes more, until set (doesn't jiggle and/or is golden on top). Remove from oven and allow to set for at least 1 hour before cutting. Serve topped with whipped cream.

8 to 10
servings

---

1 small pie pumpkin or 1¾ cups pumpkin puree

¾ cup honey

¼ teaspoon salt

1 teaspoon cinnamon

½ teaspoon ground ginger

⅛ teaspoon ground cloves

½ cup heavy cream

½ cup sour cream

2 eggs, separated

1 unbaked 10-inch pie shell (page 247)

Whipped cream

Greek Walnut Pie

1 cup honey

1 tablespoon whole wheat pastry or unbleached white flour

½ cup plus 1 tablespoon butter, melted

2 eggs

1 teaspoon vanilla extract

¾ teaspoon cinnamon

⅛ teaspoon salt

1¾ cups broken or chopped walnuts

One 1-pound package phyllo dough, defrosted (you'll need approximately 12 leaves)

Similar to baklava, this is always a favorite pie at the café. It can be put together quickly, and is delicious as well as exotic-looking.

Preheat oven to 325°.

In a medium-sized bowl, combine honey, flour, 1 tablespoon melted butter, eggs, vanilla, cinnamon, salt, and 1¼ cups walnuts. Mix and set aside.

Lay 1 phyllo leaf over a buttered 10-inch pie plate and brush lightly with melted butter. Repeat with 3 phyllo leaves, stacking them one on top of another and letting them hang over the edges of plate. Gently press phyllo into plate (fig. 1). Tightly roll up the extra overhanging phyllo dough to edge of plate to form crust (fig. 2). Pour in walnut-honey filling (fig. 3).

Brush another phyllo leaf with butter. Roll up lengthwise in a ½- to ¾-inch-wide rope by folding it over and over (fig. 4). Set coil into outside edge of pie plate, standing in the filling. Repeat brushing phyllo with butter, rolling, and laying into filling (fig. 5) until pie is covered with a tightening smaller circle and is closed. This should take around 8 leaves and the rest of the melted butter (use more if needed). When filling is covered, sprinkle remaining ½ cup walnuts on top (fig. 6) and brush any leftover butter over edges of pie. Bake 40 to 50 minutes, until golden brown, and let sit 1 hour before cutting.

10 servings

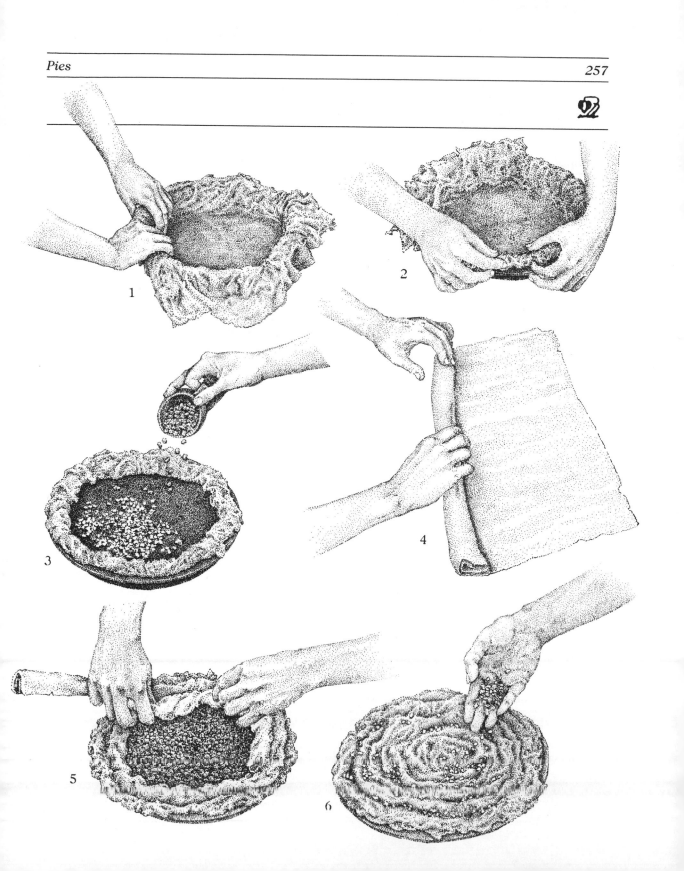

Cranberry Raisin Pie

1 double pie shell (page 247)

2 cups boiling water

2½ cups coarsely chopped raisins

2½ cups coarsely chopped cranberries

½ cup honey

1 tablespoon lemon juice (approximately ½ lemon)

2 tablespoons unbleached white flour

Dash of salt

1 teaspoon vanilla extract

Caroline, *a baker at the café, got this recipe from her mom. Their family used to have a cranberry farm in Massachusetts and discovered all kinds of wonderful things to make with cranberries.*

Make the pie dough according to the recipe. Roll out the bottom crust and fit into a 10-inch pie plate. Refrigerate the remaining dough.

Pour water into a bowl with the raisins. Soak 10 minutes, then drain well, pressing out extra water. This will plump up the raisins. Mix rest of ingredients in with the raisins. Pour filling into uncooked pie shell. Roll out top crust and place over filling, joining top and bottom crusts and fluting edges. (Lattice work is lovely if you care to make it.) Slash top for steam if you are not making a lattice crust.

Bake 30 to 35 minutes at 375°, until lightly browned on edges. Cool and allow to set at least 1 hour before serving.

8 to 10
servings

Cakes

Apricot Chocolate Almond Cake

The bottom layer of this cake is chocolate, and the top, apricot almond. Making it will produce a lot of dirty bowls, but also a moist cake that is lovely to look at and delicious to eat.

Preheat oven to 325°.

Melt chocolate in small saucepan on low heat. Set aside to cool. Beat egg whites until foamy. Add the cream of tartar and continue to beat until stiff. Add ¾ cup honey, 1 cup wheat germ, ¾ cup pastry flour, and cooled chocolate. Stir well and set aside.

Chop apricots and set in bowl with boiling water 10 minutes until softened. Drain well. In a separate bowl, beat butter, remaining ½ cup honey, and vanilla together until smooth. Stir in egg yolks and milk. Mix together the remaining 1¾ cups white and whole wheat flour, baking powder, remaining ½ cup wheat germ, and salt, and stir into batter. Fold in apricots and almonds.

Butter a 10-inch springform tube pan well. Flour pan with remaining 2 tablespoons flour, covering bottom and sides of pan. Turn pan upside down to remove excess flour. Spread chocolate mixture on the bottom and up the sides of pan up to 2 inches in a wave motion. The chocolate will be a partial upper exterior layer to the cake as well as a bottom layer. Then pour apricot mixture on top of chocolate, smoothing it evenly into the pan. Bake 1 hour until a toothpick comes clean when inserted in center of cake. Cool 10 minutes in pan. Loosen cake from pan sides with a knife. Remove sides of pan and serve.

10 servings

3 (1-ounce) squares unsweetened chocolate

4 eggs, separated

¼ teaspoon cream of tartar

1¼ cups honey

1½ cups wheat germ

1¾ cups plus 2 tablespoons whole wheat pastry flour

1 cup dried apricots

2 cups boiling water

½ cup butter, softened

2 teaspoons vanilla extract

1 cup milk

¾ cup unbleached white flour

2 teaspoons baking powder

¼ teaspoon salt

½ cup chopped almonds

Poppy Seed Cake

1 cup poppy seeds

2 cups milk

2 eggs

1 teaspoon vanilla extract

1 cup honey

½ cup butter, melted

1½ cups whole wheat pastry flour

1½ cups unbleached white flour

½ teaspoon salt

4 teaspoons baking powder

Cream Cheese Icing (page 267)

The Horn of the Moon catered my wedding and used this recipe for the wedding cake. Poppy Seed Cake is a popular dessert at the café and also makes a great birthday cake. The poppy seeds add an unusual but tasty flavor and crunch to the cake.

Preheat oven to 350°F.

In a saucepan, combine the poppy seeds and 1⅓ cups milk. Bring to a boil, then remove from heat. Let stand 20 minutes.

Beat together the eggs, vanilla, honey, butter, and remaining ⅔ cup milk. In a separate bowl, mix together the flours, salt, and baking powder.

Combine the cooled poppy seed mixture with the other liquids. Add to dry ingredients. Stir just until moist. Pour into buttered 10-inch springform pan. Bake 35 to 40 minutes.

Allow to cool in pan, then run knife around edges and remove springform sides. After it cools, cut cake in half horizontally to make 2 layers. Ice with Cream Cheese Icing in between layers and on top of cake.

10 servings

Maple Walnut Cake

M*aple Walnut Cake is a Vermont classic, and needless to say, must be made with real maple syrup. It is best when served fresh!*

Preheat oven to 375°. Butter a 10-inch springform tube pan.

Mix dry ingredients together. In a separate medium-sized bowl, combine egg yolks, maple syrup, and vanilla, adding butter last. Beat egg whites until stiff. (An electric mixer is recommended). Set aside. Add dry ingredients alternately with milk to butter mixture, stirring well after each addition (an electric mixer is okay to use for this). Stir in walnuts. Fold in egg whites gently. Pour into springform pan. Bake 35 to 40 minutes, until cake begins to turn very lightly golden on edges and toothpick comes out clean. Cool before icing.

10 servings

1½ cups whole wheat pastry flour

1 cup unbleached white flour

1 tablespoon baking powder

½ teaspoon salt

4 eggs, separated

1 cup dark amber maple syrup

1 teaspoon vanilla extract

¾ cup butter, melted

1 cup milk

½ cup finely chopped walnuts

Maple Icing (page 267)

Orange Coffee Cake

M*y good friend Sheila passed on this recipe to me. The cake has a distinctly orange taste to it that is produced from using the whole orange, skin and all.*

Preheat oven to 350°. Butter a 9- or 10-inch tube pan.

Squeeze orange and reserve juice. Put entire orange into blender along with milk and eggs. Blend on high speed until finely chopped (2 minutes).

Combine flour and baking soda in a small mixing bowl. In a separate medium-sized bowl cream butter and honey. Add orange mixture to honey-butter mixture. Then add flour, raisins, and nuts. Mix and pour into pan.

Bake 40 to 45 minutes, until top springs back. Sprinkle reserved juice over hot cake and leave in pan until almost cool. Remove from pan and allow to finish cooling.

10 servings

1 large orange (or 1½ small to medium oranges)

¾ cup milk

2 eggs

2 cups whole wheat pastry flour

1 teaspoon baking soda

½ cup butter

⅔ cup honey

1 cup golden raisins

½ cup chopped walnuts, almonds, or pecans

Mocha Tea Cake

½ cup butter

1 cup honey

2 cups whole wheat pastry flour

½ cup unbleached white flour

2 teaspoons cinnamon

½ teaspoon each nutmeg and allspice

3 tablespoons very strong brewed coffee (espresso works well)

1 cup sour cream

1 teaspoon baking soda

2 eggs

½ cup chopped walnuts

Two 1-ounce squares unsweetened chocolate, melted

Mocha Icing (page 268)

The first time I made this cake was with my old sandwich partner, David. We were to cater a lunch for a large environmental workshop where 1,000 people were expected. We baked lots of Mocha Cake for dessert, and it was moist and delicious.

The morning of the luncheon we had an incredible ice storm. Only about one third of the expected workshop participants made it to the conference. David and I froze much of the Mocha Cake and ended up selling it, eating it, and, finally, giving it away.

Preheat oven to 350°F. Butter a 10-inch springform tube pan.

Cream butter and honey. Mix in flour and spices. Then add the coffee, sour cream, baking soda, eggs, walnuts (reserve a few to sprinkle on top), and melted chocolate to the mixture. Mix well. Pour batter into pan.

Bake 35 to 40 minutes, until done. A toothpick should come out with a few crumbs on it but no batter. Don't overbake. Cool cake 15 minutes in pan before removing. Cut cake in half horizontally to make 2 layers. Ice middle and top. Garnish with a few chopped walnuts.

8 to 10
servings

Black Forest Cake

Everyone who works at the café has a cake baked for his or her birthday, and this one is a favorite among the staff. Typically, the birthday cake is presented to the birthday person on a work break or at the end of a shift.

Some of the long-term café workers had gotten quite blasé about their expected cake. Pat, the café's baker, decided to surprise a few people. Jean found her birthday cake all lit up in the café's ice freezer after she was asked to go get some ice. The candles has begun to defrost the freezer and caused it to snow inside. Jean got the ice, closed the freezer door, and came back laughing. Heidi discovered her cake all decorated in the oven she was about to light. Another worker was given a muffin with candles in it, and we all sang happy birthday. We told her we had no time to bake a cake. She believed us. The cake came out later!

Black Forest Cake is deliciously sweet with rich layers of whipped cream inside and over the top of the cake, and topped with chocolate shavings and cherries.

Preheat oven to 350°. Melt chocolate with milk and butter in a 1-quart saucepan. Cream with honey. Let cool, then add eggs, flours, and baking powder. Mix well. Bake in buttered 10-inch springform pan 40 to 45 minutes. Let cool.

Slice cake in half horizontally to make 2 layers. Just before serving, whip together the cream, vanilla, and honey until thick. Fill and cover cake with whipped cream, and garnish with fresh berries or cherries, sliced almonds, and grated chocolate.

10 servings

Cake

Four 1-ounce squares unsweetened chocolate

6 tablespoons milk

1 cup butter

1⅓ cups honey

6 eggs, well beaten

1½ cups whole wheat pastry flour

1 cup unbleached white flour

1 tablespoon baking powder

Whipped Cream

2 cups heavy cream

2 teaspoons vanilla extract

¼ cup honey

Fresh berries or cherries, sliced almonds, grated chocolate for garnish

Mandarin Orange Carrot Cake

1½ cups unbleached white flour

1½ cups whole wheat pastry flour

2½ teaspoons baking soda

2½ teaspoons cinnamon

1 teaspoon salt

1 cup grated, unsweetened coconut

2 cups grated carrot (⅔ pound carrots)

1¼ cups sunflower oil

2 teaspoons vanilla extract

1½ cups honey

One 11-ounce can mandarin oranges, drained and slightly chopped

3 eggs

Orange Walnut Frosting (page 268)

2 teaspoons grated orange peel

G uinea pig dinners took place at my house regularly on Monday nights for a few years while I was working on recipes for this book. Jackie, an old housemate of mine, took part in eating a number of experiments, which were usually quite good. She gave me this recipe and said, "Work on it, it belongs in the book!" She was right: the cake is tall, light, wonderful, and a unique variation of carrot cake.

The first time the café served it at a wedding we were catering, children lined up for seconds and thirds!

Preheat oven to 350°. Oil a 13 × 9-inch or 10-inch springform pan.

Mix dry ingredients together in large bowl. Combine wet ingredients in separate bowl. Pour wet into dry. Turn on electric mixer and mix well for 2 minutes or until well blended. Pour into pan.

Bake 40 to 45 minutes, until done. When cool, slice the cake in half horizontally to make 2 layers. Spread a thin layer of frosting on the center layer, saving most for the top of the cake. Garnish with grated orange peel over frosting.

10 servings

Carrot Cake

C arrot Cake is the traditional natural foods wedding cake. When I talk to couples about catering
*their wedding, they always have a strong opinion al-
ready formed about carrot cake. "Anything but carrot
cake!" is occasionally stated, but "Carrot cake, defi-
nitely" is the more likely response for a wedding cake.*
   *It is always a popular, moist, and delicious cake
even it if is often served at weddings!*

Preheat oven to 350°. Whip honey, butter, and oil together in a medium-sized bowl. Add eggs. Mix dry ingredients together and blend into honey-oil mixture. Add
vanilla. Fold in carrots and walnuts.

Bake in oiled 10-inch springform tube pan 45 minutes
to 1 hour, until toothpick comes out clean. Cool. Cut
cake in half horizontally to make 2 layers. Ice between
layers and on top and garnish with a few chopped walnuts.

10 servings

1¼ cups honey

½ cup butter, softened

¼ cup sunflower oil

4 eggs, well beaten

*1 cup whole wheat pastry
flour*

*1 cup unbleached white
flour*

2 teaspoons baking powder

2 teaspoons baking soda

½ teaspoon salt

2 teaspoons cinnamon

2 teaspoons vanilla extract

*3 cups grated carrot
(about 1 pound carrots)*

½ cup chopped walnuts

*Cream Cheese Icing (page
267)*

Chocolate Cheesecake

A wonderful way to end a meal!

Preheat oven to 350°. Melt chocolate on low flame in
small saucepan. Remove from heat and allow to cool a
few minutes. Beat rest of ingredients until smooth in medium-sized bowl. Add chocolate and mix well. Pour into
cooled Graham Cracker Crust. Bake 30 minutes or until
set. Cool, then refrigerate at least 2 hours before serving.

8 servings

*Two 1-ounce squares
unsweetened chocolate*

½ cup honey

*1½ cups cream cheese,
softened (12 ounces)*

1½ cups sour cream

3 eggs

2 tablespoons light rum

2 teaspoons vanilla

*1 prebaked Graham
Cracker Crust with
almonds (page 250)*

Maple Tofu Cheesecake

Crust

1½ cups granola

3 tablespoons butter, melted

¼ cup whole wheat pastry flour

1 tablespoon honey

½ teaspoon cinnamon

Filling

⅓ cup sunflower oil or melted butter

1½ cups dark amber maple syrup

1½ cups cream cheese, softened

2 squares tofu, drained and pressed (1 pound)

6 large eggs

2 teaspoons vanilla extract

¾ cup sour cream

1½ teaspoons cinnamon

3 tablespoons whole wheat pastry flour

T*his makes one very tall and filling cheesecake. Plan to have a large group of friends around to help you eat this.*

Preheat oven to 325°. Butter a 10-inch springform pan. Mix the ingredients for the crust in bowl, then put into pan. With your fingers, press the crust into the bottom and sides of pan, going up the sides about 1 inch. Bake 15 minutes at 325°. Cool. Raise oven temperature to 350°.

Combine all the filling ingredients in a large bowl. Then pour some of the ingredients into a blender, blend, and pour into another bowl. Repeat until all the ingredients have been blended. Stir well and blend again if necessary, until the filling is smooth and consistent. Pour into granola crust. (Put a plate under your pan to catch any drips.) Bake 1¼ hours at 350°, until cake is puffy, golden brown, and holds its shape when jiggled. When cool, refrigerate until set.

Before serving, run a knife around sides of pan, then remove the sides of the pan from the cake.

12 servings

Icings and Frosting

Cream Cheese Icing

This is a simple and delicious icing that we make often at the café.

Combine all ingredients in a bowl. Mix until smooth. (An electric mixer works well.) This recipe makes enough icing for a 2-layer top and bottom of a cake or 1 layer with sides iced as well (almost 2 cups).

1½ cups cream cheese, softened

½ teaspoon vanilla extract

6 tablespoons maple syrup or 4 tablespoons honey

Maple Icing

Blend ingredients in blender until smooth. Pour into saucepan and cook on low heat, stirring constantly. Bring to a boil and cook until thickened (approximately 7 minutes on medium heat), stirring constantly. Cool and refrigerate at least 15 minutes, then put onto cake. (It's thicker when it's been refrigerated and is best made ahead of time and allowed to cool.)

1½ cups

1 cup grade B (dark amber) maple syrup

½ cup cream cheese, softened

Mocha Icing

1½ cups cream cheese, softened

One 1-ounce square unsweetened chocolate, melted

¼ cup honey

2 teaspoons instant coffee or 1 tablespoon very strong brewed coffee

Blend together with electric mixer until smooth.

Almost 2 cups

Orange Walnut Frosting

1 cup cream cheese, softened

2 tablespoons butter, melted

1 teaspoon vanilla extract

1 teaspoon grated orange peel

6 tablespoons honey

1 cup chopped walnuts

Blend first five ingredients together in a bowl with electric mixer until smooth. Stir in walnuts.

2 cups

Brownies, Strudels, and Crisp

Chocolate Cream Cheese Brownies

Preheat oven to 350°. Butter a 9 × 13-inch pan.

Mix flours and baking powder together. Set aside. Melt chocolate and butter in saucepan on very low heat or in a double boiler. Set aside to cool slightly.

With electric mixer in medium-sized bowl, beat eggs until foamy. Add honey and vanilla. Beat at high speed for 4 to 5 minutes, until creamy-colored, foamy, and slightly thickened. Add chocolate-butter mixture, beat in, and turn off mixer. Stir in dry ingredients by hand until just mixed.

Set aside ¾ cup of this mixture. To the remaining mixture, add ¾ cup walnuts (save ¼ cup for the top). Stir in nuts. Spread the chocolate mixture in pan.

With electric mixer in small bowl, mix the cream cheese with butter until soft. Add honey and vanilla. Mix well. Add egg and beat until smooth. Pour cheese mixture over chocolate layer. Place the reserved ¾ cup chocolate mixture in spoonfuls on top of cheese layer (about 10 mounds). Draw a wide-bladed knife or small metal spatula through the chocolate mounds into cheese mixture to create a marble effect. Try not to cut into chocolate layer below. Don't overdo the effect. Top with remaining walnuts. Bake 25 minutes (30 if in metal rather than glass pan). Cool completely in pan and refrigerate 1 hour before cutting. These freeze well.

12 brownies

¾ cup whole wheat pastry flour

⅓ cup unbleached white flour

1 teaspoon baking powder

Six 1-ounce squares unsweetened chocolate

½ cup butter

3 eggs

¾ cup honey

1½ teaspoons vanilla extract

1 cup walnuts, cut into medium-sized pieces

Cheese Mixture

¾ cup cream cheese, at room temperature

3 tablespoons butter, at room temperature

5 tablespoons honey

¾ teaspoon vanilla extract

1 egg

Chocolate Walnut Brownies

½ cup butter

Five 1-ounce squares unsweetened chocolate

4 eggs, at room temperature *(very important!)*

1¼ cups honey, slightly warm (not cold)

¼ teaspoon salt

1 teaspoon vanilla extract

¾ cup whole wheat pastry flour

¾ cup unbleached white flour

1 cup chopped walnuts

During *the first few years of business, the café refused to bake with chocolate, and carob brownies were the only option. Chocolate contains caffeine and we felt that serving coffee was bad enough. Slowly, though, we gave in to the public demand, because chocolate is so delicious in desserts.*

The eggs for these brownies should be at room temperature before you begin. If you forget, crack them open into a bowl, where they will warm up much more quickly.

Preheat oven to 350°. Melt butter and chocolate in saucepan on very low heat or in a double boiler, stirring constantly until smooth and melted. Set aside to cool.

Beat eggs (with electric mixer if possible) until light and foamy in texture. Slowly pour in honey while mixer continues to run; add salt and vanilla. Turn off mixer. Add chocolate-butter mixture. Stir slightly, then add flours and nuts. Stir just enough to mix in, but don't overmix. Butter a 9 × 13-inch pan (I use Pyrex). Pour batter into pan. Bake 20 minutes at 350°. Cool in pan.

12 brownies

Blueberry Strudel

Preheat oven to 375°.

Put honey in a 1-quart saucepan over low heat. Add salt, allspice, cinnamon, and lemon juice, and stir well. When honey begins to boil, add arrowroot and flour. Cook until thick. Add blueberries, stir well, and cook 1 minute. Remove from heat and set aside.

Lay out a sheet of phyllo dough on a counter. Lightly brush with melted butter. Lay another sheet of phyllo on top of the first piece and again brush with butter. Repeat 2 more times. Spread half the blueberry filling evenly along the shorter side of the dough, leaving a 2-inch border on either side and the end closest to you. Fold ends of dough in over the filling. Now gently roll the dough up. (See illustration on page 231 for phyllo technique.) Be careful not to roll the dough up too tightly or it will burst when baking (but too loose a roll will harm the strudel appearance).

Repeat this procedure once more, using up the remaining sheets of phyllo dough and filling. Set strudels on a buttered cookie sheet and brush them with remaining butter. Sprinkle tops with maple sugar. Bake 20 minutes. Cool 30 minutes before serving, and then cut into slices at an angle.

8 servings

¼ cup honey

⅛ teaspoon salt

¼ teaspoon allspice

¼ teaspoon cinnamon

2 teaspoons lemon juice

2 tablespoons arrowroot

1 tablespoon unbleached white flour

1 pint fresh blueberries (2 cups)

8 phyllo dough leaves

3 tablespoons butter, melted

1 teaspoon maple sugar

Apricot Strudel

4 cups dried apricots

2 cups boiling water

½ cup honey

½ teaspoon cinnamon

Dash of cloves

10 leaves (½ box) phyllo dough

¼ cup butter, melted

1 teaspoon wheat germ

Chop apricots finely. Put them into a medium-sized bowl, and pour boiling water over them. Let sit 10 minutes, stirring occasionally until soft. Drain very well, pressing excess water out of apricots. Mix in honey and spices.

Preheat oven to 350°.

Spread out a leaf of phyllo dough on a flat surface. With pastry brush, lightly butter the dough. Spread another sheet of dough directly on top of the first one, butter, and repeat 3 more times until 5 sheets of dough are one on top of another. Spread half the apricot mixture lengthwise across the lower half of the phyllo dough (see illustration on page 231 for phyllo technique). Leave a 2-inch border on either end of dough. Fold over edges onto filling. Roll up like a jelly roll. Lay on buttered cookie sheet. Repeat the phyllo dough layering once again, using up remaining apricot mixture. Place both strudel logs on buttered cookie sheet and brush with remaining butter. Sprinkle tops with wheat germ. Bake 20 minutes. Cool for 10 to 15 minutes, then cut into slices at an angle.

8 to 10
servings

Peach Berry Crisp

Delicious alone or with some vanilla ice cream on top!

Place peaches in a bowl. Pour lemon juice over them, stir, and then add berries and stir again. Melt butter and honey together in saucepan over low heat. Mix remaining ingredients together in a medium-sized bowl and combine with honey-butter mixture. Spread half this mixture into oiled 9 × 13-inch pan. Cover with fruit (it will shrink down a bit when cooked). Spread remaining topping over fruit mixture. Bake approximately 30 to 35 minutes at 375°, or until browned on top.

8 to 10
servings

3 cups sliced peaches
(about ¼-inch-thick slices)

2 tablespoons lemon juice
(about 1 lemon)

3 cups whole berries (your choice)

1 cup butter

⅔ cup honey

4 cups raw rolled oats

1½ cups whole wheat pastry flour

½ cup chopped walnuts

1 teaspoon allspice

2 teaspoons cinnamon

½ teaspoon salt

Cookies

Moon Cookies

1½ cups butter, softened (3 sticks)

¾ cup honey

1 teaspoon vanilla extract

⅔ cup very finely ground almonds

1¾ cups whole wheat pastry flour

1¾ cups unbleached white flour

Jam for center of cookies (optional)

On the Horn of the Moon's first day of business we gave away these moon-shaped cookies. We made hundreds; they didn't last long. It has become a café tradition to bake and give away Moon Cookies on Christmas and on our anniversary. They are a delicious buttery shortbread cookie, and customers are always asking for the recipe.

Using electric mixer if available, cream softened butter, honey, and vanilla together until smooth. Add almonds, then flours. Work in with hands and knead on floured board until well mixed. If there is time, refrigerate dough 1 hour before cutting into shapes.

Roll out dough approximately ⅛ to ¼ inch thick on large floured board. (Be generous with the flour: it will save you the frustration of finding cookies stuck to your rolling surface.) Cut into shapes with cutters or an upside-down glass. If filling with jam, make a thumbprint in the center of each cookie and put a dab of your favorite jam in it after you place the cookies on a cookie sheet. Bake on oiled cookie sheets 7 to 12 minutes at 325°, depending on cookie size and thickness. (The thinner the cookie, the quicker it bakes.) Bake until the edges of cookies are light brown. Let cool on racks. Both the cookies and dough freeze well.

5 to 7 dozen
small cookies

Carob Chip Cookies

These cookies are a favorite of kids who come into the café. One day during a busy lunch hour a small child tipped over the chair he was sitting on and began to cry very loudly. The café hushed as everyone turned to see if the child was all right. I grabbed a cookie out of the cookie jar, ran over to the table, and said loudly, "Anyone who falls out of their chair is entitled to a free cookie!" The child grabbed it and began munching. Then a friend of mine sitting at a nearby table fell off his chair and onto the floor. The whole café laughed, and the atmosphere was lightened and relaxed once again.

Cream butter with honey; stir in vanilla. In separate bowl, mix together flour, baking soda, salt, and cinnamon. Add this mixture to honey mixture. When flour is mixed in, add chips and stir until smooth. Form into balls, using about 1 tablespoon mixture per ball. Place on oiled cookie sheet and bake at 325° 10 minutes, until golden. Allow to cool a few minutes on sheet before removing to finish cooling.

About 45 cookies

Chocolate Chip Cookies. Omit cinnamon and replace carob chips with chocolate chips. Add ½ cup chopped walnuts if you like.

⅔ cup butter, softened (if unsalted, add salt in recipe; if salted, skip salt)

1⅓ cups honey

1 teaspoon vanilla extract

4 cups whole wheat pastry flour

2 teaspoons baking soda

¼ teaspoon salt

1 teaspoon cinnamon

1½ cups unsweetened carob chips

Butter Pecan Cookies

1½ cups butter, softened

¾ cup honey

2 teaspoons yogurt

1½ cups unbleached white flour

1 cup whole wheat pastry flour

2 cups chopped pecans

½ teaspoon baking soda

¼ teaspoon each ginger and nutmeg

½ teaspoon cinnamon

These are a favorite cookie of mine. The first time I made them I decided to use up a jar of unshelled pecans that I had. Shelling the pecans was very tedious work, and it took me nearly an hour to end up with 2 cups of nuts. The cookies, however, were worth it, though I have bought only shelled nuts since.

Preheat oven to 375°. Oil 2 to 3 cookie sheets.

In large mixing bowl, cream butter and honey until smooth. Stir in yogurt. Mix remaining ingredients together in medium-sized bowl. Add to honey-butter mixture and stir until smooth. Drop by rounded tablespoons onto cookie sheets. Flatten slightly with hand before baking. Bake 8 to 10 minutes. Cool.

3 dozen cookies

Peanut Butter Cookies

⅔ cup butter, softened

⅔ cup honey

1¼ cups peanut butter

3 tablespoons milk

1 teaspoon vanilla extract

2¾ cups whole wheat pastry flour

1 teaspoon baking soda

½ teaspoon salt

In the early days of the restaurant, Chris made many experimental batches of these cookies. Replacing the sugar with honey threw everything off. But he finally got it just right!

Cream butter and honey with electric mixer. Add peanut butter, milk, and vanilla and mix with beater until smooth. In separate bowl, mix dry ingredients together. Slowly add to peanut butter mixture. Stir in by hand (the batter will get too thick for mixer). Then oil 3 cookie sheets. Use 1 tablespoon batter per cookie. Roll into balls and set on cookie sheets 3 inches apart. Set tines of a fork across cookie and gently push down. Then cross the cookie with the fork again. Do this to all the cookies. Bake 12 to 15 minutes at 325°. Rotate sheets in oven halfway through baking from upper shelf to lower and back to front. Bake until *lightly* browned on edges and tops. Remove from cookie sheets and cool on a rack.

45 cookies

Chocolate Peanut Butter Cookies

*W*e have to keep refilling the cookie jar when these
are made.

Melt chocolate on very low heat in saucepan or double
boiler along with the butter. With electric mixer, blend
chocolate-butter mixture and honey. Add vanilla. Gradually add flours. Mix well and set aside.

In separate bowl, cream butter and peanut butter,
using clean beaters. Beat in honey, then flour.

Divide chocolate mixture in half. Set 1 bowl aside.
Drop teaspoons of chocolate batter onto *ungreased*
cookie sheet 2 inches apart. Top each mound with a
small spoonful of peanut butter mixture. Then top once
again with a spoonful of the reserved chocolate mixture.
Bake 10 to 12 minutes at 350°. Reverse cookies from top
and bottom shelves midway through baking if using 2
shelves, otherwise use higher rack. Don't overbake.
Watch bottoms. Cookies will become crisp as they cool.

2 dozen
cookies

Chocolate Mixture

*Two 1-ounce squares
unsweetened chocolate*

1/2 cup butter

1/2 cup honey

1 teaspoon vanilla extract

*3/4 cup whole wheat pastry
flour*

*1/2 cup unbleached white
flour*

Peanut Butter Mixture

2 tablespoons butter

1/3 cup peanut butter

1/4 cup honey

*2 tablespoons unbleached
white flour*

Chocolate Currant Cookies

2 (1-ounce) squares
unsweetened chocolate

1 cup boiling water

1 cup currants or raisins

1¼ cups whole wheat
pastry flour

1¼ cups unbleached white
flour

1 teaspoon baking powder

½ teaspoon baking soda

¼ teaspoon salt

½ cup plus 2 tablespoons
butter, softened

1¼ cups honey

1 teaspoon vanilla extract

½ cup sour cream

Melt chocolate carefully in saucepan over very low heat or in double boiler. Set aside. Pour boiling water over currants or raisins. Let sit 10 minutes, then drain well.

Mix dry ingredients together in a bowl. In large bowl, using electric mixer, cream butter, then add honey and vanilla. Mix in well. Mix in chocolate, then sour cream. On low speed, add dry ingredients to chocolate mixture. Turn off mixer and stir in currants or raisins. On oiled cookie sheet put 1 tablespoon mixture for each cookie 3 inches apart. Bake approximately 10 to 15 minutes at 375°, until they have just begun to brown lightly and bounce back to the touch. Don't overbake. They will harden as they cool.

40 cookies

Poppy Seed Cookies

½ cup milk

1 cup poppy seeds

¾ cup whole wheat pastry
flour

½ cup unbleached white
flour

Dash of salt

1 teaspoon baking powder

½ cup raisins

½ cup butter

½ cup honey

½ teaspoon vanilla extract

Poppy seeds are a favorite for baking at the café. We use them for muffins, pancakes, Danish, coffee and dessert cakes, and cookies. They have caused many a black-toothed smile from customers.

Heat milk in saucepan. When it is just about to boil, turn off heat and add poppy seeds. Stir and set aside. Mix dry ingredients together. Chop raisins. Using electric mixer, cream butter in medium-sized bowl. Add honey and vanilla. On low speed, add dry ingredients. Turn off mixer. Stir in poppy seed-milk mixture and raisins. Place on oiled cookie sheets 2 inches apart in heaping teaspoons. Bake 15 minutes at 350°, until lightly brown and semifirm to the touch. They will become crisp as they cool.

3 dozen
cookies

Oatmeal Raisin Walnut Cookies

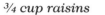

Pour boiling water over the raisins and allow to soak for 15 minutes. Then drain and squeeze dry.

Cream butter and honey together until light and fluffy. In a small bowl, mix the flours, baking powder, salt, and spices. Stir in honey-butter mixture, alternating with milk. Stir in oats, walnuts, and raisins. Roll into balls, using 1 tablespoon mixture per cookie. Place on oiled cookie sheet and flatten slightly with hand. Bake 10 minutes at 350° until lightly golden.

3 dozen
cookies

¾ cup raisins

¾ cup boiling water

½ cup butter, softened (1 stick)

¾ cup honey

¾ cup whole wheat pastry flour

¾ cup unbleached white flour

2 teaspoons baking powder

¼ teaspoon salt

2 teaspoons cinnamon

¼ teaspoon each cloves and ginger

⅓ cup milk

1¾ cups rolled oats

½ cup chopped walnuts

Hermit Cookies

1½ cups whole wheat flour

1 cup whole wheat pastry flour

1 teaspoon baking soda

1 teaspoon cinnamon

½ teaspoon allspice

¼ teaspoon nutmeg

¼ teaspoon salt

½ cup butter, softened

1¼ cups honey

2 eggs

1 cup currants

1 cup raisins

1 cup coarsely chopped pitted dates

2 cups coarsely chopped walnuts

Cookies at the café are traditionally made without eggs. We have found it to be easily done and unnoticeable to taste or consistency. These cookies are the exception. They are so chock-full of fruit and nuts that eggs are needed. The results are quite delicious.

Mix dry ingredients together in bowl and set aside. In large bowl using electric mixer, cream butter, then add honey, then eggs. Slowly mix in dry ingredients. Turn off mixer. Stir in the fruits and nuts well.

Use 1 tablespoon dough per cookie. Form into a ball and lay on oiled cookie sheets approximately 3 inches apart. Bake 12 to 15 minutes at 375°, until they slightly (barely) spring back to the touch. Cool.

4 dozen
cookies

Celebrations, or Cooking for the Masses

Weddings, birthdays, reunions, holidays, the first day of spring, an abundant garden harvest, and an exciting new job are all good reasons for having a celebration. Gathering together friends, family, neighbors, or co-workers brings festivity, warmth, sharing, and pleasure to our lives, and breaks up daily routines. No celebration can be a total success, though, without delicious food and drink.

Food is always an attraction that guests look forward to. It's an important part of any festivity no matter whether it's a casual get-together, wedding, office party, or a dusk-to-dawn contra dance. The tradition of breaking bread with those around you often unites a diverse group of people.

Cooking for fifty, however, is quite a bit different than planning a meal for four. The café has prepared the fare for many special events, ranging from music festivals to business luncheon meetings. This experience has taught us which foods are best served together. When planning a menu, you must also consider the kind of event, as well as the time of day, the season, and where it will be served.

A large summer brunch might be set out in a flowering backyard. The menu might include mimosas, stuffed melon fruit salad, assorted quiches, tossed green salad, Poppy Almond Coffee Cake, and fresh Danish or muffins. A small spring luncheon could offer Asparagus Nests along with Creamy Broccoli Soup, or plates of delicious cheeses, breads, and sliced vegetables along with a hearty Tomato Corn Chowder. A Christmas party menu might have eggnog, Broccoli Cheese Tiropitas, Hummus, Guacamole, and Bleu Cheese Dip as well as cookies and Cranberry Bread. A large summer wedding could include champagne, cheeses, dips, three or four salads, and Spinach Mushroom Strudel with Two Cheeses.

On the morning of an affair catered by the café, workers assigned to the job always end up competing for counter and oven space with the regular staff. They are also preparing food which will be served at the restaurant that day. This situation leads us into preparing ingredients for a large event in advance. We chop, slice, and grate many of the foods ahead of time, but mix and bake them the day they are to be served. Generally, this is a good idea, no matter what your circumstances are, and it can make the entire process calmer and more manageable.

Such planning will allow you to serve selections like fresh, green, crispy salads, flaky piecrusts, and hot quiches while still maintaining some resemblance of sanity in your life. To make preparation easier, borrow a food processor if you do not own one. It saves huge amounts of time and can prevent the inevitable soreness that comes from doing more chopping, grating, and mincing than you are used to. Hummus and Guacamole will have a smoother, creamier consistency, pie doughs quickly mix together, and vegetables are sliced in seconds.

If possible, use a kitchen with plenty of counter space. You will usually need one or two large cutting boards, along with a number of varied-sized mixing bowls, sharp knives, and an oven in good working order.

What follows is a typical menu to be served at a summer wedding for 100 guests. This will give you an idea of quantities needed and tell you what to prepare ahead of time. Even if you are planning a smaller, less involved event you will still benefit from reading up on kitchen tactics for cooking for large numbers.

Menu for a Summer Wedding

Serves 100

Appetizers

Hummus with pita bread and vegetable dippers

Assorted cheeses, breads, and crackers

Bleu Cheese Dip with vegetable dippers

Guacamole and corn chips

Drinks

Nonalcoholic Fruit Punch

Champagne

Wine and beer

Salads

Stuffed Watermelon Fruit Salad

Marinated Potato Salad

Tabouli

Tossed Green Salad with Vinaigrette Dressing

Main Courses

Quiches, assorted varieties
　　　or
Spinach Mushroom Strudel with Two Cheeses
　　　or
Mushroomkopita
　　　　　　　　(Pick two)

Dessert

Mandarin Orange Carrot Cake

Coffee and tea

Appetizers

I f time and money budgets allow, it's always best to serve snacks initially at a celebration while the guests arrive, mill around, and talk. Some people may have driven for hours with no time to stop and eat and they will lunge at whatever food is set out. But if you serve too large a quantity of appetizers, guests will fill up on these, leaving no room for the main course. A happy compromise is offered here.

Offer a selection of your favorite cheeses. A popular combination includes a quarter wheel of Brie and a few pounds each of Swiss, cheddar, and Gouda cheeses. Display the cheeses on a large cutting board on trays covered with lettuce leaves or kale, along with a crock of spicy mustard.

Slicing cheese in advance will dry it out. Leftover sliced cheese is also less useful because it cannot be easily grated. The alternative to slicing is to serve the cheese with cheese slicers and sharp paring knives nearby.

Breads should be cut just before serving. Have them set out on a tray along with crackers.

Assorted Cheeses, Breads, and Crackers

Multiply the Hummus recipe (page 142) by five. The Hummus can be made a few days in advance and refrigerated. It can also be prepared weeks ahead of time and frozen. Defrost the Hummus thirty-six hours before serving and allow to thaw in the refrigerator. Using a food processor will greatly speed up the preparation time involved.

Sliced vegetables should be cut up the day of your event to preserve freshness. Set the vegetable dippers out on trays after you have transported them. Otherwise, your lovely arrangements are likely to fall into one another. Peeled carrot sticks, celery sticks, and broccoli and cauliflower florets are best for serving with Hummus as dippers. Pita bread can be sliced into eight triangles and served alongside the Hummus on a tray. Garnish the bowl of Hummus with parsley sprigs and thinly sliced lemon twists.

Hummus

Bleu Cheese Dip — Multiply the Bleu Cheese Dip recipe (page 144) by five. The dip can be made up to two days in advance. The vegetable dippers should be cut up the day you plan to serve the dip. Include in the assortment mushrooms (sliced in halves or quarters if they are large), cherry tomatoes, zucchini, carrot and celery sticks, and broccoli florets.

Guacamole and Corn Chips — Multiply the Guacamole recipe (page 129) by eight. Guacamole does not store well and should be served on the same day it is made. Set the dip on a large tray in a medium-sized bowl. Surround the bowl with corn chips. Corn chips are usually quite popular, so have a bag or two extra to avoid running out.

Drinks

Fruit Punch — A nonalcoholic punch is a good idea for parties, where it is likely to be drunk by children and adults alike. This punch is quick and easy to prepare, as well as delicious. It combines three juices with sparkling water, and people always ask me, "What's in it?"

In a very large mixing bowl, combine 2 gallons apple cider or juice with 3 quarts sparkling water, 3 quarts grape juice, and 3 quarts pineapple coconut juice. Stir well and transfer to a punch bowl. Add plenty of ice and garnish with sliced strawberries and thin slices of oranges and limes. Label the punch nonalcoholic, and if no alcohol is being served, have backup ingredients for another full recipe on hand.

Champagne

Champagne is a traditional and popular drink at weddings. Have enough on hand to allow everyone to drink a toast with it and enough additional bottles for those who would like a little more. Two cases of fifths of champagne should be enough; have up to three cases if you have many champagne-drinking guests.

The price and quality of champagne vary tremendously. Much of what is sold as champagne in this country is actually sparkling wine. If you plan on buying an inexpensive champagne, don't purchase the commonly known brands that your guests will recognize immediately. Instead, find a lesser-known and possibly better-tasting brand. There are some good California sparkling wines available that are reasonably priced. Spain and Italy are also getting into the traditionally French market with some good quality sparkling wines and champagnes.

Wine and Beer

If you plan on serving hard liquor in addition to wine and beer, adjust your amounts accordingly. Much less wine and beer will be needed. Quantities of beer and wine drunk at celebrations vary tremendously. When speculating how much to buy, consider whether the party might go late. A larger amount of alcohol will be drunk the later the party continues.

Beer is a popular drink during hot summer weather. For a winter event you should opt for smaller amounts. Beer is much less expensive when bought in a keg. But once a keg is open the beer will quickly go flat within a day or two. You must also have a container large enough to sit the keg in so that ice can be packed all around it. Smaller half and quarter kegs of beer are also options.

Wine can also be bought in kegs, but it is a less popular drink and bottles are the better choice. White wine is drunk the most, with red coming in second and rosé a slow third. France, Italy, and California produce some inexpensive but good table wines sold in fifths, magnums, and liters. Avoid the really inexpensive wines. Their flavor is poor, quite often too sweet, and there is always the risk of hidden additives. Some cheap Italian wines were exposed in early 1986 for having methanol included in their ingredients.

Salads

Stuffed Watermelon Fruit Salad

Select a large, long green watermelon. Slice the melon in half lengthwise. Follow directions for Stuffed Honeydew Melon (page 132), increasing the proportions accordingly by eight. Use both halves of the melon.

Ideally, it is best to have two people working on each half of melon. Two melon ballers are then a necessity, for this is the most tedious part of the job. Seeds must be separated and discarded from the melon.

The stuffed melon fruit salad must be made on the day it is to be served or the fruit will lose its freshness and vitality. All of this work is worth it; the melons will be beautiful as centerpieces on your serving table, as well as irresistible to eat.

Marinated Potato Salad

Since this salad should marinate, it is best when made a day in advance. This will allow the vegetables to mix and absorb the flavors. Multiply the Marinated Potato Salad recipe (page 130) by six. Put all of the ingredients for the salad in a large bowl except the tomatoes, which should be included in the salad the day you serve it. Garnish the salad with parsley sprigs and cucumber slices.

Tossed Green Salad

Wash six to eight heads of assorted lettuce and greens. This can be done a day in advance if the lettuce can be well dried and stored in airtight containers that will not be crushed or packed too full. Grated carrots and sliced red cabbage can also be prepared ahead of time—a food processor will do this work quickly.

The salad should not be tossed together until the day it will be served. At that time, add any other vegetables that you like, including sliced cucumbers, sprouts, sliced red onions, tomatoes, etc.

Don't mix the dressing into the salad or the greens will wilt in a few hours. Instead, have a decanter of one or two dressings on the side. Multiply the salad dressing recipes in the book by five if you are making two kinds of salad dressing or by ten if you are making only one.

Multiply the Tabouli recipe (page 116) by six. This salad can be prepared a day in advance, adding the tomatoes the day the salad will be served. Garnish the Tabouli with tomato wedges and parsley sprigs.

Tabouli

Main Courses

Two varieties of main dishes should be offered to your guests. This will prevent someone who doesn't like spinach, for example, from being faced with Spinach Mushroom Strudel with Two Cheeses as their only option.

Choose two different main courses or make two or more varieties of the same entrée. Broccoli Mushroom and Avocado Tomato Scallion Cheddar Quiches could be offered, or Spanikopita and Mushroomkopita. Have labels by the dishes so that your guests will be aware of their choices.

Mushroomkopita

Mushroomkopita is a popular and delicious main dish but a more costly one to make. A compromise is to have quiche as well as Mushroomkopita for main dishes. If you multiply the Mushroomkopita recipe (page 225) by six and the quiche by eight, there should be plenty of food for everyone. Each pan of Mushroomkopita will serve eight.

The phyllo dough must be defrosted in the refrigerator for six to eight hours before you use it. Buy six 9 × 12-inch aluminum disposable baking pans. If two people will be preparing the dish together, have two pastry brushes on hand.

The filling may be prepared a day in advance but the pie should not be put together and baked until the day you serve it.

Quiche   Quiche is always popular and easy to warm up and serve. If the quiche will be your only main dish, plan on each pie serving six, making a total of eighteen quiches. However, if there is an additional main dish, each quiche will serve eight to ten, and then eight quiches should be ample.

For convenience you may want to buy disposable aluminum pie pans, which come in a nine-inch size only. If you choose to do this, roll out two extra pie shells for the excess filling cause by the smaller pie tin size. Your other option is to buy pie pans or borrow them from friends. (A nine-inch pie can be cut into six small pieces, a ten-inch pie into eight small slices.)

Piecrust mix can be made up a few days in advance, excluding the water, until you are ready to roll out your shells. The crusts can be rolled out a day ahead of time but should be wrapped tightly and refrigerated to prevent drying out.

The quiche filling of cheese, eggs, and sour cream or heavy cream can be prepared one or two days prior to the celebration. The vegetables may also be sliced in advance but are at their best if not cooked until the day you bake and serve the quiche.

To reheat the quiche, place in a 350° oven 15 minutes.

**Spinach
Mushroom Strudel
with Two Cheeses**

This recipe (page 230) should be multiplied by seven and the quiche by seven to serve 100 guests. Each strudel recipe will make two strudels, serving a total of eight people.

The filling may be made a day in advance, but the strudels should be rolled and baked the day they are to be served. Remember to defrost the phyllo dough six to eight hours in advance, allowing it to thaw in the refrigerator. The strudels can be baked on seven cookie sheets or in seven disposable aluminum baking tins.

Dessert

The wedding cake can be the most difficult part of
the meal to prepare yourself. Traditional wedding
cakes are tiered cakes that have separated layers
which get progressively smaller. Baking the cake is the
easy part: you can buy the correct-sized cake pans and
they will fit in a standard home oven.

Building and icing the cake can be a challenging job.
The cake must be well constructed; special building
sets can be bought at bakeries and baking supply
houses.

I suggest, however, that if you desire a lovely tiered
wedding cake, you hire a professional to bake it for
you. Once a cake is decorated, it must be carefully
transported to the celebration site. Driving with a wedding cake in the back of a car can be risky business.
Our Vermont back roads have wounded more than one
wedding cake that we were delivering from the café.

The second and easier option is to make a rectangular sheet cake. This can best be done if you have ac-
cess to a commercial-sized 18 × 24-inch cake pan and
a large baker's oven. You can also try to make smaller
9 × 12-inch cakes, arranging them beside and on top
of one another after baking so that when iced it will
ideally look like one cake.

The Mandarin Orange Carrot Cake recipe (page
264) multiplied by five will produce one tall 18 × 24-
inch sheet pan cake or five tall 9 × 12-inch cakes.
This will be the right amount of cake for sixty to sev-
enty people. The cake can be cut in half through the
center lengthwise and iced in the center layer, top,
and sides. To serve 100 to 150 people, you will need to
multiply the recipe by ten, making two 18 × 24-inch
sheet pan cakes. Stack one cake on top of the other
with icing between to form three layers of icing plus
one on top.

When icing this cake, make sure that the cake is
perfectly cool. Spread a thin coating of icing over the
first layer of cake. It will be easier to set the second
layer of cake on top of the first if you cut the second
layer in half first. This will make the positioning of the
cake more manageable and cracking will be less likely.

You will need a tremendous amount of icing to cover

Mandarin Orange Carrot Cake

the whole cake. For a cake that will serve 100 people the Cream Cheese Icing recipe (page 267) should be multiplied by twelve. This should leave you with some extra icing available for repairs if needed. See if you can locate three-pound logs of cream cheese instead of all those small individually wrapped eight-ounce packages. It will be more economical and convenient. The icing can be made the day of the event or one to two days before. In either case, the cream cheese or icing should be softened at room temperature two hours to make it more manageable to work with.

To ice the cake, you will need a wide sandwich spreader, along with a cake decorating pastry bag. The pastry bag will have various decorating tube design options and you can get as fancy or simple as you wish. Practice with the bag a few times before you attempt to decorate the cake. Have fresh flowers for placing on and around the base of the cake. Baby roses, miniature carnations, irises, and even wild flowers can dress up a cake nicely.

Transport the cake very carefully (ideally a hatchback car, station wagon, and van are the best vehicle options). Always bring extra icing for repairs, along with your spreader and pastry bag. If it is a particularly hot and humid day of 80° or more, you may want to frost the sides and top of the cake after you have gotten to your destination. Cream Cheese Icing is less firm in hot weather and can be jiggled off a cake in the heat.

To avoid any possibility of icing that is too soft, the frosting can be sweetened with confectioners' sugar instead of honey. The sugar acts as a binder, holding the icing together.

Coffee and Tea

Rent or borrow a large coffeepot with a fifty- to eighty-cup capacity. Also have a smaller twenty-five-cup pot filled with hot water for tea. Include an assortment of herbal and black teas, as well as a coffee substitute.

You will also want to bring two extension cords, coffee filters, cream pitcher and cream, honey or sugar, as well as your coffee and teas.

How to Serve It

S erving food buffet-style has become common for most large events, and it is certainly the easiest option. You will need a minimum of two people to be in charge of the kitchen, with volunteers coming to their aid when needed. The staff's duties should include setting out the appetizers and refilling trays, preparing and serving the champagne, clearing dishes, plates, and cups, serving the salads and hot main dishes, making coffee, serving the cake once the ceremonial cutting has been done, and basically doing whatever needs to be done.

Paper and plastic goods are the simplest options for dishes and cutlery. They have come a long way and no longer begin to bend or wilt when hot food is set on them. Buy the best of a quality line of paper goods from a supplier. You will have many color and design choices in plates, glasses, and cutlery. Paper table coverings are also available.

Renting china is almost as costly as paper goods and will involve much more work. The dishes must be returned clean and breakage must be paid for. Unless china is available in the hall you are renting, buy paper goods.

And Finally

T here are bound to be some leftovers, so be prepared and bring some empty containers and plastic wrap to divide the food up among those interested in taking some home.

Hire someone to do your cleanup if you rent a hall or have the celebration in your home. You deserve it after all the hard work you have been through!

Menu Planning

Everyone has experienced difficulty in planning a meal. Deciding which foods to serve depends upon various circumstances. Consider whether you are entertaining or preparing a simple meal for yourself or your household. If guests are coming, check to see if anyone has a restricted diet. Cost and availability of ingredients must also be included in your decision.

After these influences are considered, special attention should be given to providing a meal that is well balanced and nutritious, as well as aesthetically pleasing. Repeating the same food groups in a menu can be a bad idea.

At the café an occasional customer will order something like a Lentil Burger and Lentil Vegetable Soup, or Creamy Tomato Soup and green salad. One meal offers protein and few vegetables, while the other has no protein and only vegetables. These kinds of meals involve poor judgment, which can easily be avoided by paying attention to a few basic principles and learning which foods go well together.

Ideally, a full day of meals should include raw greens, different-colored cooked vegetables, fruits, starches, and a variety of protein sources such as grains, legumes, nuts, eggs, and/or dairy products. This will produce complete amino acid combinations. Keep this in mind when you are making up a shopping list for a trip to the store, as well as for individual menus.

Listed below are a number of menu ideas, beginning with simple meals that can be put together quickly. Next are main dishes that need only a salad to complete the dinner. Finally, a listing of various menus for entertaining are included that in many cases have a soup or appetizer, main dish, salad, and dessert to complete the meal.

These are only a few suggested recipe combinations from the many that can be made from this book. But it may help you to plan a meal when you simply cannot decide what to prepare or do not have the time to think about it.

Simple, Casual Meals

Lentil Vegetable Soup
Herb Stuffed Eggs
Bedouin Bread

Chili
Corn Bread
Tossed Green Salad

Canadian Split Pea Soup
Sea Vegetable Chapati

Garden Bean Soup
Lemon Couscous Salad
  with Macadamia Nuts

Miso Vegetable Soup
Lentil Burgers

Butternut White Bean
  Ginger Soup
The Hot Greek Pita

Creamy Tomato Soup
Tofu Burgers

Chilled Avocado
  Cucumber Soup
Tofu Chapatis

Alphabet Vegetable Soup
Broccoli Mushroom
  Sandwich with Three
  Cheeses

Rice, Tofu, and Vegetables
  or Florentine Omelette
Basic Green Salad with
  Tahini Dressing

Tempeh Reuben
Greek Salad

Tomato Barley Soup
Farmer Cheese Melt

Marinated Rice Salad
Hummus with Bread

Black Bean Soup
Carrot Walnut Raisin
  Muffins
Spinach Salad

Chilled Spicy Tomato
  Avocado Soup
Tabouli with Pita Bread

Gypsy Vegetable Stew
Poppy Seed Muffins

Main Dishes to Serve with a Tossed Green Salad

Pasta Dishes

Ricotta Fettuccine

Pasta Florentine

Lasagne Primavera

Mushroom Tofu
  Stroganoff

Blue Moon Asparagus
  Fettuccine

Basil Cream Pasta

Linguine with Mushroom
  and Garlic Sauce

Three-Herb Pesto

Mexican Dishes

Bean and Vegetable
  Burritos

Moon Burritos

Baked Mexican
  Vegetable Pie

Black Bean Enchiladas

Avocado Tortillas

Garbanzo Chimichangas

Tortitas

And

Baked Stuffed Squash

Quiches

Broccoli Feta Pie

Asparagus, Mushrooms,
  and Rice with a Zesty
  Dijon Cheddar Sauce

Sesame Lo Mein

Greek Vegetable Pie

Tofu Mushroom Pie

Pizza Alfredo

Miso Tofu Pizza

Meals for Entertaining

Creamy Broccoli Soup
Luna Pie
Greek Salad
Carrot Cake

Tofu Stuffed Mushrooms
French Lasagne
Green Salad with Herb
   Dressing
Apple, Blueberry, or
   Peach Pie

Mushroom Bisque
Greek Vegetable Pie
White Bean Salad
Poppy Seed Cake

Indian Split Pea Soup
Mushroom, Spinach, and
   Potato Curry
Chapatis
Yogurt Cheese Pie

Hummus with Vegetable
   Dippers and Pita Bread
Shish Kebabs with
   Couscous
Green Salad with Sour
   Cream and Garlic
   Dressing
Greek Walnut Pie

Creamy Tomato Soup
Mushroomkopita
Three-Bean Salad
Strawberry Cheese Pie

Creamy Green Bean Soup
Tofu "No Meat" Balls
   served with Linguine
   and Basic Tomato
   Garlic Sauce
Spinach Salad with
   Creamy Italian
   Dressing
Apple, Peach, Blueberry,
   or Pumpkin Pie

Guacamole with Corn
   Chips
Layered Enchiladas
Green Salad with Herb
   Dressing
Raspberry Pie

Tofu Cutlets with
   Mushroom Sauce
Wild Rice with Pine Nuts
   Salad
Apricot or Blueberry
   Strudel

Chilled Avocado
   Cucumber Soup
Spinach Ricotta Deep-
   Dish Pizza
Triple Pepper Salad
Chocolate Walnut
   Brownies

Florentine Stuffed
   Mushrooms
Broccoli Walnut Crepes
Tossed Green Salad with
   Green Vinaigrette
   Dressing
Cranberry Raisin Pie

Flautas with Salsa
Refried Beans
Guacamole
Peach Berry Crisp

Black Bean Soup
Avocado Tortillas with
   Salsa
Green Salad with Dilly
   Vinaigrette Dressing
Strawberry Rhubarb Pie

Nachos
Baked Mexican
   Vegetable Pie
Refried Beans
Green Salad with Spicy
   Tomato Dressing
Mandarin Orange Carrot
   Cake

Chilled Fruit Soup
Chalupas with Salsa,
   topped with Guacamole
Chocolate Cheesecake

Index